POCKET GUIDE
TO

THE
POPES

THE
POCKET GUIDE
TO

THE
POPES

RICHARD P. McBRIEN

HarperSanFrancisco
A Division of HarperCollinsPublishers

HarperCollins books may be purchased for educational,
business, or sales promotional use. For information please
write: Special Markets Department, HarperCollins Publishers,
10 East 53rd Street, New York, NY 10022.

HarperCollins Web site: http://www.harpercollins.com

HarperCollins®, 📖®, and HarperSanFrancisco™
are trademarks of HarperCollins Publishers.

FIRST EDITION

Book design by rlf design

Library of Congress Cataloging-in-Publication Data
    McBrien, Richard P.
        The pocket guide to the Popes / Richard P. McBrien.
    — 1st ed.
        p.   cm.
    Includes bibliographical references and index.
    ISBN-13: 978-0-06-113773-0
    ISBN-10: 0-06-113773-1
        1. Popes—Biography.   2. Papacy—History.   I. Title

BX955.3.M33   2006
282.092'2—dc22
[B]   2006043422

06 07 08 09 10   (WE)   10 9 8 7 6 5 4 3 2 1

THE
POCKET GUIDE
TO

THE
POPES

INTRODUCTION

*T*his book contains the abridged profiles of all of the popes of the Catholic Church organized chronologically according to the dates of their respective terms of office. For the complete profiles, readers should consult the full edition, originally published in hard cover by HarperSanFrancisco in 1997, subsequently released in paperback in 2000, and finally issued in an updated edition that includes Pope Benedict XVI in 2006. The full edition contains many original features; this abridged edition is limited to profiles of individual popes that rely upon secondary source material for their factual and historical content. For a listing of these sources and an explanation of how they were incorporated into the profiles, the reader should consult the Preface and the Select Bibliography of the full edition.

WHAT IS A POPE?

The office occupied by the pope is known as the papacy. The pope's principal title is Bishop of Rome. In addition to his immediate pastoral responsibilities as Bishop of Rome, the pope also exercises a special ministry on behalf of the universal Church. It is called the Petrine ministry, because the Catholic Church considers the pope to be the successor of the Apostle Peter. As such, he has the duty to preserve the unity of the worldwide Church and to support all of his brother bishops in the service of their own respective dioceses.

The title "pope," which means "father" (Lat., *papa*), was in earlier centuries of church history applied to every bishop in the West, while in the East it seems to have been used of priests as well. In 1073, however, Pope Gregory VII formally prohibited the use of the title for all except the Bishop of Rome. In addition to Bishop of Rome, the pope has several other titles: Vicar of Peter, Vicar of Jesus Christ, Successor of the Chief of the Apostles, Supreme Pontiff of the Universal Church, Primate of Italy, Archbishop and Metropolitan of the Roman Province, Sovereign of Vatican City State, and Servant of the Servants of God.

According to traditional Catholic belief, the papacy was established by Jesus Christ himself when he conferred its responsibilities and powers upon the Apostle Peter at Caesarea Philippi: "And so I say to you, you are Peter, and upon this rock I will build my church, and the gates of the netherworld shall not prevail against it. I will give you the keys of the kingdom of heaven. Whatever you bind on earth shall be bound in heaven; and whatever you loose on earth shall be loosed in heaven" (Matt. 16:18–19).

WHY ROME?

It is because of the ancient tradition that the two principal leaders of the apostolic church, Sts. Peter and Paul, were martyred and buried in Rome that the papacy, from its beginnings, has been linked with this former imperial city. St. Ignatius of Antioch (d. ca. 107) is traditionally regarded as the first major witness to the primacy of Rome. In his famous letter to the church at Rome not long before he himself was martyred there, he addressed "the church holding chief place in the territories of the district of Rome—worthy of God, worthy of honor, blessing, praise, and success; worthy too in holiness, *foremost in love*" (emphasis added).

It would have been extraordinary, in fact, if Rome had *not* been singled out for a special role and position of authority in the early Church. Not only was it the city traditionally regarded as the site of the martyrdoms and burials of both Peter and Paul; it was also the center of the Roman Empire. Gradually Rome did emerge as an ecclesiastical court of last resort, the local church to which other local churches and their bishops would appeal when disputes and conflicts could not be settled between or among themselves. The Bishop of Rome intervened in the life of distant churches, took sides in theological controversies, was consulted by other bishops on doctrinal and moral questions, and sent delegates to distant councils.

The connection between Peter and the Bishop of Rome, however, did not become fully explicit until the pontificate of Leo I (also known as Leo the Great) in the mid-fifth century (440–61). Leo insisted that Peter continued to speak to the whole Church through the Bishop of Rome. But prior to the East-West schism of 1054, the Bishop of Rome had been viewed primarily as patriarch of Rome alongside the patriarchs of Constantinople,

Antioch, Alexandria, and Jerusalem. After the split, a merger occurred in which the papal office completely absorbed the Roman patriarchal office. In the eyes of many Eastern Christians, Western Christianity became thereby a papal church, that is, a church that relates so predominantly to the see of Rome that the pastoral autonomy of the local churches and their bishops is all but lost. The Bishop of Rome came to regard himself, and be regarded by others, as the universal primate of the entire Church. It was as if he were the bishop of every diocese and the local bishops functioned simply as his vicars or delegates.

Following a long and complex history, the Second Ecumenical Council of Lyons in 1274 claimed for the Roman church "the supreme and full primacy and authority over the universal Catholic Church." That formal declaration laid the foundation, in turn, for the dogmatic definition of the First Vatican Council in 1870 that "in the disposition of God the Roman church holds the preeminence of ordinary power over all the other churches."

WHAT IS THE ROLE OF A POPE?

The evolution of the doctrine of papal primacy has not proceeded in a direct, unbroken line from the time of the New Testament to the present day. During the first Christian millennium, and particularly before the pontificate of Gregory VII (1073–85), popes functioned largely in the role of mediator. They did not claim for themselves the title Vicar of Christ. They did not appoint every bishop. They did not govern the universal Church through the Roman Curia. They did not impose or enforce clerical celibacy. They did not write encyclicals or authorize catechisms for the whole Church. They did not retain for themselves alone the power of canonizing saints. They did not even convene ecumenical councils as a rule—and certainly not the major doctrinal councils of Nicaea (325), Constantinople (381), Ephesus (431), and Chalcedon (451).

The Second Vatican Council (1962–65) brought the Church's understanding of the papacy more in line once again with that of the first millennium. The council viewed the papacy in increasingly communal and collegial terms. The pope is no longer to be conceived of as an absolute monarch—an impression clearly left by the First Vatican Council (1869–70). According to Vatican II, the pope exercises supreme authority over the whole Church, but the other bishops also share in that authority.

To be sure, the supreme authority vested in the college of bishops cannot be exercised without the consent of the pope. "This college, insofar as it is composed of many, expresses the variety and universality of the People of God, but insofar as it is assembled under one head, it expresses the unity of the flock of Christ" (Dogmatic Constitution on the Church, n. 22). Although the pope retains "full, supreme, and universal power over the Church," the other bishops are no longer perceived as simply his stand-ins or delegates. They also receive from Christ "the mission to teach all nations and to preach the gospel to every creature" (n. 24). They govern their own dioceses not as "vicars of the Roman Pontiff, for they exercise an authority which is proper to them" (n. 27). Whatever authority the pope and the other bishops enjoy, it is always to be exercised within a communion of local churches through the faithful preaching of the gospel, the administration of the sacraments, and pastoral service.

The papal office serves the unity of the whole Church as "the perpetual and visible source and foundation of the unity of the bishops and of the multitude of the faithful" (n. 23). Papal primacy, therefore, is a primacy of service—in the service of unity. Insofar as the universal Church is a communion of local churches, the papal office must respect the legitimate diversity of these churches and practice a collegial mode of decision making (n. 23). The bishops, therefore, truly collaborate with the pope in the work of the Holy Spirit, which is the work of unity. They do so in their collegial confession of one faith, in their common celebration of divine worship, especially the Eucharist, and in their promotion of the loving harmony of the family of God (Decree on Ecumenism, n. 2).

IS THE POPE INFALLIBLE?

In addition to its reaffirmation of the doctrine of papal primacy, the First Vatican Council solemnly defined the dogma of papal infallibility. Infallibility means, literally, immunity from error. Theologically it refers to a charism, or gift, of the Holy Spirit that protects the Church from fundamental error when it solemnly defines a matter of faith or morals. Catholic theologians are careful to point out, however, that the charism is a negative charism, that is, it only guarantees that a particular teaching is not erroneous. The charism of infallibility does not ensure that a particular teaching is an adequate, appropriate, or opportune expression of faith or morals. Furthermore, papal infallibility is a dimension of the infallibility of the whole Church, not vice versa. The pope's infallibility is the same infallibility "with which the divine Redeemer willed His Church to be endowed" (Dogmatic Constitution on the Church, n. 25).

The formal concept of infallibility was not applied to the papacy until the fourteenth century, during a controversy over poverty in the Franciscan order. Advocates of a rigorist position (that Franciscans must divest themselves of all property, regardless of practical need) employed the term "infallibility" to defend the binding authority of statements by earlier popes against the more liberal decisions of their successors. Under the impact of the Reformation, the concept of infallibility gained wider currency among the theologians of the Counter-Reformation (St. Robert Bellarmine [d. 1621] and others). There were also appeals to infallibility in the condemnations of Jansenism and Gallicanism (two largely French dissident movements) in the seventeenth and eighteenth centuries. Under strong personal pressure from a beleaguered Pope Pius IX (1846–78), the First Vatican Council formally defined the dogma of infallibility in 1870.

The key words of the Vatican I text placed certain restrictions on the exercise of papal infallibility: "When the Roman Pontiff speaks *ex cathedra* [Lat., "from the chair"], that is, when . . . as pastor and teacher of all Christians in virtue of his highest apostolic authority he defines a doctrine of faith and morals that must be held by the Universal Church, he is empowered, through the divine assistance promised him in blessed Peter, with that infallibility with which the Divine Redeemer willed to endow his Church." Thus: (1) The pope must be speaking formally as earthly head of the Church (*ex cathedra*). (2) He must be speaking on a matter of faith or morals (not governance or discipline). (3) He must clearly intend to bind the whole Church. Indeed, the revised Code of Canon Law (1983) stipulates that "No doctrine is understood to be infallibly defined unless it is clearly established as such" (can. 749.3).

Infallibility is not a personal prerogative of the pope. It would be inaccurate to say, without qualification, that "the pope is infallible." A pope is only infallible, according to Vatican I, when he is in the act of defining a dogma of faith or morals under the conditions specified.

Neither does the dogma of infallibility mean that the pope is somehow above the Church. Vatican I's declaration that the definitions of popes are "irreformable by themselves (*ex sese*) and not by reason of the agreement of the Church (*non autem ex consensu ecclesiae*)" was added to the definition in order to oppose Gallicanism, an attitude prevalent in France that maintained that papal definitions and other decisions did not go into effect unless and until they were subsequently ratified by the Church. On the other hand, the official presenter of the dogma of papal infallibility at Vatican I, Bishop Vincenz Gasser (d. 1879), made it clear during the debate that the consent of the Church can never be lacking with an infallible pronouncement.

Nor did Vatican I intend to say, in using the word "irreformable," that infallible teachings can never change. They are formulated in human language and are expressive of human concepts. As such they are historically conditioned (*Mysterium Ecclesiae*, Congregation for the Doctrine of the Faith, 1973).

Like the doctrine of papal primacy, the dogma of papal infallibility was set in a larger context by the Second Vatican Council. The charism of infallibility can be exercised by the whole college of bishops, in communion with the pope, either when assembled in an ecumenical council or when scattered throughout the world. In principle, the whole Church, not just the pope and the other bishops, is infallible (Dogmatic Constitution on the Church, n. 25).

To be sure, not all of Rome's bishops effectively fulfilled their important ministry. Pope Marcellinus (296–304) complied with imperial orders to hand over copies of Sacred Scripture and to offer incense to the gods, for which he was probably deposed. Liberius (352–66) was a weak pope who at first opposed the excommunication of St. Athanasius (d. 373), the great enemy of Arianism, but then relented under pressure. Vigilius (537–55) vacillated on the teaching of the Council of Chalcedon (451) and was even excommunicated by a synod of African bishops. Honorius I (625–38) became an unwitting adherent of Monothelitism, a heresy that held there is only one (divine) will in Christ, and after his death was formally condemned by the Third Council of Constantinople (680). Certain Western metropolitans (archbishops with some form of jurisdiction over suffragan dioceses in the same geographical area) even in the early Middle Ages sometimes contradicted papal decisions. Prophetic voices, including those of saints like Bernard of Clairvaux (d. 1153) and Catherine of Siena (d. 1380), were also raised against the style and practice of the papal ministry centuries before the Reformation. Medieval theologians and canonists admitted that individual popes had erred in matters of doctrine and even conceded that a pope could deviate from the faith.

Nevertheless, the formula "Rome has never erred" survived and over the course of time came to be understood as "Rome *cannot* err." The legal maxim "The first see is judged by no one" appeared initially in the sixth century and was later interpreted to mean that the pope's teaching authority is supreme. Alas, that principle has been interpreted differently in various periods of church history, including our own. And therein lies much of the drama found in the lives of the popes.

THE POPES

1 PETER, APOSTLE, ST.

Galilean,* d. ca. 64

Peter, Jesus' chief apostle, whom Catholic tradition regards as the first pope, was born in the village of Bethsaida on the Sea of Galilee. (The first succession lists, however, identified Linus, not Peter, as the first pope. Peter was not regarded as the first Bishop of Rome until the late second or early third century.)

That Peter was married and remained so even after becoming a disciple of Jesus is clear from the account of Jesus' healing of Peter's mother-in-law (Mark 1:29–31) and from Paul's reference to the fact that Peter and the other apostles took their wives along on their apostolic journeys (1 Cor. 9:5). The pious belief that the apostles, including Peter, "put away" their wives once

---

*Unless otherwise indicated, the ethnic background or nationality of an individual pope is Italian.

they received the call from Jesus has no historical basis. Rather, it arises from the mistaken and essentially unchristian assumption that celibacy is more virtuous than marriage because sexual intimacy somehow compromises one's total commitment to God and the things of the spirit.

Peter's Singular Role in the New Testament

Catholic tradition has regarded Peter as the first pope because of the special commission he received from Jesus Christ and because of his unique status and central role within the college of the twelve apostles. He was the first disciple to be called by Jesus (Matt. 4:18–19). He served as spokesman for the other apostles (Mark 8:29; Matt. 18:21; Luke 12:41; John 6:67–69). According to the tradition of Paul and Luke (1 Cor. 15:5; Luke 24:34), he was the first to whom the Lord appeared after his Resurrection. Peter is also the most frequently mentioned disciple in all four Gospels and is regularly listed first among the Twelve (Mark 3:16–19; Matt. 10:1–4; Luke 6:12–16). This latter point alongside others is of particular significance because, in the ancient world, respect and authority resided in the first of a line, the first born or the first chosen.

Peter's activities are not reported following the Council of Jerusalem, where he exercised an important, though not necessarily "papal," role in opening the mission of the Church to the Gentiles (Acts 15:7–12). Significantly, it was James, not Peter, who presided over the council and ratified its decisions. However, there is increasing agreement among historians and biblical scholars that Peter did go to Rome and was martyred there (by crucifixion, according to the North African theologian Tertullian [d. ca. 225]). However, there is no evidence that before his death Peter actually served the church of Rome as its first bishop, even though the "fact" is regularly taken for granted by a wide spectrum of Catholics and others. Indeed, there is no evidence that Rome even had a monoepiscopal form of ecclesiastical government until the middle of the second century. By the late second or early third century, however, Peter did become identified in tradition as the first Bishop of Rome. But tradition is not a fact factory. It cannot make something into a historical fact when it is not.

Peter and the Primacy

In the Catholic tradition, the biblical basis for associating the primacy with Peter is embodied in three texts: Matthew 16:13–19; Luke 22:31–32; and John 21:15–19. The fact that Jesus' naming of Peter as the "rock" occurs in three different contexts in these three Gospels raises a question about the original setting of the incident itself. Scholars are not sure if the naming occurred during Jesus' earthly ministry or after the Resurrection with what is called a subsequent "retrojection" into the accounts of Jesus' earthly ministry.

Scholars, however, point to a significant trajectory of images relating to Peter and his ministry as an independent basis for the primatial claims. He is spoken of as a fisherman (Luke 5:10; John 21:1–14), an occupation that, in fact, he and his brother Andrew had practiced; as the shepherd of Christ's sheep (John 21:15–17); as a Christian martyr (John 13:36; 1 Pet. 5:1); as an elder who addresses other elders (1 Pet. 5:1); as a proclaimer of faith in Jesus as the Son of God (Matt. 16:16–17); and, of course, as the rock on which the Church is to be built (Matt. 16:18).

Peter's unique importance as Jesus' first and chief disciple and as the leader of the college of the twelve apostles is clear enough. No pope in history has achieved his status, and it is no accident that none of the more than 260 individuals whom Catholic tradition regards as his successors have taken the name Peter II, including two whose own baptismal names were Peter (John XIV, elected in 983, and Sergius IV, elected in 1009). What can be said, however, about Peter's enduring significance for the papacy and for the Church itself?

Petrine Succession

History provides a long list of popes following Peter, beginning with Linus (ca. 66–ca. 78) and continuing into the twenty-first century and the beginning of the third Christian millennium with such popes as Pius XII (1939–58), John XXIII (1958–63), Paul VI (1963–78), John Paul I (1978), John Paul II (1978–2005), and Benedict XVI (2005–). Catholic tradition regards all of these popes as successors of Peter. In what sense are they his successors, and in what sense are they not?

In at least two of his apostolic roles, Peter could not have had successors: first, as the traditional cofounder with Paul of the Apostolic See of Rome; and, second, as one of the Twelve, who were personal witnesses of the Risen Lord. These are unique, nonrepeatable, and nontransmittable aspects of Peter's apostleship. On the other hand, the bishops of Rome do continue Peter's ministry of evangelizing the world and of maintaining the unity of the whole Church. They also continue to exercise within the college of bishops the same kind of pastoral authority Peter exercised within the original company of the Twelve. The word "continue" is important. The popes do not succeed Peter in the sense of replacing him, as a newly inaugurated president of the United States, for example, replaces his predecessor. The popes carry on Peter's ministry, but Peter as such is irreplaceable. He alone is the rock on which the Church is built.

Petrine Ministry

According to Catholic tradition, the ministry that the Bishop of Rome exercises in his capacity as Vicar of Peter (see below) is a continuation of Peter's own ministry on behalf of the universal Church. As such it is called the Petrine ministry. The ministry of pastoral leadership exercised by Peter in the first part of Acts is the model and the norm for the Petrine ministry exercised by the pope. It involves witnessing to the faith, overseeing the way in which local churches preserve and transmit this faith, providing assistance and encouragement to fellow bishops in their own local and universal ministry of proclaiming and defending the faith, speaking in the name of the bishops and their local churches when the need arises, and articulating the faith of the Church in the name of the whole communion of local churches which together constitute the universal Church.

Vicar of Peter

The most traditional title accorded the pope (from the end of the fourth century) is Vicar of Peter. The Bishop of Rome does not take the place of Peter. Unlike Peter, the pope is neither an apostle nor an eyewitness of the Risen Lord. These are qualities that cannot be transmitted to those who follow. The popes can only continue Peter's ministry by keeping alive the faith that has been handed on to them. The closest English word to "vicar" is "substitute." Like a substitute teacher in a classroom, the pope stands in for Peter, but does not replace him. The pope is Vicar of Christ insofar as he is a bishop, not insofar as he is a pope. The title that captures his distinctive Petrine responsibilities is that of Vicar of Peter. Feast day (with St. Paul): June 29.

2 LINUS, ST.

ca. 66–ca. 78 (67–76 in the Vatican's official list)

Because it was not until the late second or early third century that Catholic tradition came to regard Peter as the first Bishop of Rome, it was Linus, not Peter, who was considered in the earliest succession lists to be the first pope. Very little is known about Linus. Early sources, including Eusebius, claim that Linus held office for about twelve years, but they are not clear about the exact dates or about his exact pastoral role and authority. It should be remembered—contrary to pious Catholic belief—that the monoepiscopal structure of church governance (also known as the monarchical episcopate, in which each diocese was headed by a single bishop) still did not exist in Rome at this time. For almost the entire first Christian millennium the pope was elected by the clergy and people of Rome, since his immediate and primary pastoral office was that of Bishop of Rome.

There is no evidence to support the legend that Linus died as a martyr and was buried on Vatican Hill close to St. Peter, nor for the tradition that he decreed, in keeping with 1 Corinthians 11:1–16, that women should keep their heads covered in church. His name occurs after those of Peter and Paul in the ancient Canon of the Mass. Feast day: September 23.

3 ANACLETUS [CLETUS], ST.

Greek (?), ca. 79–ca. 91
(76–88 in the Vatican's official list)

The name of the second successor of Peter, Anacletus, is really Anencletus, a Greek adjective meaning "blameless." Since it was also a common name for a slave, it may be indicative of his social origins. Anacletus evidently exercised a position of pastoral leadership in Rome. One unconfirmed tradition is that, during his pontificate, he divided Rome into twenty-five parishes. The church historian Eusebius of Caesarea (d. ca. 339) reports that he died in the twelfth year of the Emperor Domitian's reign (81–96). The tradition that he died a martyr is also unattested. His former feast day, April 26, was dropped in the course of Pope Paul VI's reform of the liturgical calendar in 1969.

4 CLEMENT I, ST.

ca. 91–ca. 101 (88–97 in the Vatican's official list)

Also known as Clement of Rome, he is best known for his likely authorship of the letter referred to as *1 Clement,* the most important first-century Christian document outside the New Testament and treated by some in the ancient Church as if it were, in fact, part of the New Testament canon. A second letter attributed to him (*2 Clement*) is not authentic.

The Roman community at this time was probably divided into a number of small house churches scattered throughout the city and its neighboring districts, each presided over by a presbyter (and possibly more than one). There would have been no united and coordinated leadership within the city's Christian community as a whole, but it was otherwise the case in the community's relations with the Christian communities of other cities. One presbyter, like Clement, was charged with corresponding with these other communities and probably also with dispensing aid to those in need.

This first letter of Clement was sent ca. 96 from the church in Rome to the church in Corinth, instructing the Corinthians to reinstate elders (presbyters, or senior priests) who had been improperly deposed and to exile the younger persons who had instigated the rebellion. Significantly, Clement offered no defense for his intervening in the pastoral affairs of the Corinthian church (he had not been invited to do so by the Corinthians), but neither did he appeal to any special Roman privilege. The form of Clement's intervention seems to have been modeled on the relations of the imperial capital of Rome (its Senate and emperor) with its outlying provinces. When some Catholic theologians and historians today suggest that the hierarchical structures of the Church, including the papacy, owe more to the Roman Empire than to Jesus, they do not exaggerate.

There is no historical evidence to support the claim that Clement died a martyr. Clement is mentioned in Eucharistic Prayer I between Cletus (Anacletus) and Sixtus I (ca. 116–ca. 125). Feast day: November 23 (in the West); November 24 or 25 (in the East).

5 EVARISTUS, ST.

Greek, ca. 100–ca. 109
(97–105 in the Vatican's official list)

Evaristus is regarded by Catholic tradition as the fourth successor of Peter. The early succession lists, however, differ about the length of his pontificate and even about his exact place on the list. There is little or no reliable information about him. Specifically, there is no basis for the claim that he died as a martyr and was buried on Vatican Hill near St. Peter. The fact that he is on the early succession lists indicates, at the very least, that he exercised a prominent role of leadership in the Roman church, although not as its only bishop, or overseer. The monoepiscopal structure did not come to Rome until the middle of the second century, with the pontificate of St. Pius I (ca. 142–ca. 155). Feast day: October 26.

6 ALEXANDER I, ST.

ca. 109–ca. 116 (105–115 in the Vatican's official list)

Alexander is regarded by Catholic tradition as the fifth successor of Peter. As in the case of his predecessors, the length of Alexander's pontificate is a matter of guesswork. The estimates of the early sources range from seven to ten years. When information about an early religious figure is sparse to nonexistent, as in this case, pious legend too often fills the vacuum. Thus, the *Liber Pontificalis,* a collection of papal biographies that began to take shape in the sixth century, attributes to Alexander the insertion of the eucharistic institution narrative from the Last Supper into the Canon of the Mass and also repeats a Roman tradition that Alexander was beheaded on the Via Nomentana, a road leading out of Rome. The tradition evidently had confused him with an actual martyr of the same name whose tomb was discovered along that road in 1855. Feast day: May 3.

7 SIXTUS [XYSTUS] I, ST.

ca. 116–ca. 125
(115–125 in the Vatican's official list)

Sixtus I is regarded by Catholic tradition as the sixth successor of Peter; thus the Latin name Sixtus (meaning "sixth"), although he is more correctly known as Xystus. The dates of his pontificate are as uncertain as those of his immediate predecessors. The early sources generally agree that it lasted about ten years. Little or nothing else is known about him. The *Liber Pontificalis* (a collection of papal biographies first compiled in the mid-sixth century) indicates that he was the son of a priest and attributes to him, without historical basis, a decree that sacred vessels should only be touched by clergy. Feast day: April 3.

8 TELESPHOROS, ST.

Greek, ca. 125–ca. 136
(125–136 in the Vatican's official list)

Telesphoros is the only second-century pope whose martyrdom is historically verifiable. Although the exact dates of his pontificate are uncertain, early sources are in agreement that it lasted eleven years. St. Irenaeus (d. ca. 200) notes that Telesphoros always observed Easter on Sunday rather than on whatever day of the week Passover happened to fall (which was the practice of those Christians who were known as the Quartodecimans—the Latin word for "fourteenth"—because they observed Easter on the fourteenth day

of the Jewish month of Nisan). Feast day: January 5 (in
the West); February 22 (in the East).

9 HYGINUS, ST.

Greek, ca. 138–ca. 142
(136–140 in the Vatican's official list)

Hyginus is regarded by Catholic tradition as the eighth
successor of Peter. Estimates of the length of this pontificate range from as many as twelve years to as few
as four (the more credible figure). According to the
Liber Pontificalis (a collection of papal biographies first
compiled in the mid-sixth century), Hyginus was a
Greek from Athens with a background in philosophy.
St. Irenaeus (d. ca. 200) reports that during Hyginus's
pontificate the Gnostic teachers Valentinus (d. ca. 175)
and Cerdo came to Rome from Egypt and Syria, respectively, indicating that Rome was becoming a major Christian center. Hyginus was regarded as a martyr,
but there is no historical evidence to substantiate that
belief or the pious tradition that he was buried on Vatican Hill near St. Peter. Feast day: January 11.

10 PIUS I, ST.

ca. 142–ca. 155 (140–155 in the Vatican's official list)

Pius I was the first of the listed popes to have functioned as the single, or sole, Bishop of Rome. Before his
pontificate, the Roman church seems to have been governed by a council or group of presbyters or presbyter-
bishops. Those regarded by Catholic tradition as popes

before Pius I may simply have been the most prominent members of those governing groups.

The early sources are confused about the dates of this pontificate. Some place Pius I after his successor, Anicetus (ca. 155–ca. 166). Nothing much is known of Pius's pontificate except that the Gnostics Valentinus (d. ca. 175), Cerdo, and Marcion (d. ca. 160) were actively promoting their views in Rome, specifically that the Old Testament had been completely supplanted by the New Testament so that Christianity is in no sense a fulfillment of Judaism, but rather its replacement. It is thought that Pius presided over a synod of presbyters that excommunicated Marcion in July 144. There is no evidence that Pius was martyred or that he was buried on Vatican Hill near St. Peter. Feast day: July 11.

11 ANICETUS, ST.

> Syrian, ca. 155–ca. 166
> (155–166 in the Vatican's official list)

Anicetus was Bishop of Rome at a time when the city was becoming a flourishing center of Christian activity, attracting some of the leading figures of the ancient Church, including the great anti-Gnostic Syrian scholar St. Hegesippus (d. ca. 180) and St. Justin Martyr (d. ca. 165). Although the *Liber Pontificalis* (a collection of papal biographies first compiled in the mid-sixth century) reports that Anicetus forbade clerics to wear long hair, he is perhaps best remembered for his serious but amicable discussions with one of the most revered figures in the early Church, St. Polycarp (d. ca. 155/6), bishop of Smyrna (in present-day Turkey), who had been a disciple of St. John the Evangelist.

Already in his eighties, Polycarp had come to Rome to urge the pope to adopt the common liturgical practice in Asia Minor of observing the feast of Easter, regarded as the Christian Passover, on the fourteenth day of the Jewish month of Nisan (the day of the Jewish Passover), regardless of the day of the week on which it fell. Anicetus denied Polycarp's request, insisting that he felt bound by his predecessors' custom of celebrating the Resurrection every Sunday. The discussion remained friendly, and Anicetus invited Polycarp to preside at the Eucharist. They departed in peace, but Rome and the East continued their separate practices. It was probably Anicetus who erected a memorial shrine for St. Peter on Vatican Hill that was familiar to visitors at the turn of the century (ca. 200). Feast day: April 17.

12 SOTER, ST.

ca. 166–ca. 174 (166–175 in the Vatican's official list)

The most significant development in Soter's pontificate was the introduction of Easter as an annual liturgical feast in Rome. Until this time, the Roman church had no separate feast of Easter, but instead regarded every Sunday as a celebration of the Resurrection. The date agreed upon for the new feast was the Sunday following the fourteenth day of the Jewish month of Nisan (in other words, the Sunday following the day of Passover). This contrasted with a common

Christian practice in Asia Minor of celebrating Easter on the day of Passover itself, no matter what day of the week it fell on. Those who followed this practice were called Quartodecimans (Lat., "fourteenth," for the fourteenth day of Nisan).

The *Liber Pontificalis* (a collection of papal biographies first compiled in the mid-sixth century) reports that Soter ordered nonordained monks not to touch altar cloths or offer incense in church—an indication that pastoral micro-management is not an exclusively modern phenomenon. Although Soter was later venerated as a martyr, there is no evidence that he died a martyr's death. Feast day: April 22.

13 ELEUTHERIUS [ELEUTHERUS], ST.

Greek, ca. 174–ca. 189
(175–189 in the Vatican's official list)

Eleutherius is regarded by Catholic tradition as the twelfth successor of Peter, having served as a deacon (assistant) to Pope Anicetus (ca. 155–ca. 166) before being elected to the papacy himself. In 177 or 178, he received a visit from St. Irenaeus of Lyons (d. ca. 200) bearing a letter from the Christians of Lyons (in southern Gaul, or modern-day France) that set out their highly critical views on Montanism, a new religious movement that was prophesying a speedy end of the world and preaching the need to impose severe ascetical practices upon the Church. Although the historical record is not completely clear, it seems that Eleutherius failed to see the danger of Montanism and declined to pass judgment on its prophetic claims. Eleutherius is first mentioned as a martyr in the somewhat unreliable ninth-century martyrology compiled by St. Ado of Vienne (d. 875). Feast day: May 26.

14 VICTOR I, ST.

African, 189–198

The first African pope, whom St. Jerome (d. ca. 420) identified as the first Latin ecclesiastical writer, Victor is best known for his firm resolution of the controversy over the celebration of Easter. With his urging, synods were held in Rome and in other Christian centers from Gaul (modern-day France) to Mesopotamia (present-day Iraq). Although the great majority sided with the pope, the churches of Asia Minor held fast to their practice of celebrating Easter on the fourteenth day of the Jewish month of Nisan (the day of Passover), whether it fell on Sunday or not. They were called Quartodecimans, after the Latin word for "fourteenth," because of their preference for the fourteenth day of Nisan. By contrast, the Roman church observed Easter on the Sunday following the day of Passover.

When the Quartodecimans, under the leadership of Polycrates, bishop of Ephesus, refused to bend to his will, Victor declared them out of communion (excommunicated) not only with the Roman church, but with the universal Church. His harsh action evoked a storm of protest, even from those who accepted his ruling on Easter. The fact that the churches of Asia

Minor remained in communion with Rome may indicate that he later withdrew the sentence of excommunication. But the incident shows the growing belief of the popes at this time that the Roman church enjoyed some kind of primatial status within the universal Church.

Victor is also the first pope known to have had dealings with the imperial household, supplying the emperor's mistress, herself a Christian, with a list of Christians condemned to the mines of Sardinia and thereby securing their release. Though later venerated as a martyr, there is no evidence that Victor suffered a martyr's death or that he was buried on Vatican Hill near St. Peter. Feast day: July 28.

15 ZEPHRYNUS, ST.

198/9–217 (199–217 in the Vatican's official list)

Although his pontificate lasted more than seventeen years, relatively little is known about Zephrynus except for the sharp criticisms he received, especially from St. Hippolytus (d. ca. 236), a leading and learned Roman presbyter. Hippolytus and others, including the North African theologian Tertullian (d. ca. 225), were frustrated with the pope because of his apparent weakness and vacillation in the face of new challenges to the historic faith from Montanism (a religious movement that was prophesying a speedy end of the world and preaching the need to impose severe ascetical practices upon the Church), Adoptionism (a Christological theory that Jesus was an ordinary human being who became the "adopted" Son of God at his baptism), and Sabellianism (also known as Modalism and Monarchianism, a theory holding that in God there is, in effect, only one divine Person with three different modes or manifestations of divine activity). In the light of the modern emphasis on the papal office as the guardian and defender of orthodoxy, such criticisms are truly remarkable. Early popes like Zephrynus and Eleutherius were accused of actually being too easy on doctrinal dissidents rather than too censorious. Zephrynus may have been buried in his own cemetery near that of Callistus on the Appian Way. Feast day: August 26.

16 CALLISTUS [CALIXTUS] I, ST.

217–222

Callistus is the first pope, after Peter, whose name is commemorated as a martyr in the oldest martyrology of the Roman church, the *Depositio Martyrum* (ca. 354). Much of the information that survives about Callistus comes filtered through the highly derogatory writings of St. Hippolytus (d. ca. 236), a leading and learned Roman presbyter who also had been a persistent critic of Callistus's predecessor, Zephrynus. In his youth Callistus had been a slave of a Christian who set him up in banking, but eventually he became Pope Zephrynus's deacon. Because of Zephrynus's own intellectual and administrative limitations, Callistus exerted enormous influence and was elected to succeed him. Hippolytus, however, refused to accept the election and seems to have sought and received election as bishop by a schismatic group, thereby becoming the Catholic Church's first of thirty-nine antipopes.

Callistus's five-year pontificate was defined in large part by his constant battles with Hippolytus and his faction, who accused the pope of doctrinal deviations (Modalism in particular, the view that in God there is only one divine Person with three modes of activity) and laxity in discipline, especially in regard to readmitting heretics and schismatics. Both charges were unfair. Callistus was clearly not a Modalist, but neither did he support Hippolytus's teaching that the Word (Logos) is a distinct Person, a view the pope regarded as ditheistic (positing two Gods). And Callistus's approach to sinners was actually closer to that of Jesus than to that of the new rigorists in the Church. Although his name appears in the oldest Roman martyrology, it is questionable whether he was, in fact, a martyr. Feast day: October 14.

17 URBAN I, ST.

222–230

Urban had a generally peaceful pontificate, because it fell within the imperial reign of Alexander Severus (222–35), in which there were no persecutions of Christians. The schism in the Roman church provoked by the bitter opposition of St. Hippolytus (d. ca. 236) to Urban's two immediate predecessors, Zephrynus (198/9–217) and Callistus (217–22), continued during Urban's pontificate, albeit in less acute form. However, there is no historical record of the relationship between Urban and Hippolytus. Contrary to pious belief, Urban did not die a martyr's death. According to the fifth-century martyrology of St. Jerome, he is buried in the cemetery of Callistus on the Appian Way. A tomb slab bearing his name in Greek letters has been discovered there. Feast day: May 25.

18 PONTIAN [PONTIANUS], ST.

d. October 235,
pope July 21, 230–September 28, 235

Pontian was the first pope to abdicate the papal office. He did so only because he had been deported by the new, anti-Christian emperor Maximinus Thrax to labor in the mines on the island of Sardinia, known as the "island of death," from which few ever returned alive. Pontian did not want there to be a vacuum of leadership in the Roman church. All except the last few months of his pontificate had been peaceful because the tolerant Emperor Severus was still reigning. After succeeding Severus in March 235, however, Maximinus Thrax abandoned his predecessor's policy of toleration and initiated a violent campaign against Christian leaders. He arrested Pontian and the antipope Hippolytus (d. ca. 236), a strong critic of popes Zephrynus (198/9–217) and Callistus (217–22) and the apparent leader of a schism in the Roman church. Both were imprisoned in Rome and then exiled to Sardinia. According to the fourth-century *Liberian Catalogue*, Pontian abdicated on September 28, 235, the first precisely recorded date in papal history. Neither Pontian nor Hippolytus survived the harsh conditions on Sardinia. A fourth-century martyrology lists Pontian as the first Roman bishop-martyr (after Peter). Feast day (with St. Hippolytus): August 13.

19 ANTERUS, ST.

Greek, November 21, 235–January 3, 236

Because his pontificate was less than two months long (he died a natural death), there is nothing to be said of Anterus except that he was the first pope to be buried in the newly completed papal crypt in the cemetery of Callistus on the Appian Way. Large fragments of the inscription over his tomb have been found there. Anterus's predecessor, Pontian, was also buried in the papal crypt some months later, after his body was returned from the island of Sardinia, where he had died in exile. Feast day: January 3.

20 FABIAN, ST.

January 10, 236–January 20, 250

Fabian was one of the most respected and accomplished popes of the earliest Christian centuries. St. Cyprian of Carthage (d. 258), one of the leading bishops in the contemporary Church, described him as honorable and praised the integrity of his administration. With unusual administrative skill, Fabian reorganized the local clergy, dividing the growing Roman church into seven ecclesiastical districts with a deacon, assisted by a subdeacon and six junior assistants, in charge of each district. He also supervised numerous building projects in the cemeteries and arranged for the bodies of Pope Pontian (d. 235) and the antipope Hippolytus (d. 236) to be returned from their Sardinian exile and buried properly in Rome. Most of Fabian's fourteen-year pontificate was peaceful (two emperors, Gordian III and Philip the Arab, were generally tolerant of the Church), but after Decius ascended to power (249), a new and vicious persecution was initiated. Fabian was arrested and was among the first to die, probably as a result of brutal treatment in prison. Feast day (with St. Sebastian): January 20.

21 CORNELIUS, ST.

March 251–June 253

Cornelius's pontificate was marked by his constant and often bitter battles over the question of the validity of baptism by heretics and schismatics. The Roman practice, upheld and enforced by Cornelius, recognized the validity of such baptisms and did not require the rebaptism of those wishing to enter or be reconciled with the Catholic Church.

It had taken more than a year to elect Cornelius as successor to Fabian. The Roman clergy had postponed the election because of the violent persecution under the emperor Decius. During the interregnum of fourteen months, the Roman church was governed as it had been during the first century of its existence, that is, collegially, with the presbyter Novatian acting as spokesman. The following spring the emperor left Rome to fight the Goths, and the persecution subsided. Novatian fully expected to be elected, but the clergy voted instead for Cornelius, whom Cyprian (d. 258), bishop of Carthage, described as an unambitious priest who had come up through the ranks. Novatian reacted bitterly to the election and had himself ordained a bishop, setting himself up as a rival (antipope) to Cornelius. What was clearly at the basis of Novatian's opposition was Cornelius's readiness to readmit to communion, albeit after suitable penance, those Christians who had lapsed during the persecution.

Novatian tried to persuade the bishops of other Christian centers to accept his own title to the Roman see, and in Rome itself a faction of rigorist clergy and laity refused to recognize Cornelius's authority. However, Cornelius's election was upheld by Cyprian and Dionysius (d. 264/5), bishop of Alexandria. Cyprian also supported Cornelius when, in October 251, he excommunicated Novatian and his followers at a synod in Rome attended by sixty bishops and many presbyters and deacons.

When the new emperor, Gallus, resumed the persecutions in June 252, Cornelius was arrested and deported to Centumcellae (present-day Civitavecchia, the port of Rome). He died there the following June, and his body was later taken back to Rome and buried in the cemetery of Callistus on the Appian Way. Feast day (with St. Cyprian): September 16.

22 LUCIUS I, ST.

June 25, 253–March 5, 254

Almost immediately after his election, Lucius was banished from Rome by the emperor Gallus. His place of exile, like that of his predecessor, may have been Centumcellae (present-day Civitavecchia, the port of Rome). Upon the death of Gallus and the accession of Valerian, who seemed at first favorably disposed to Christians, Lucius managed to make his way back to Rome with other exiled Christians. After his return, he received a congratulatory letter from Cyprian (d. 258), bishop of Carthage. Another of Cyprian's letters to him suggests that Lucius maintained the moderate policy of his predecessor, Cornelius, toward those who had lapsed in time of persecution and who sought reconciliation with the Church. Because he suffered for the faith in exile, Lucius can be regarded as a confessor (the technical name for one who suffers for the faith, short of death). There is no evidence, however, that he died as a martyr. Feast day: March 4.

23 STEPHEN I, ST.

May 12, 254–August 2, 257

Stephen is best known for his theologically important dispute with St. Cyprian (d. 258), bishop of Carthage, over the question of whether those who had been baptized by heretics and schismatics had to be rebaptized upon entrance or return to the Catholic Church. Cyprian held that they had to be rebaptized; Stephen insisted they did not. This dispute, however, had been preceded by two others.

The first clash with Cyprian occurred after two Spanish bishops who had lapsed under persecution went to Rome and persuaded Stephen to restore them to the Church and to their bishoprics. The Spanish churches appealed the pope's decision to Cyprian, who convened a council of North African bishops. The council confirmed the deposition of the two bishops from their sees, but excused Stephen from any blame for his action because he obviously did not have all the facts.

A second clash between Stephen and Cyprian occurred over Bishop Marcian of Arles, who had adopted the rigorist views of the antipope Novatian and was refusing even deathbed reconciliation to Christians who had lapsed in time of persecution. The local bishops of Gaul (modern-day France) had written to Stephen, urging him to depose Marcian. When the pope took no action, the bishops appealed to Cyprian, who urged the pope to depose Marcian and arrange for the election of a new bishop.

The third clash was over the rebaptism of those who had been baptized already by heretics and schismatics. Cyprian, along with most of the churches of North Africa, Syria, and Asia Minor, generally held that the first baptism was invalid, since baptism could only be validly administered within the Church. Stephen represented the tradition of Rome, Alexandria, and Palestine, which held that the first baptism was valid and that a second baptism would be illicit (i.e., sinful). Cyprian ultimately held three synods that supported his position.

With the danger of a major rift in the universal Church looming large, Dionysius (d. 264/5), bishop of Alexandria, himself an opponent of rebaptism, wrote to Stephen, imploring him to adopt a more conciliatory approach. One can only speculate as to how the situation might have deteriorated even further had not Stephen died in the midst of the controversy and had Cyprian himself not been martyred a year later.

These events, however, underscore the growing recognition of the Roman church as a court of appeal, certainly for the churches of Gaul and Spain, and as a church with which other churches are desirous of being in communion. Stephen seems to have been the first pope to have appealed to Matthew 16:18 as the basis of the primacy of the Roman church and its bishop. He died a natural death and was buried in the papal crypt in the cemetery of Callistus on the Appian Way. Feast day: August 2.

24 SIXTUS [XYSTUS] II, ST.

Greek, August 30, 257–August 6, 258

More correctly known as Xystus, Sixtus II is one of the Church's most highly venerated martyrs. He was elected just as the emperor Valerian abandoned his policy of toleration toward Christians, ordering them to participate in state-sponsored religious ceremonies and forbidding them to gather in cemeteries. He managed to avoid personal trouble with the authorities until Valerian issued a second, more severe edict ordering the execution of bishops, priests, and deacons and imposing assorted penalties on laypersons. On August 6, 258, while the pope was seated in his episcopal chair addressing the congregation at a liturgical service in the private (and presumably safe) cemetery of Praetextatus, imperial forces rushed in and seized and beheaded the pope and four deacons.

Before his death, however, Sixtus II successfully devoted his energies to healing the breach between Rome and the churches of North Africa and Asia Minor created by the issue of the rebaptism of those who wished to enter the Church and, in particular, by the intransigent approach taken by his predecessor, Stephen I. Although he too upheld the Roman policy of accepting the validity of baptisms administered by heretics and schismatics, he restored friendly relations with St. Cyprian (d. 258), bishop of Carthage, and the estranged churches of Asia Minor. The name of Sixtus II was included in the Eucharistic Prayer, or Canon of the Mass, situated between those of Popes Clement and Cornelius. Feast day: August 6.

25 DIONYSIUS, ST.

July 22, 260–December 26, 268

Dionysius (also known as Dionysius of Rome, perhaps to distinguish him from Dionysius [d. 264/5], bishop of Alexandria) was one of the most important popes of the third century because of his organizational and charitable activities and his clarification of the Church's doctrine of the Trinity. His election to the papacy had been delayed for nearly two full years because of the emperor Valerian's severe persecution of Christians, which included the execution of many presbyters. During that period, the Roman church was governed by the remaining presbyters (all seven deacons had been martyred along with Sixtus II). Not until word was received that Valerian had died in captivity in Edessa (in modern-day Turkey) did the presbyters consider it safe to hold an election.

Some Christians in Alexandria had written to Pope Dionysius to complain about their bishop's views on the Trinity, charging that he separated the Son from the Father by speaking of the Son as a creature and by refusing to affirm that the Son is of the same divine essence as the Father (doctrinal aberrations known as Sabellianism and Subordinationism). Dionysius convened a synod in Rome in 260 that struck a fine balance between the need to preserve the distinction between the three divine Persons, on the one hand, and the need to preserve their unity and equality, on the other. Contrary to one tradition, Dionysius was not a martyr. He is buried in the papal crypt in the cemetery of Callistus on the Appian Way. Feast day: December 26.

26 FELIX I, ST.

January 5, 269–December 30, 274

Felix I is one of the least known of the popes. The only matter for which he has received any attention from historians concerns a letter he received from a synod in Antioch announcing its decision to depose Bishop Paul of Samosata for his heretical teachings on the Trinity. But even this letter affords Felix only the weakest of footholds on historical durability because it was addressed originally to Felix's predecessor, Dionysius, who died before it reached Rome. In his reply to the letter, Felix seems to have accepted the synod's decision and recognized the new bishop. When the deposed Paul refused to vacate the premises, the local church leaders appealed to the emperor Aurelian (and not to the pope), who ordered the premises to be handed over to "those with whom the bishops of Italy and of Rome were in communication." Contrary to one tradition, Felix did not die a martyr. He is buried in the papal crypt in the cemetery of Callistus on the Appian Way. Feast day: May 30.

27 EUTYCHIAN, ST.

January 4, 275–December 7, 283

No reliable information about Eutychian or his pontificate (which occurred wholly within a period of peace) survived the devastation wrought by the emperor Diocletian's persecution of the Church beginning in 303. It is conjectured that the Roman church may have flourished under him because of the expansions of its official cemeteries undertaken at the time. We do know that Eutychian is the last pope to be buried in the papal crypt in the cemetery of Callistus on the Appian Way, where fragments of his epitaph, in ill-formed Greek letters, were discovered. The tradition that he died a martyr is without foundation, however. Feast day: December 7.

28 CAIUS [GAIUS], ST.

December 17, 283–April 22, 296

The pontificate of Caius, more accurately known as Gaius, occurred during a continued period of peace when the Roman church seems to have consolidated its position. Although he was in office for more than twelve years, there is no reliably specific information about his pontificate. By the time of his death, the papal crypt in the cemetery of Callistus must have been full, because he was buried in a section nearby. Fragments of his epitaph, in Greek letters, were discovered there in the nineteenth century. The first letter of his name was clearly a gamma ("G"). Pope Urban VIII transported his body to the church of St. Caius (San Caio) in Rome in 1631. After the church's destruction in 1880, the pope's remains were placed in a private chapel of the Barberini princes. Feast day: April 22.

29 MARCELLINUS, ST.

June 30, 296–October 25, 304

During the Diocletian persecution launched in 303, Marcellinus complied with imperial orders to hand over copies of Sacred Scripture and other sacred books and to offer incense to the gods. Some historians think that he was deposed or abdicated before his death. For a time, his name was actually omitted from the official list of popes.

There is little reliable information about him. On February 23, 303, the emperor Diocletian issued his first edict against the Christians, ordering the destruction of churches, the handing over of sacred books, and the offering of sacrifice to the gods by those attending courts of law. Sometime around May of that same year, Marcellinus seems to have complied with the second and the third items. It is not clear when, and if, Marcellinus either voluntarily abdicated his office or was formally deposed. The *Annuario Pontificio*, an official Vatican publication, identifies the date of his termination from office with his date of death (October 25, 304). His actions, however, would have automatically disqualified him from the priesthood and, therefore, from the papacy as well, as of about May 303. If he was deposed or voluntarily abdicated, we have no date for either event.

Because of various reports of his execution by the emperor after allegedly repenting of his actions, Marcellinus came to be venerated as a martyr and his name was included in the ancient Roman Canon of the Mass. However, he is not mentioned in the martyrology of St. Jerome or in the Gelasian Sacramentary. Feast day (with St. Peter, exorcist and martyr): June 2.

30 MARCELLUS I, ST.

> *November/December 306–January 16, 308*
> *(May 27 or June 26, 308–January 16, 309,*
> *in the Vatican's official list)*

Marcellus is best known for his severe attitude toward those Christians who had lapsed in time of persecution. There is some confusion, however, about his real identity and the dates of his pontificate. Some have confused him with his predecessor, Marcellinus (Marcellus is not mentioned, for example, in Eusebius of Caesarea's history of the Church), and the *Annuario Pontificio,* an official Vatican publication, gives his dates as May/June 308–January 16, 309. Whatever the case, he seems to have governed the Roman church during the period between Marcellinus's death in 304 and the election of Eusebius (not Eusebius of Caesarea) in 310.

Because of the losses suffered during the Diocletian persecution and the internal divisions it created within the Roman church itself, the election of a successor to Marcellinus was delayed for more than three and a half years. Marcellus, a leading presbyter during Marcellinus's pontificate and the one who probably held the church together during the intervening period, was elected. However, the severe penances he imposed on lapsed Christians provoked a backlash in the church. There was public disorder and even bloodshed. So serious did the situation become that the emperor Maxentius banished him from the city for the sake of public peace. Marcellus died shortly thereafter. His body was later brought back to Rome and buried in the private cemetery of St. Priscilla. Feast day: January 16.

31 EUSEBIUS, ST.

*Greek, April 18–October 21, 310 (April 18, 309–August 17,
309 or 310, in the Vatican's official list)*

Eusebius's exceedingly brief pontificate was completely dominated by the issue of the reconciliation
of those who had compromised their faith during the
Diocletian persecution (they were known as *lapsi*, "the
lapsed"). Eusebius adopted a pastoral approach, offering full reconciliation to those who repented of their
sin and performed an appropriate penance. He was
condemned by a faction, this time under the leadership of Heraclius, for not being severe enough. The
internal discord within the Christian community was
so bitter and so disruptive that the emperor Maxentius
once again intervened and deported both the pope
and Heraclius to Sicily. Eusebius died soon thereafter.
His body was brought back to Rome and buried in the
cemetery of Callistus on the Appian Way. Feast day:
August 17.

32 MELCHIADES [MILTIADES], ST.

African (?), July 2, 311–January 11, 314

Also known as Miltiades, Melchiades was Bishop of
Rome when the emperor Constantine granted favored status to the Church via the Edict of Milan (313).
Although the *Liber Pontificalis*, a collection of papal
biographies that began to take shape in the sixth century, identifies him as an African, it is more likely that
he was a Roman.

Even before the Edict of Milan (also known as the Edict of Constantine), the emperor Maxentius had promulgated an Edict of Toleration at Nicomedia on April 30, 311, and later ordered the return of church lands and buildings that had been confiscated during the Diocletian persecution. On October 28, 312, the emperor Constantine defeated his brother-in-law Maxentius at the Milvian Bridge and then conquered Rome itself. The following year he and his coemperor in the East, Licinius, granted religious toleration to everyone and restored all remaining confiscated property to Christians.

An incident in North Africa otherwise defined Melchiades' pontificate. Caecilian was consecrated bishop of Carthage in 311. He was immediately rejected by the rigorist party, which opposed readmission of those who had compromised their faith under persecution. Caecilian had supported the more tolerant approach of the previous bishop of Carthage. The rigorists thereupon consecrated a rival bishop, Majorinus, who was soon succeeded by Donatus. The rigorists appealed to the emperor Constantine to mediate the dispute and he, in turn, asked Melchiades to hear the case and to report to him. Melchiades convened a synod, meeting at the Lateran Palace, which rendered a verdict in favor of Caecilian, and excommunicated Donatus. At the same time, Melchiades offered full communion to other North African bishops, allowing them to retain their episcopal sees. The Donatists were bitterly resentful of the verdict and appealed once again to Constantine, who summoned a council of representatives from all the Western provinces to meet at Arles on August 1, 314. Melchiades died several months before the council actually met, but it is significant that the emperor, in calling the council, did not regard the pope's decision as final and that neither Melchiades nor his successor took exception to the emperor's action. Melchiades was buried somewhere in the cemetery of Callistus on the Appian Way. Feast day: December 10.

33 SYLVESTER [SILVESTER] I, ST.

January 31, 314–December 31, 335

In spite of the length of Sylvester I's pontificate (twenty-two years) and the importance of the Constantinian period in which he served, the pope seems to have made little or no lasting impact on the Church or on the papacy itself. Indeed, it is what he did not do as pope that is more significant than what he did do.

Constantine, who occasionally assumed the title "bishop of external affairs," called a special council of some 130 bishops at Arles in August 314 to hear another appeal from the Donatists, who were contesting the consecration of Caecilian as bishop of Carthage. (The Donatists were rigorist opponents of readmitting to the Church those who had compromised their faith during the Diocletian persecution.) Significantly, the emperor did not convene the council in Rome, nor did he appoint the Bishop of Rome to preside over it. When the council ended, however, it transmitted its decisions to him in a letter that acknowledged his primacy over the West (although not over the whole

Church) and asked him to circulate the decisions to the other churches.

Also during Sylvester's pontificate, the first ecumenical council, consisting of some 250 bishops, was held at Nicaea, the emperor's summer residence (in modern northwest Turkey), in July 325. This was the council that first defined the divinity of Jesus Christ, teaching that he is of the same being, or substance (*homoousios*), as God the Father (against the Arians, who held that Jesus Christ was the greatest of creatures, but not equal to God). And yet, significantly, the pope played no part in the proceedings of this ecumenical council.

Sylvester was buried in the private cemetery of St. Priscilla on the Via Salaria, but his remains (perhaps only his head) seem to have been moved by Pope Paul I in 762 to the church of San Silvestro in Capite within the city walls. Feast day: December 31.

34 MARK [MARCUS], ST.

January 18–October 7, 336

During his exceedingly brief pontificate, Mark saw the tide turn strongly against the orthodox teaching of the Council of Nicaea (325) on the divinity of Jesus Christ. Although the emperor Constantine had been a vigorous supporter of the council's teaching against Arianism (which held that Jesus Christ was the greatest of creatures, but not equal to God), he wavered under the influence of his Arian half sister, Constantia. A few months before Mark's election, St. Athanasius (d. 373), bishop of Alexandria, was deposed by the Council of Tyre and forced into exile to the city of Trier. Other orthodox bishops were also deposed at the same time. Arius himself would have been rehabilitated had he not died suddenly. There is no evidence, however, that Pope Mark played any role at all in these developments or in their immediate aftermath. Mark was buried in the cemetery of Balbina on the Via Ardeatina, in a basilica that was probably built under his direction. Feast day: October 7.

35 JULIUS I, ST.

February 6, 337–April 12, 352

Julius I is best known for his forceful defense of the Council of Nicaea's teaching on the divinity of Jesus Christ (325) and of those Eastern bishops, including especially St. Athanasius of Alexandria (d. 373), who remained faithful to that teaching in the face of determined opposition, even to the point of deposition from office and exile. When the emperor Constantine died in 337, the orthodox bishops were allowed to return to their dioceses. The Arian bishops, however, appealed to Julius to prevent this and to recognize Athanasius's replacement in Alexandria. Julius rejected their request, having already offered support and protection to the orthodox bishops.

After the second expulsion of Athanasius from Alexandria in 339, Julius convened a synod in Rome, in June 341, which exonerated the orthodox bishops of doctrinal errors attributed to them by the Arians. It is significant that Julius justified his intervention not on the basis of the Petrine primacy, to which later popes would appeal, but on the basis of ecclesiastical custom and the collegiality of the episcopate. The following summer the Arian bishops met and adopted a creed that ostentatiously omitted the language of Nicaea that the Son is "one in being with the Father." Julius thereupon asked the two emperors to convene a general council of East and West at Sardica (modern Sofia, Bulgaria) in 343. (Julius himself did not attend the council.) The Easterners, however, withdrew when the Western bishops insisted on seating Athanasius and other bishops who had been deposed in the East. The council proceeded without them, reaffirming the validity of Athanasius's claim to the see of Alexandria and ratifying the teaching of the Council of Nicaea.

We know little about the remainder of Julius's pontificate. He was buried in the cemetery of Calepodius on the Via Aurelia. Feast day: April 12.

36 LIBERIUS

May 17, 352–September 24, 366

Liberius is the first pope not to be listed among the saints and is generally regarded as a weak pope. Liberius was elected to the papacy at a time when pro-Arian bishops enjoyed a dominant position in the East and when the pro-Arian emperor Constantius II, now the sole emperor, was putting increasing pressure on the Western bishops to join in the condemnation of

Athanasius, bishop of Alexandria. Athanasius, whom Liberius supported, had become the primary symbol of Nicene orthodoxy, that is, of support for the teaching of the Council of Nicaea (325) that Jesus Christ is "one in being with the Father" and not simply the greatest of creatures, as the Arians held.

Under pressure from the pro-Arian bishops and lacking the strength of character of his predecessor, Liberius asked Constantius II to convene a council at Aquileia to settle the dispute regarding Athanasius and the see of Alexandria. The emperor did hold a synod there and then at Arles. Responsive to the imperial will, both assemblies reaffirmed the condemnation of Athanasius. The papal legates also agreed to the decision. The pope was appalled by the weakness of his own envoys and demanded a general council to uphold not simply Athanasius, but the Council of Nicaea itself. But when the council met in Milan in October 355, the emperor's will again prevailed. Liberius continued to resist but was sent into harsh exile in Thrace and eventually accepted the condemnation of Athanasius as well as the ambiguous first Formula of Sirmium (351), which omitted the Nicene language "one in being with the Father," but did not explicitly reject it. He also personally submitted to the emperor. He was then allowed to return to Rome, but forced to rule for a time with the antipope Felix II (d. 365), who had been elected during his absence. (However, riots broke out and Felix withdrew to the suburbs.) Only after the death of the emperor in 361 did Liberius return to orthodoxy and make an effort to restore the Nicene faith to the universal Church.

Liberius was commemorated on September 23 in the fifth-century martyrology of St. Jerome, but his name does not appear in subsequent liturgical calendars. Later tradition remembered him as a betrayer of the faith. Feast day: July 29.

37 DAMASUS I, ST.

ca. 304–84, pope October 1, 366–December 11, 384

One of the most aggressive advocates of the primacy of Rome in the early Church, Damasus promoted the cult of martyrs by restoring and decorating their tombs with his own marble inscriptions and authorized his secretary, St. Jerome (d. ca. 420), to compose a new Latin translation of the New Testament (later known as the Vulgate) based on the original Greek.

Born in Rome, the son of a priest, Damasus was ordained a deacon and accompanied Pope Liberius into exile in 355. He soon returned to Rome, however, and was in the service for a time of the antipope Felix II. After Liberius was allowed to return from exile, he and Damasus reconciled. After Liberius died, a bitter and violent controversy erupted over the choice of a successor. Bloody fighting occurred between those loyal to Liberius and their candidate, Ursinus, and those loyal to Felix II and Damasus. Damasus dispatched his own forces to attack Ursinus's supporters, who had taken refuge in the Liberian Basilica (now St. Mary Major). A contemporary historian reported that some 137 died in the battle.

Although Damasus had badly blotted his ecclesiastical copybook, he enjoyed much favor with the court and the aristocracy, especially women of wealth. Roman gossips nicknamed him "the matrons' ear-tickler." His grand lifestyle and lavish hospitality endeared him to upper-class pagan families. At the same time, he was relentless in opposing heresies and other dissident movements in the Church. He was harsh in his repression of Arianism and achieved condemnations of Apollinarianism (which denied that Jesus had a human soul) and Macedonianism (which denied the divinity of the Holy Spirit) at successive Roman synods.

Damasus was tireless, in fact, in promoting the primacy of Rome, referring to it frequently as "the Apostolic See" and insisting that the test of a creed's orthodoxy is papal approval. He was buried in a church he had built on the Via Ardeatina, but his body was later moved to another of his churches, that of San Lorenzo in Damaso. Feast day: December 4.

38 SIRICIUS, ST.

December 384–November 26, 399 (December 15 or 22 or 29, 384, in the Vatican's official list)

Siricius was the first pope to issue decretals, that is, legally binding directives formulated in the style of imperial edicts. The oldest surviving decretal, dated February 11, 385, was addressed to Himerius, bishop of Tarragona, in response to fifteen questions on matters of church discipline. It begins with the claim that the Apostle Peter is present in the Bishop of Rome and then proceeds to offer directives on such items as the readmission of heretics to the Church (they were not to be rebaptized), the requirement of celibacy for priests and deacons, and penitential discipline. Siricius asked that these decrees be circulated to churches in the neighboring provinces of Africa, Spain, and Gaul (modern-day France).

Siricius was elected to office unanimously in spite of the candidacy of the antipope Ursinus. The emperor Valentinian II was delighted with the show of support for Siricius and officially confirmed his election, perhaps to ward off any residual opposition from the supporters of Ursinus. Although Siricius was as much opposed to heresies and other dissident movements as his predecessor, Damasus, he urged lenient treatment of those who repented. Although honored as a saint in earlier centuries, his name was omitted from the first edition of the Roman Martyrology (1584) because of his personal conflicts with St. Jerome, in whose expulsion from Rome he had concurred, and St. Paulinus of Nola (d. 431), who complained of the pope's haughtiness. His name was added to the martyrology in 1748 by Pope Benedict XIV. Feast day: November 26.

39 ANASTASIUS I, ST.

November 27, 399–December 19, 401

Best known for his condemnation of the great third-century theologian Origen (d. ca. 254), with whose writings he was not even familiar, Anastasius was also the father of his own successor, Innocent I. Those who disliked his predecessor, Siricius, approved of him, namely, St. Jerome (d. ca. 420), who still had a circle of influential friends in Rome, and St. Paulinus of Nola (d. 431), both of whom thought Anastasius more sympathetic than Siricius to the practice of strict asceticism in the Church. When the African bishops, for example, asked the pope to relax the ban on Donatist clergy returning to the Church because of the shortage of priests, Anastasius wrote to the Council of Carthage (401) and urged the bishops to continue their struggle against the heresy. Anastasius was buried in the cemetery of Pontian on the Via Portuensis. Feast day: December 19.

40 INNOCENT I, ST.

December 22, 401–March 12, 417

One of the early Church's staunchest defenders of the prerogatives of the Apostolic See in matters of doctrine and ecclesiastical discipline, Innocent I was actually the son of Anastasius I. This is the first instance of a son succeeding his father to the papacy.

As the Western empire was buckling under the relentless onslaughts of the migrating Germanic tribes, Innocent asserted papal claims with ever greater frequency and emphasis. He laid down laws for churches (all in the West, however) regarding the Canon of the Mass, Eucharistic Prayer, the sacraments of Penance, Extreme Unction, and Confirmation, and the canon of Sacred Scripture (he excluded several apocryphal books).

Innocent also exercised his authority in the North African churches' efforts against Pelagianism, a heretical movement that held that one can be saved by human effort alone without the aid of divine grace. Two African councils had reaffirmed the condemnation of Pelagius (originally issued in 411), following an effort at the Palestinian synod at Diapolis (415) to pardon him. The bishops, out of deference to the pope, asked him, in 416, to add his own condemnation to theirs. In one of three letters written in reply, the pope praised the African bishops for referring the matter to him (when, in fact, they had not). He appealed to an ancient (but hardly unequivocal or consistent) tradition that bishops everywhere should submit disputed matters of faith to Peter and his successors. Contrary to the pious belief, however, that Christ conferred supreme teaching authority on Peter and through him to every successor, Innocent I was really the first pope to make this claim so clearly.

Midway through his pontificate, Innocent was faced with another kind of pastoral challenge: the siege of Rome by Alaric the Visigoth, with attendant famine and despair throughout the city. In 410 he led a delegation to see the emperor Honorius at Ravenna in order to arrange a truce. The negotiations failed, and Alaric stormed and sacked Rome on August 24, 410, while Innocent was away. He did not return to the city until 412. After his death five years later, he was buried in the same cemetery as his father, Anastasius I, on the Via Portuensis. Feast day: July 28.

41 ZOSIMUS, ST.

Greek, March 18, 417–December 26, 418

Temperamentally impulsive, politically inept, and culturally unprepared for the office, Zosimus was a presbyter who had been recommended to Innocent I by St. John Chrysostom (d. 407), the deposed and exiled bishop of Constantinople. Unfamiliar with Western ways, as pope Zosimus appointed a maverick bishop, Patroclus of Arles (who may have had a hand in manipulating the papal election), as metropolitan of Arles, with full authority to consecrate all bishops of the provinces of Vienne and the two Narbonnes and to decide all cases not subject to Roman review (making him, in effect, papal vicar of Gaul). The pope ignored the subsequent protests from bishops and clergy alike, taking his cue always from Patroclus himself.

Zosimus's handling of matters in North Africa was even worse. He reopened the question of the condemnation of Pelagius and his disciple Celestius. After reading Pelagius's profession of faith sent originally to Innocent I (but arriving after Innocent's death) and after a personal meeting with Celestius in Rome, he wrote to the African bishops to inform them that both men had cleared themselves and to reproach the bishops for having acted in haste against them. The African bishops, including St. Augustine (d. 430), were outraged. They firmly informed the pope that his predecessor's decision must stand. Zosimus backed off. After another council at Carthage in 418 and at the insistence of Augustine, Zosimus addressed a lengthy document (known as the *Epistola Tractoria*) to the bishops of East and West in which he condemned the Pelagians and their teachings.

Zosimus died in 418 and was buried in the basilica of San Lorenzo outside the walls on the road to Tivoli. The ninth-century martyrology of Ado was the first to list him as a saint, a title that in these early centuries seemed to be attached automatically to virtually every pope, without regard for evidence of the special sanctity of their lives. Feast day: December 26.

42 BONIFACE I, ST.

December 28, 418–September 4, 422
(December 28 or 29, 418, in the Vatican's official list)

A dedicated opponent of Pelagianism (which held that salvation can be attained by human effort alone without the aid of grace) and a vigorous advocate of papal authority, Boniface I is the author of the axiom *Roma locuta est; causa finita est* ("Rome has spoken; the cause is finished").

Almost immediately after the burial of Zosimus, the deacons of the Roman church along with a few presbyters barricaded themselves in the Lateran Basilica and elected Eulalius, Zosimus's chief deacon, who was probably also a Greek. The next day the great majority of the presbyters and many laypersons assembled in the Basilica of Theodora and elected the aged and frail presbyter Boniface, who was himself the son of a priest. On the day after that, both were consecrated separately. Boniface had many friends and supporters in Rome and at court, including the emperor's sister. The emperor convened a council at Spoleto on June 13, 419, to finally decide the matter. During the deliberations he required both Boniface and Eulalius to leave Rome. Boniface complied, but Eulalius refused. This caused civil disorder in Rome and infuriated the emperor, who ordered Eulalius banished from the city and declared Boniface the lawful bishop.

Boniface proceeded to undo the damage created by his predecessor, Zosimus, in establishing a papal vicariate in Arles. He restored metropolitan rights to Marseilles, Vienne, and Narbonne. When Boniface died, the antipope Eulalius made no effort to claim the see. Feast day: September 4.

43 CELESTINE I, ST.

September 10, 422–July 27, 432

Among the events that occurred during Celestine's pontificate was the third ecumenical council of the Church, held at Ephesus in 431. Significantly, the emperor Theodosius II, not the pope, convened the council, and the pope himself did not attend. He sent three legates to represent the interests of the Roman church. The acts of the council were not submitted to the pope for his approval, but in subsequent letters he expressed his satisfaction with its accomplishments.

After his unanimous election as Bishop of Rome following his term as chief deacon (archdeacon) of the church, Celestine confiscated the churches of the

large Novatianist community in Rome (who favored
the rebaptism of individuals who were originally baptized by heretics or schismatics) and began the restoration of the Julian Basilica (Santa Maria in Trastevere),
which had been severely damaged in the sack of the
city by the Visigoth Alaric in 410. Like his predecessor Zosimus (417–18), he got into difficulty with the
bishops of North Africa for meddling in their affairs.
He ordered the rehabilitation of the priest Apiarius,
who had been excommunicated by his bishop. However, at a council in Carthage (ca. 426), the priest admitted his guilt and the papal legate was forced to disavow
him. This gave the African bishops an opportunity to
chastise the pope for failing to respect their autonomy
and for entering into communion with persons they
had excommunicated, a practice, they reminded him,
that was expressly forbidden by the Council of Nicaea
(325).

   Celestine nonetheless continued to press the point
that, as Bishop of Rome and successor of Peter, he had
pastoral authority beyond the Roman church and, indeed, over the universal Church, in the East as well
as the West. Toward the end of his pontificate, he
plunged into the debate between Nestorius of Constantinople (d. ca. 451) and St. Cyril of Alexandria (d.
444) concerning the relationship between the divinity and the humanity of Jesus Christ. Nestorius held
that there were two distinct persons in Christ and that
Mary was the mother of the human person, Jesus of
Nazareth, and not of the divine Person, the Son of
God. Cyril held, on the contrary, that there is a fun-

damental personal unity in Christ, in such wise that Mary can be called the Mother of God (Gk. *Theotokos*). When both individuals submitted their views to Celestine, he received them as an appeal from the East to Rome. With Cyril's encouragement, the pope condemned Nestorius's position and demanded that Nestorius recant within ten days or be excommunicated. Meanwhile the Byzantine emperor Theodosius II convened a general (ecumenical) council at Ephesus to settle the matter. Nestorius was excommunicated.

Celestine was buried in the private cemetery of Priscilla on the Via Salaria. His mausoleum was decorated with paintings recalling the ecumenical council at Ephesus, which he neither convened nor attended. Feast day: April 6.

44 SIXTUS [XYSTUS] III, ST.

July 31, 432–August 19, 440

Also known as Xystus and himself the son of a priest, Sixtus III acted as peacemaker in the aftermath of the Council of Ephesus (431) and, aided by funds from the imperial family, directed a major rebuilding program in Rome in the aftermath of the invasion by the Visigoths under Alaric in 410. True to his Petrine ministry of maintaining the unity of the Church by healing wounds of division and by building bridges between alienated groups, Sixtus reached out to John of Antioch (d. 441), whom the ecumenical Council of Ephesus (431) had deposed and excommunicated. Sixtus asked only that John accept the teaching of

Ephesus and disavow Nestorius (who held that there are two persons in Jesus Christ, one human and one divine, and that Mary is only the mother of the human person, not the mother of God). As part of his program to repair the damage wrought by the Visigoths, Sixtus III rebuilt the Lateran baptistery into its present octagonal form. He was buried somewhere in the cemetery of St. Lawrence. Four centuries passed before a cult developed in his honor. The name of Sixtus III first appeared in the ninth-century martyrology of Ado. Feast day: March 28.

45 LEO I, "THE GREAT," ST.

September 29, 440–November 10, 461

Elected to the papacy while still only a deacon and while away from Rome on a diplomatic mission in Gaul (modern-day France), Leo is one of only two popes in all of church history to have been called "the Great" (the other was Gregory I [590–604]). He was a strong advocate of papal authority and of the teachings of the Council of Chalcedon (451) on the humanity and divinity of Jesus Christ. So forcefully articulated were Leo's claims for the pope's universal and supreme authority over the Church, in fact, that his own pontificate constitutes a major turning point in the history of the papacy.

Leo himself exercised firm control over the bishops of Italy, including those of Milan and the northern region, enforcing uniformity of pastoral practice, correcting abuses, and resolving disputes. In replying to appeals from the bishops of Spain to help in their fight against Priscillianism, a heresy that regarded the human body as evil, he laid down precise instructions for action. Although ecclesiastical Africa was traditionally jealous of its pastoral autonomy, especially against any encroachments upon it by Rome, Leo's rulings on irregularities in African elections and other regional conflicts were eagerly sought after and embraced.

The East was much less disposed than the West to accept Leo's papal claims. In June 449, for example, he sent an important letter (*Letter 28*), or *Tome*, to Bishop Flavian of Constantinople condemning the Monophysite teaching that in Christ there is only one divine nature, Christ's human nature having been absorbed by the divine. The emperor Theodosius II called a council at Ephesus in August (not to be confused with the ecumenical Council of Ephesus, held in 431). Pope Leo was represented by three delegates who had with them a copy of the *Tome*, which Leo expected to be read aloud and approved. But the council disregarded it and condemned Bishop Flavian. Leo refused to recognize the council, referring to it as a "robber council." Two years later another ecumenical council reversed the decisions made at the "robber council" of Ephesus and endorsed the Christological teaching of Leo and others; namely, that in Jesus Christ there are two natures, one divine and one human, hypostatically united in one divine Person. Leo's *Tome* was respectfully received and approved as a standard of orthodoxy and an expression of the "voice of Peter."

Leo is also celebrated for his courageous personal confrontation with Attila the Hun near Mantua in 452, when the warrior was laying waste to northern Italy and preparing to move south toward Rome. Heading a delegation from the Roman Senate, Leo persuaded Attila to withdraw beyond the Danube. Upon his death, Leo was buried in the portico, or porch, of St. Peter's. His body was moved to the interior of the basilica in 688. He was made a Doctor of the Church in 1754. Feast day: November 10 (in the West); February 18 (in the East).

46 HILARUS [HILARY], ST.

November 19, 461–February 29, 468

The pontificate of Hilarus was generally uneventful. Having served as Leo the Great's archdeacon and one of his representatives at the "robber council" of Ephesus in 449, from which he barely escaped unharmed because of his support of Flavian, the patriarch of Constantinople, Hilarus attempted to follow in his predecessor's footsteps, but he never quite approximated his stature. Unlike Leo, he had almost no dealings with the Church in the East except for a decretal he may have circulated to Eastern bishops confirming the ecumenical councils of Nicaea (325), Ephesus (431), and Chalcedon (451) and Leo's *Tome,* condemning various heresies, and reasserting Roman primacy. He did not hesitate, however, to exercise his authority in the ecclesiastical affairs of Spain and Gaul; his letters indicate how dependent those bishops had become on Rome. Hilarus founded a monastery at St. Lawrence Outside the Walls, where he was buried. Feast day: February 28.

47 SIMPLICIUS, ST.

March 3, 468–March 10, 483

Simplicius's pontificate saw the last of the Western emperors, Romulus Augustulus, succeeded by a German general as king of Italy and the establishment of barbarian kingdoms in the rest of the Western empire. It is ironic that his pontificate, coming so soon after Leo the Great's, was also marked by a further erosion of papal prestige and influence in the East. Faithful to Leo's firm opposition to the Council of Chalcedon's canon 28, granting Constantinople ecclesiastical status roughly equivalent to Rome's, Simplicius resisted the effort by the patriarch Acacius (d. 489) to honor the canon. He also strongly opposed the new concessions being made jointly by emperor and patriarch to Monophysitism, the heresy, condemned by the Council of Chalcedon (451), that denied that Christ had a human as well as a divine nature. Until 479 his letters show him struggling unsuccessfully to influence developments. After 479, however, Acacius deliberately kept the pope in the dark, and his already minimal influence declined even further. Simplicius died after a long illness and was buried near Leo the Great in the portico, or porch, of St. Peter's. Feast day: March 10.

48 FELIX III (II), ST.

March 13, 483–March 1, 492

Felix III (so identified because, at the time of his election, the antipope Felix II [355–65] had not yet been removed from an early official list of popes) is famous for his rejection of the *Henoticon* and for his excommunication of Acacius, the patriarch of Constantinople who supported it. The *Henoticon*, developed jointly in 482 by the emperor Zeno and Acacius, was a statement attempting to reconcile Chalcedonian orthodoxy (which taught that in Christ there are two natures, one human and one divine, united in one divine Person) and Monophysitism (which denied that Christ had a human as well as a divine nature).

The son of a priest, Felix III was himself a widower with at least two children, from one of whom Pope Gregory the Great (590–604) was descended. Immediately after his election, Felix demanded the deposition from office of the new Monophysite bishop of Alexandria and the observance of the teaching of the Council of Chalcedon (451) on the two natures of Christ. He reproached Acacius, the patriarch of Constantinople, for supporting the new bishop of Alexandria and the *Henoticon* and summoned him to Rome to defend himself. But the pope's legates did their job badly, failing to protest when the Monophysite bishop's name was included in the Canon, or Eucharistic Prayer, of the Mass, thereby giving the impression that Rome actually approved of him. Upon the return of the legates to Rome, the pope excommunicated them as well as

Acacius at a synod held in 484 and dispatched his sentence of excommunication upon Acacius to Constantinople by special messenger. The only immediate effect the excommunication had was on the pope himself. His name was removed from the prayers of the Mass in Constantinople. The longer-term effect on the Church was more serious. It precipitated the Acacian Schism, which lasted for thirty-five years (484–519) and was the first serious breach of unity between East and West. Felix was buried in a family crypt in St. Paul's Basilica, close to his father, his wife, and his children. Feast day: March 1.

49 GELASIUS I, ST.

African, March 1, 492–November 21, 496

Gelasius was the first pope to be called Vicar of Christ, although the title was not exclusively attached to popes until the pontificate of Eugenius III (1145–53). After Leo the Great (440–61), Gelasius was the outstanding pope of the fifth century. An African by birth, he is remembered for his strong stand against both the emperor and the patriarch of Constantinople in the Acacian Schism (484–519) and for his defense of papal primacy by appealing to the theory of "two powers" or "two swords" (the spiritual and the temporal).

Having served as archdeacon under his predecessor, Felix III, Gelasius faced a very difficult situation upon his election to the papacy. The so-called barbarian kings, all Arian (those who held that Christ was the greatest of creatures, not the Son of God), now ruled what was left of the Western empire. The Ostrogoths under Theodoric, also an Arian, were in control of most of Italy. Refugees and shortages, of clergy as well as of supplies, abounded. Gelasius befriended Theodoric, encouraging him to stay out of ecclesiastical affairs, and used his own money to assist the poor and ease the famine. But in dealing with the Acacian Schism he proved more intransigent. Gelasius insisted that no reconciliation was possible until Acacius's name and those of others associated with the attempt to reconcile orthodoxy and Monophysitism were removed from the prayers of the Mass. Some influential groups in Rome began to murmur against the pope and applied pressure for a more reasonable approach to the schism. At the Roman synod of 494, in a gesture of goodwill, Gelasius revoked Felix III's excommunication of one of the legates blamed for mishandling the original mission to Constantinople that began the schism. It was at a synod the following year that Gelasius was first referred to as the Vicar of Christ.

In a famous letter to the emperor and in other documents, Gelasius advanced a theory that would have profound influence in the Middle Ages, namely, that two powers govern the world: the one spiritual (the "consecrated authority of bishops"), centered in the pope, and the other temporal (the "royal power"), centered in the emperor. Each power has its source in God, and each is independent in its own sphere. But the spiritual power is intrinsically superior to the temporal because it mediates salvation to the temporal.

Although his public performance in office was that of an authoritarian and severe pastoral leader, contemporaries pointed out that Gelasius was, in private, a humble person, given to mortification and the service of the poor. He was buried somewhere in St. Peter's Basilica. Feast day: November 21.

50 ANASTASIUS II

November 24, 496–November 19, 498

Following a pattern that one sees repeated again and again in the history of papal elections, Anastasius II was elected to the papacy because of dissatisfaction with the policies of the two previous popes, Felix III (483–92) and Gelasius I (492–96). Both had been unyielding in their approach toward the Acacian Schism (484–519), the forerunner of the major East-West Schism that would occur in the eleventh century.

Anastasius II immediately sent two legates to Constantinople carrying a conciliatory letter for the emperor, in which the pope announced his election to the papacy and expressed his desire for the restoration of church unity. The pope was even prepared to recognize the validity of baptisms and ordinations performed by Acacius, but insisted that Acacius's name be removed from the list of those to be prayed for at Mass. The emperor (who was also named Anastasius) suggested a compromise: he would recognize Theodoric the Ostrogoth as king of Italy if the pope would accept the *Henoticon,* a doctrinally ambiguous formula of union between orthodox Catholics and Monophysites drawn up in 482. The pope accepted this. A number of Roman clergy felt betrayed and, in turn, broke communion with their own bishop, the pope. At the height of the crisis, the pope died suddenly, and with his death perhaps the last hope of restoring unity between East and West also died.

Anastasius II's name is not found in any of the ancient martyrologies, and there is no evidence of any cult or devotion to him following his death. The medieval tradition regarding him as a traitor to the Holy See because of his efforts at East-West reconciliation is manifestly unjust.

51 SYMMACHUS, ST.

November 22, 498–July 19, 514

Elected while still a deacon by a majority of the Roman clergy who were dissatisfied with the conciliatory attitude of his predecessor, Anastasius II, toward the East, Symmachus confronted a schism in Rome from the outset of his pontificate. But a smaller number of clergy who favored Anastasius's approach met on the same day in the basilica of St. Mary Major and, with the support of most of the Roman Senate and the Roman aristocracy, elected the archpriest Lawrence. Both sides appealed to Theodoric, the Ostrogothic king of Italy, even though he was himself an Arian (a heretic who believed that Jesus Christ was the greatest of creatures, but not the Son of God). Theodoric ruled in favor of the one who was ordained first and had the largest amount of support. That was Symmachus.

But peace lasted only a short time. The aristocrats reported the pope to Theodoric for having celebrated Easter according to the old Roman calendar rather than the Alexandrian calendar. The king summoned Symmachus to his residence in Ravenna, but after the pope reached Rimini and learned that he was also being charged with unchastity and the misuse of church property, he returned immediately to Rome. The king was displeased with the pope's action and called a synod of Italian bishops (known as the Palmary Synod) to adjudicate the matter in 501. The synod decided that no human court could judge the pope.

Displeased with the verdict, the king immediately invited Lawrence back to Rome, where he functioned as Bishop of Rome (from the official Catholic point of view as antipope) for four years. By the year 506, Theodoric had become alienated politically from Byzantium and its allies in Rome and therefore confirmed the synodal verdict of 501 that exonerated Symmachus. Lawrence withdrew, settling on a farm owned by his patron Festus.

In 514, riots in Constantinople and Antioch and a revolt in Thrace induced the emperor, Anastasius I, to seek some sort of reconciliation with the pope. He invited Symmachus to preside over a general council at Heraclea in Thrace in order to settle the doctrinal issues behind the schism. But the pope was already dead before the invitation arrived in Rome. He was

buried in the portico, or porch, of St. Peter's. Feast
day: July 19.

52 HORMISDAS, ST.

July 20, 514–August 6, 523

Married before ordination, Hormisdas had a son,
Silverius, who later succeeded him as pope. A peacemaker at heart, from a rich, aristocratic family, he moved
immediately to restore harmony to the Church.

When the pope received an invitation from the
emperor Anastasius I (originally intended for Hormisdas's predecessor, Symmachus) to preside over a
general council at Heraclea in Thrace, Hormisdas sent
legates to Constantinople on two occasions, in 515 and
517, carrying his conditions for reunion: public acceptance of the anti-Monophysite teaching of the Council of Chalcedon (451) and of Pope Leo I's *Tome* on the
two natures of Christ; the condemnation of Acacius,
the deceased patriarch of Constantinople, and of others who were considered "soft" on Monophysitism;
and the retrial by Rome of all deposed or exiled bishops, thereby establishing the jurisdictional primacy of
the pope in the East. But the emperor was now politically stronger than at the time he extended the invitation to the pope to preside over a general council,
and he refused to yield. Within a year, however, the
emperor was dead. He was succeeded by Justin I, an
orthodox Catholic who fully embraced the teaching
of Chalcedon and made it the official faith of the empire. When Hormisdas resubmitted his demands, an

agreement known as the *Formula of Hormisdas* was signed (519) in the imperial palace by John II, patriarch of Constantinople, and by all the bishops and abbots present, thereby ending the Acacian Schism.

Some historians have noted a shadow across Pope Hormisdas's achievement in the East. First, the pope could not have accomplished anything without the support of Justin I and his successor, Justinian, his nephew. They restored the exiled orthodox bishops to their sees on their own imperial authority, prior to any negotiations with Rome, making the point that the pope had no jurisdictional primacy in the East. Hormisdas was buried in the portico, or porch, of St. Peter's. Feast day: August 6.

53 JOHN I, ST.

August 13, 523–May 18, 526

Already elderly and sick when elected, John I was the first pope to travel to the East, albeit under pressure from the king of Italy. (It was also under John I that the practice began of numbering the years from the birth of Christ instead of the unwieldy custom of listing them according to the era of Diocletian.) Just before John's election, the emperor Justin I, headquartered in Constantinople, revived a number of laws directed against the Arians (heretics who held that Jesus Christ was the greatest of creatures, but not the Son of God). The emperor's campaign against the Arians, many of whom were Goths, had infuriated Theodoric, the king of Italy, because he was both a Goth and an Arian himself. Therefore, he summoned the pope to the royal residence in Ravenna and dispatched him on a mission to Constantinople.

Although his was a humiliating mission, John I was received in Constantinople with extraordinary enthusiasm and respect in October or November 525. In subsequent discussions, however, the emperor refused to yield to Theodoric's demand that the Arians not be required to renounce their Arian faith. Believing that they could achieve no more than that, the pope and the rest of the delegation returned to Ravenna, only to face the king's fury. Already exhausted by his long journey and terrified by the prospect of severe punishment, the elderly pope collapsed and died. His body was taken back to Rome, where it was venerated as that of a martyr's and as possessing miraculous powers. John I was buried in the nave of St. Peter's. Feast day: May 18.

54 FELIX IV (III), ST.

July 12, 526–September 22, 530

Because there was an antipope who took the name Felix II in 355 and whose name was included for a time on the official list of popes, Felix IV is really the third Pope Felix in the official line of successors of St. Peter. His pontificate is best known for its support of Caesarius, bishop of Arles, against the semi-Pelagians, a heretical group who held that, although grace is necessary for salvation, the first move toward salvation is an act of human freedom without grace.

Felix IV is also remembered for the manner in which he left the papacy. As death approached, he named his archdeacon Boniface as his successor. The majority of the Senate, however, rejected the pope's action and published an edict forbidding both discussion of a papal successor during a pope's lifetime and the acceptance of a nomination as successor.

It was Felix IV who, with the support of the queen-regent of Italy, converted two pagan temples into a church dedicated to Sts. Cosmas and Damian. A mosaic portrait of the pope in the apse is the first contemporary papal likeness to have survived, although in a highly altered state. He was buried in the portico, or porch, of St. Peter's. Feast day: September 22.

55 BONIFACE II

September 22, 530–October 17, 532

Though born in Rome, Boniface II was the first pope of Germanic stock. Archdeacon under his predecessor, John I, he had been picked by the dying pope as his successor. This action precipitated a reaction in the Roman Senate, which forbade any discussion of a successor during a sitting pope's lifetime or the acceptance of a nomination as successor. Most of the Roman clergy agreed with the Senate's action. When they met in the Lateran Basilica to elect a new pope, they elected the deacon Dioscorus of Alexandria. The defeated minority withdrew to an adjacent hall and elected Boniface. Both were consecrated on the same day, September 22, 530. Dioscorus, however, died twenty-two days later and his supporters, bereft of their leader, acknowledged Boniface as pope. Although Dioscorus is not officially recognized as a legitimate pope, there is little or no doubt that, according to the church law of the day, he, not Boniface, was the rightly elected pope. Although Boniface II is buried in St. Peter's, there is no evidence of any cult devoted to him.

56 JOHN II

January 2, 533–May 8, 535

Because his name from birth was that of a pagan god, Mercury, John II was the first pope to take a different name upon his election to the papacy. He was also famous for contradicting, under pressure from the Eastern emperor, the teaching of a previous pope (Hormisdas) on a matter of doctrine.

An elderly priest, John II was a compromise choice, elected after an extremely corrupt process that included bribery. Following a synod, the new pope formally accepted a dogmatic decree the emperor had published in March 523. The decree acknowledged the teaching of the first four ecumenical councils, but it also included the so-called Theopaschite formula ("One of the Trinity suffered in the flesh"), which Pope Hormisdas had rejected as both unnecessary and open to misunderstanding. Pope John II wrote to the emperor Justinian to inform him that his decree was orthodox. The emperor, in turn, incorporated the pope's letter and his own (in which he acknowledged the Apostolic See as "the head of all the Churches") in his famous Code of Justinian. The whole episode, however, is remembered mainly as an example of one pope's contradicting another in a matter of doctrine. John II died on May 8, 535, and was buried in the portico, or porch, of St. Peter's.

57 AGAPITUS I, ST.

May 13, 535–April 22, 536

The son of a priest who had been killed by supporters of the antipope Lawrence in 502, Agapitus I was strongly opposed to the practice of a pope's designating his successor and, therefore, began his pontificate by having Pope Boniface II's (530–32) condemnation of the antipope Dioscorus of Alexandria publicly burned (see Boniface II, number 55).

As pope, Agapitus also took a forceful stance against former Arians (heretics who held that Jesus Christ was not the Son of God, but only the greatest of creatures) in North Africa and in the East. At the same time, the pope was forced to pawn sacred vessels in order to pay for his trip to Constantinople, under explicit threats from the last Ostrogothic king of Italy, Theodahad. The king had learned of the emperor's plans to invade Italy in order to reincorporate it into the empire after almost sixty years as a Germanic kingdom. Although given a triumphal welcome in Constantinople, the pope's mission failed. The emperor explained that his plans for the invasion could not be called off.

While in Constantinople, however, Agapitus I did persuade the emperor to remove Anthimus, the patriarch of Constantinople, on the grounds that he was a Monophysite (a heretic who held that in Jesus Christ there is only a divine nature, and not a human nature as well). The pope died in Constantinople on April 22, 536; his body was brought back to Rome in a lead casket and buried in the portico, or porch, of St. Peter's. Feast day: September 20 (in the West); April 17 (in the East).

58 SILVERIUS, ST.

d. December 2, 537,
pope June 1 or 8, 536–November 11, 537

The son of Pope Hormisdas (514–23), Silverius was the first (and only) subdeacon to be elected pope and one of only three (or perhaps five) popes to resign their office.

The Monophysite empress Theodora, upset with the previous pope's deposing of the Monophysite patriarch Anthimus of Constantinople, urged Pope Silverius to step down in favor of the Roman deacon Vigilius, the papal nuncio to Constantinople, with whom she had made a pact to restore Anthimus to Constantinople. When Silverius refused, he was summoned to the headquarters of the emperor's general, Belisarius, and accused of plotting with the Goths, who were then laying siege to the city. The pope was degraded to the status of a monk and deposed on March 11, 537. He was deported to Patara, a seaport town in Lycia, whose local bishop directly interceded on his behalf with the emperor Justinian himself. The emperor ordered the pope back to Rome to face trial. If found innocent, he would be restored to the papal throne.

By this time, however, Vigilius had already been elected the new pope. When Silverius reached Rome, Vigilius arranged to have him taken to Palmaria, an island in the Gulf of Gaeta, where he resigned from the papacy under threat on November 11. Silverius died less than a month later, on December 2, probably from physical abuse and starvation designed to avoid a potentially embarrassing trial. From the eleventh century he has been venerated as a martyr, but not until the fourteenth century was he venerated in Rome itself. Feast day: June 20.

59 VIGILIUS

March 29, 537–June 7, 555 (The Vatican's official list also recognizes Vigilius as pope from March 29, 537, even though his predecessor, Silverius, had not yet formally abdicated until November 11 of that same year.)

Vigilius was clearly one of the most corrupt popes in the history of the Church. As papal nuncio to Constantinople, he entered into a secret pact with the Monophysite empress Theodora to restore the Monophysite patriarch Anthimus to the see of Constantinople and to disavow the Council of Chalcedon (451). (The Council of Chalcedon had condemned Monophysitism as a heresy because it denied that Jesus Christ had a human as well as a divine nature.) In return for his cooperation, she showered him with gifts and assured his election to the papacy upon the death of Agapitus I (535–36).

When Justinian published an edict condemning the "Three Chapters," that is, the writings of three theologians whose work the Council of Chalcedon had not questioned, he demanded that the pope sign it along with the other patriarchs. When Vigilius resisted, the emperor had him arrested while he was saying Mass on November 22, 545, and taken to Sicily. After a long stay there, the pope was brought to Constantinople in January 547. While there, he and Mennas, the patriarch of Constantinople, excommunicated one another. But by June Vigilius relented. He resumed communion with Mennas and promised the emperor and empress that he would condemn the "Three Chapters." When he did so, however, his *Iudicatum* ("decision" or "judgment") was interpreted throughout the West as a betrayal of Chalcedon.

A synod of African bishops at Carthage excommunicated the pope in 550. The crisis became so severe that a council would be necessary to resolve it. Vigilius was allowed to withdraw his edict condemning the "Three Chapters," but soon thereafter the emperor issued a fresh edict of condemnation. After further threats and conflicts between the pope and the imperial forces, there was, in June 552, a reconciliation initiated by the emperor Justinian himself. The pope returned to Constantinople, where the emperor decided a synod would be held. The pope refused to attend because of the tiny representation of Western bishops. The emperor had the council condemn the "Three Chapters" and then placed the pope under house arrest. After six months, the ill and isolated pope gave in and, on December 8, 553, wrote to the new patriarch, revoking his earlier defense of the "Three Chapters" and admitting they needed to be condemned.

When Vigilius finally left for Rome in the spring, he suffered another of many attacks of gallstones and died in Syracuse, Sicily. When his body was brought back to Rome, it was not buried in St. Peter's because of his unpopularity. He was buried instead in San Marcello on the Via Salaria.

60 PELAGIUS I

April 16, 556–March 4, 561

Because of the circumstances surrounding his election to the papacy, Pelagius I's pontificate was marred from the outset. Upon the death of Pope Vigilius, the deacon Pelagius, the papal nuncio in Constantinople, returned to Rome as the emperor Justinian's personal choice to be the new pope. The Roman clergy were very unhappy about having to accept Pelagius without even an election and gave him a very hostile reception when he reached Rome.

As pope, Pelagius acted with determination to restore law and order to Rome and to Italy generally after the wars. He was especially devoted to the alleviation of poverty and famine and to the ransoming of war prisoners. He reformed papal finances and reorganized papal properties in Italy, Gaul, Dalmatia, and North Africa, diverting their income to the poor. But resentment and hostility toward him were still deeply rooted and widely dispersed. Already elderly when consecrated as pope, Pelagius died after five years in office and was buried in St. Peter's.

61 JOHN III

July 17, 561–July 13, 574

Little is known about the thirteen-year pontificate of John III. Known as a pro-Easterner, he was elected with the support of the emperor Justinian and of Narses, the imperial exarch (viceroy) in Italy. Seven years into John III's reign, the Lombards invaded large sections of Italy. This crisis helped to ease the schism that had existed between Rome and the great churches of the West during the pontificate of Pelagius I, as some of those churches now deemed it politically prudent to renew communion with Rome. Relations with North Africa had already improved after the death of Justinian in 565.

As the Lombards moved south, John III rushed to Naples to persuade the unpopular imperial viceroy, Narses, to return to Rome and take charge of the crisis. But the Roman people were displeased, and Narses' unpopularity began to contaminate the pope as well. To avoid being drawn deeper into the conflict between the Romans and Narses, John withdrew from the city until Narses died. But soon thereafter the pope himself died and was buried in St. Peter's.

62 BENEDICT I

June 2, 575–July 30, 579

Very little is known about the pontificate of Benedict I. Because of the breakdown in the lines of communication between Rome and Constantinople, he had to wait eleven months before receiving imperial confirmation of his election to the papacy. During his reign, the Lombards continued their push southward, finally laying siege to Rome itself in the summer of 579. Appeals to the emperor for help were of little avail. The troops he sent were too few in number. As the siege intensified and famine spread, Benedict died. He was buried in the sacristy of St. Peter's.

63 PELAGIUS II

August 579–February 7, 590 (The Vatican's official list begins his pontificate on November 26, the date of his imperial confirmation, but theologically he became pope as soon as he was ordained Bishop of Rome in August.)

Elected when the Lombard siege of Rome was at its height, Pelagius II, the second pope of Germanic extraction, was ordained as Bishop of Rome immediately, without waiting for the emperor's formal approval. The new pope immediately sent his deacon (the future Gregory the Great) to Constantinople as his representative to explain the departure from precedent and to beg for military aid. But the emperor did not have the necessary forces to dispatch. Appeals to the Franks also failed. In 585, however, the imperial exarch (viceroy) in Ravenna arranged a truce with the Lombards, which lasted for four years.

During Pelagius II's pontificate, yet another controversy with Constantinople erupted over the patriarch's use of the title "ecumenical patriarch," a custom dating back to the previous century. When Patriarch John IV assumed the title at a synod in 588, the pope refused to endorse the acts of the synod because of his conviction that the title infringed upon papal supremacy. Pelagius ordered Gregory, his nuncio, to break communion with John until the latter repudiated the title. When a plague broke out in the aftermath of flooding caused by the overflow of the Tiber River, Pelagius II was among its first victims. He was buried in the portico, or porch, of St. Peter's.

64 GREGORY I, "THE GREAT," ST.

ca. 540–604, pope September 3, 590–March 12, 604

Only the second pope in all of church history to be called "the Great" (Leo I [440–61] was the first), Gregory I was the first pope to have been a monk and was one of the papacy's most influential writers. His *Pastoral Care,* which defined the episcopal ministry as one of shepherding souls, became the textbook for medieval bishops. Although only a junior deacon at the time of Pelagius II's death, he was unanimously elected to the papacy.

Because of the general breakdown of civil order at the time, Gregory found himself drawn as deeply into temporal and political affairs as into spiritual and ecclesiastical concerns. He immediately organized the distribution of food to the starving, and, in order to expand the reservoir of resources, he reorganized the papal territories in Italy, Sicily, Dalmatia, Gaul, and North Africa. He admonished each rector of the papal estates "to care for the poor" and "to promote not so much the worldly interests of the Church but the relief of the needy in their distress."

When the imperial exarch (viceroy) in Ravenna proved incapable of doing anything about the Lombard threat, the pope took the lead and fashioned a truce with the duke of Spoleto. When the exarch broke the truce and the Lombards moved against Rome, Gregory saved the city by bribing the Lombard king and promising yearly tributes. As a result of all these efforts, Gregory became virtually the civil as well as the spiritual ruler of Rome.

He imposed a detailed code for the election of bishops in Italy, enforced clerical celibacy, secured better relationships with the churches of Spain and Gaul, and dispatched Augustine and forty other monks to England in 596 to evangelize the Anglo-Saxons. Given his own monastic background, Gregory was a vigorous promoter of monasticism and of the liturgy, particularly of liturgical music. Indeed, his name was so closely identified with plainsong that it came to be known as Gregorian chant. Many prayers recited in the Eucharist are attributable to Gregory, and he is credited with the placement of the "Our Father" in the Mass. His support of monasticism and of monks, however, created divisions within the ranks of the

Roman clergy (between pro-monastic clergy and pro-diocesan clergy) that were to last for many years and would affect several subsequent papal elections. His many writings had a wide influence on the Church, and he was eventually included with Ambrose, Augustine, and Jerome as a Doctor of the Church.

Gregory's spirituality was marked by a vivid sense of the imminent end of the world, intensified perhaps by the ill health that hindered him throughout his pontificate. He was so racked with gout that, by the time of his death, he could no longer walk. He died on March 12, 604, and was buried in St. Peter's with the epitaph "consul of God." Feast day: September 3.

65 SABINIAN

September 13, 604–February 22, 606

Sabinian was one of the most unpopular popes in history. In fact, his funeral procession had to make a detour outside the city walls to avoid the hostile demonstrations. How did this pope come to such an end? Having fallen out of favor with Gregory the Great for his unsatisfactory performance as nuncio to Constantinople, Sabinian was elected to the papacy as a reaction to Gregory, who had himself become unpopular with the Roman populace by the time of his death.

Sabinian reversed Gregory's policy of favoring monks and promoted diocesan, or secular, clergy instead. But he reversed another Gregorian policy as well. With the renewal of hostilities with the Lombards and the return of famine, Sabinian maintained tight control over food supplies and, unlike Gregory, sold them to the people rather than giving them away freely. Accused of profiteering, he was as despised in death as in life. He was buried in a secret location in the Lateran.

66 BONIFACE III

February 19–November 12, 607

It was Boniface III who, following a Roman synod, forbade under penalty of excommunication all discussion of a successor to a pope or bishop during that pope's or bishop's lifetime and until three days after his death. His action may have been prompted by the rivalries (between pro- and anti-monastic factions) that preceded his own election. Indeed, a full year passed before the vacancy created by Sabinian's death was even filled. A second interesting point about Boniface III's brief pontificate was the declaration of the new emperor Phocas (actually a repeat of a declaration by the emperor Justinian) that the see of St. Peter was the head of all the churches, thereby putting to a temporary end the patriarch of Constantinople's use of the title "ecumenical patriarch." Boniface died on November 12, 607, and was buried in St. Peter's.

67 BONIFACE IV, ST.

August 25, 608–May 8, 615

A disciple and imitator of Pope Gregory the Great (590–604), Boniface IV converted his house in Rome into a monastery upon his election to the papacy and, like Gregory, favored monks and promoted monasticism. The ten-month vacancy in the papal office was caused by a delay in receiving imperial approval from Constantinople for his consecration as Bishop of Rome. The new pope held a synod (at which the first bishop of London was present) in 610 to regulate monastic life and discipline. The pope enjoyed good relations with the emperor, Phocas, and his successor, Heraclius, but his pontificate was constantly disturbed by famine, plagues, and natural disasters. Like Gregory, he was especially devoted to the poor. He was buried in St. Peter's. Feast day: May 25.

68 DEUSDEDIT [ADEODATUS I], ST.

October 19, 615–November 8, 618

Deusdedit (later Adeodatus I) was the first priest to be elected pope since John II in 533. All the intervening popes were deacons when elected (except for Silverius in 536, who was the first subdeacon elected to the papacy). Already elderly when elected, Deusdedit was the choice of the clerical faction opposed to the pro-monastic policies of Gregory the Great and Boniface IV. As a diocesan priest himself, he promoted diocesan clergy over religious to offices. Almost nothing is known about his pontificate except that during it Rome was hit with an earthquake and another plague. On his deathbed he gave the first recorded bequest by a pope to his clergy, the equivalent of a year's salary to each. He was buried in St. Peter's. Feast day: November 8.

69 BONIFACE V

December 23, 619–October 25, 625

Like his predecessor, Deusdedit, Boniface V was elected by the clerical faction opposed to the pro-monastic policies of Gregory the Great and Boniface IV. And like Deusdedit, he had to wait almost a year for imperial confirmation of his election and approval of his consecration as Bishop of Rome. He promoted policies favorable to the diocesan clergy, decreeing, for example, that only priests could transfer the relics of martyrs, and he took a special interest in the English church, conferring the pallium (a woolen vestment worn around the neck of an archbishop as a symbol of pastoral authority) on Justus when he became arch-bishop of Canterbury in 624. The pope also estab-lished the principle of asylum in churches.

Boniface V was known for his compassion and gen-erosity, having distributed his entire personal fortune to the poor. Buried in St. Peter's, he is described in his epitaph as "generous, wise, pure, sincere, and just." One only wonders why he was not eventually recog-nized as a saint, since the title had been conferred on many less deserving popes in the past.

70 HONORIUS I

October 27, 625–October 12, 638

Honorius is one of the few popes in history to have been condemned by an ecumenical council (the Third Council of Constantinople in 680–81) for doctrinal deviation. One source indicates that Honorius, elected on October 27, 625, only two days after the death of Boniface V, did not await imperial approval of his consecration, that he was ordained Bishop of Rome on November 3. If that were the case, the beginning of his pontificate would be November 3 rather than October 27. But the *Annuario Pontificio,* which contains the official Vatican list of popes, indicates the beginning of his pontificate as October 27. The *Annuario* obviously accepts the judgment of other sources that Honorius had indeed received imperial confirmation of his election from the exarch Isaac, who was in Rome at the time, and immediate consecration as Bishop of Rome. The matter is not a small point. Theologically, a person does not become pope until he is Bishop of Rome.

In 634 Honorius I received a letter from Sergius I, the patriarch of Constantinople, proposing that the second Person of the Trinity, the Word of God, was the subject of every "operation," human and divine, in the God-man, Jesus Christ. Sergius pointed out that the formula "two distinct natures but one operation" had been found useful in the East to win over the Monophysites (heretics who held that in Christ there was no human nature, only a divine nature). Sophronius, the new bishop of Jerusalem, and others branded the formula as Monophysitism in disguise. Nevertheless, Honorius not only accepted the formula, but took it a step further. Since the Word of God acted through both natures (human and divine), he had only one will. Because Honorius's formula of the "one will" was incorporated in Emperor Heraclius's decree on the subject, called the *Ecthesis* (638), which came to be regarded as the classic expression of Monothelitism, the council censured Pope Honorius (along with others) by name. The condemnation, or anathema, was explicitly ratified by Pope Leo II in 683 when he approved the acts of the council in a letter to the emperor Constantine IV.

Otherwise, Honorius was a reasonably successful pope. He was such an efficient administrator of the papal estates that he never lacked for funds for the building, maintenance, and improvement of the churches of Rome, including the complete restoration of St. Peter's, where he was eventually buried with the epitaph "leader of the common people."

71 SEVERINUS

May 28–August 2, 640

Already elderly at the time of his election, Severinus had to wait almost twenty months before receiving imperial approval for his consecration because he refused to accept the emperor's *Ecthesis* (638), the classic expression of Monothelitism (a heresy that held that in Christ there is only one will, not two). In the meantime, the pope-elect was subject to brutal treatment. The imperial troops surrounded the papal residence at the Lateran Palace for three days, demanding to be paid. The papal treasury was subsequently plundered and the contents divided between the soldiers and

civic officials. Severinus died two months after his consecration, before having to take a definitive stand on
the *Ecthesis*. He was buried in St. Peter's.

72 JOHN IV

Dalmatian, December 24, 640–October 12, 642

Although he was the son of the legal adviser to the imperial exarch at Ravenna, John IV refused to endorse
the imperial line on Monothelitism (the heresy that
held that in Christ there is only one divine will, and not
a human will as well). In January 641 he held a synod in
Rome to condemn Monothelitism as heretical. When
the new patriarch of Constantinople, Pyrrhus I, appealed to Pope Honorius's endorsement of Emperor
Heraclius's *Ecthesis* (the classic expression of Monothelitism, which the emperor himself later repudiated
before his death), John IV wrote to the new emperor,
Constantine III, to express his disgust at the patriarch's
attempt to link his predecessor with heretical views
and to demand that copies of the *Ecthesis* be taken
down from their public postings in Constantinople.

There is one interesting development connected
with his election to the papacy. While he was awaiting
official confirmation from the emperor, the Roman
church sent an official letter to certain Irish bishops
and abbots having to do with doctrinal matters. What
is striking about this document is that the pope-elect
was the second signatory, not the first, and that the
first signatory, the archpriest Hilarus, and the chief
secretary (also named John) described themselves as

"vicegerents of the Apostolic See." For a long period of church history, election to the papacy was sufficient for validity. If that were the case in this time period, John IV would have already been pope and would have functioned as such. But apparently it was not: since the pope is Bishop of Rome, John could not be pope unless and until he was ordained a bishop. That is once again the present canonical requirement: election and ordination as a bishop, if the one elected is not already a bishop (can. 332.1). John IV died on October 12, 642, and was buried in St. Peter's.

73 THEODORE I

Greek, November 24, 642–May 14, 649

Theodore I was an implacable foe of Monothelitism (the heresy that held that in Christ there is only one divine will, not two, divine and human). A Greek, born in Jerusalem and the son of a bishop, Theodore probably came to Rome as a refugee from the Arab invasions of the Holy City. The choice of an Easterner with close ties to opponents of Monothelitism indicated the electors' desire to resist the imperial pressure in support of this heresy. One of the new pope's first acts was to write to the boy-emperor Constans II to ask why the *Ecthesis* (the imperial decree in support of Monothelitism) was still in force despite its repudiation by Pope John IV and even by its author, the emperor Heraclius, before his death on February 11, 641.

The emperor promulgated a decree known as the *Typos* ("Rule"), which abrogated the *Ecthesis*, prohibited all further discussion of the number of wills in Christ, and ordered that official church teaching should be limited to what had been defined by the first five ecumenical councils (thereby excluding the Third Council of Constantinople, which had condemned Monothelitism as heretical). Pope Theodore died on May 14, 649, before issuing an official response to the *Typos*, which surely would have been strongly negative. He was buried in St. Peter's.

74 MARTIN I, ST.

> *d. September 16, 655, pope July 5, 649–August 10, 654*
> *(The Vatican's official list ends his pontificate September 16, 655, the day of his death in exile, rather than August 10, 654, the day a successor, Eugenius I, was elected.)*

Martin I was the last pope to be recognized as a martyr. He was also the first pope in decades to be consecrated without waiting for imperial approval, an act that infuriated the emperor, Constans II, who refused to recognize him as a legitimate pope. A strong and resolute opponent of Monothelitism (the heresy that held that in Christ there is only one divine will, not two, human and divine), Martin I paid a heavy personal price for his defense of Catholic orthodoxy.

Three months after his election, the new pope held a synod, attended by 105 Western bishops and a number of exiled Greek clergy, that affirmed the doctrine of the two wills in Christ and condemned both Monothelitism and the emperor's *Typos* (the decree banning further discussion of the number of wills in Christ). The emperor, in turn, sent Olympius as exarch to Italy with orders to arrest the pope and bring him to Constantinople (others say it was to assassinate the pope). But Olympius soon discovered that such a move was impossible because of the widespread support for the pope. He subsequently joined the pope against the emperor.

In the summer of 653 a new exarch, Theodore Calliopas, seized the pope, bedridden from gout, in the Lateran Basilica, where he had taken sanctuary. The exarch handed the clergy an imperial decree declaring that Martin was not the legal pope and was therefore deposed. The exarch smuggled the ailing pope out of Rome and forced him onto a ship to Constantinople on June 17, 653. The ship arrived in September 653 and, after three months of solitary confinement, the pope was tried for treason. He was found guilty, condemned to death, and publicly flogged. However, the dying patriarch of Constantinople, Paul II, pleaded for Martin's life and the sentence was commuted to exile. After three more months in prison under terrible conditions, the pope was taken by ship to Chersonesus in the Crimea, where he died on September 16, 655, from the effects of starvation and harsh conditions and treatment. He was buried there in a church dedicated to the Blessed Virgin Mary. The Roman church came to venerate Martin I as a martyr, and he is mentioned by name in the Mass in the *Bobbio Missal* (an eighth-century collection of liturgical texts). Feast day: April 13 (formerly November 12).

75 EUGENIUS [EUGENE] I, ST.

August 10, 654–June 2, 657

Eugenius I is best known for the dubious circumstances under which he was elected to the papacy. His predecessor, Martin I, was still alive in exile. Eugenius was elected and consecrated on August 10, 654, but Martin I did not die until September 16 of the following year. There is no evidence that Martin resigned the papacy, although he did know that someone had been elected to succeed him and, in a letter to a friend in Constantinople, acknowledged that he was praying for the one placed over the Roman church. The Vatican's official list of popes, given in the *Annuario Pontificio*, places the end of Martin I's pontificate on September 16, 655, and the beginning of Eugenius I's on August 10, 654. According to the *Annuario*, therefore, there were two legitimate popes occupying the Chair of Peter simultaneously! It seems theologically appropriate to characterize Martin I's lengthy exile as tantamount to a resignation and Eugenius I's election, therefore, as pastorally prudent and canonically valid.

A mild, elderly priest (presbyter) at the time of his election, the new pope immediately sent envoys to Constantinople to restore friendly relations between Rome and the emperor. The emperor insisted that they recognize Peter, the new patriarch of Constantinople, who proposed to them a compromise formula stating that, although each of Christ's two natures had its own will, the divine Person possessed only one will. The patriarch handed the envoys his profession of faith to be taken back to the pope. When it was read aloud in the basilica of St. Mary Major, however, the clergy and laity were so outraged that they prevented the pope from continuing with Mass until he promised to reject the formula. Eugenius I relented, and a schism was begun once again between Rome and Constantinople. Eugenius I died on June 2, 657, and was buried in St. Peter's, but his name was not included in the martyrologies until inserted into the Roman Martyrology by the church historian Caesare Baronius (d. 1607). Feast day: June 2.

76 VITALIAN, ST.

July 30, 657–January 27, 672

Unlike some of his immediate predecessors, Pope Vitalian adopted a conciliatory attitude toward imperial and ecclesiastical Constantinople on the question of Monothelitism (the heresy that posited only one will, not two, in Jesus Christ). In return, the emperor Constans II sent the pope elaborate gifts and officially confirmed various privileges for the Roman church, and the patriarch Peter included the pope's name among those to be prayed for at Mass, the first pope to be so included since Honorius I (625–38). When the emperor was assassinated in 668, Pope Vitalian gave his strong support to the emperor's son Constantine IV. In gratitude, the new emperor did not enforce his father's decree (the *Typos*), leaving the pope free to teach orthodox doctrine.

Pope Vitalian had a deep concern for the church in Britain and supported the efforts of the king of

Northumbria, following the Synod of Whitby (664), to establish in England the Roman, as opposed to the Celtic, date for Easter (that is, the Sunday after the Jewish Passover, rather than the day of Passover itself) and other Roman practices as well. In Rome Vitalian supported the music school at the Lateran in order to train singers for the more elaborate Byzantine-style rites. The chanters were called "Vitaliani." Vitalian died on January 27, 672, and was buried in St. Peter's. Feast day: January 27.

77 ADEODATUS II

April 11, 672–June 17, 676

Very little is known about the pontificate of Adeodatus II. An elderly monk when elected, he rejected the synodical letters and profession of faith sent to him by Constantine I, the new patriarch of Constantinople, who like several of his predecessors was a Monothelite (a heretic who held that in Jesus Christ there is only one divine will, and not a human will as well). The pope did have a reputation for kindness and generosity to the poor, to pilgrims, and to his clergy. He was buried in St. Peter's.

78 DONUS

November 2, 676–April 11, 678

Like many other early pontificates, Donus's pontificate was generally wrapped in obscurity. Already elderly when elected in August (he had to wait about three months for imperial approval of his consecration), he did reach an understanding with the archbishop of Ravenna whereby the latter abandoned his see's claim to be completely independent of Rome in terms of governance and the appointment of bishops, a privilege granted by the emperor in 666. It is said that Donus was an active builder and restorer of churches and that he laid down a marble pavement in the atrium of St. Peter's. He died on April 11, 678, and was buried four days later in St. Peter's.

79 AGATHO, ST.

June 27, 678–January 10, 681

Agatho's pontificate was marked by the end of imperial support for Monothelitism (the heresy that held that in Jesus Christ there is only one divine will rather than two wills, one divine and one human) and by the restoration of friendly relations between Rome and Constantinople. It was soon after his election (date unknown) and consecration that Agatho received a letter from the emperor Constantine IV proposing a conference at which the whole issue of the wills of Christ could be discussed and by which unity between Rome and Constantinople might be restored.

The emperor decided to upgrade the conference to a general council (the Third Council of Constantinople), to meet in the imperial palace (November 7, 680–September 16, 681) and to be presided over by the emperor himself. At the council's thirteenth session it condemned (anathematized) the Monothelite leaders, including Pope Honorius I (625–38) for his approval of the Monothelite formula "two distinct natures but one operation," but only after overcoming the objections of the understandably reluctant papal delegates. The condemnation, or anathema, was explicitly ratified by Pope Leo II in 683 when he approved the acts of the council in a letter to the emperor Constantine IV. Pope Agatho had died eight months before the council ended, but his contribution was acknowledged in the council's congratulatory address to the emperor, which acknowledged that Peter had spoken through Agatho.

Widely regarded as a kindly, cheerful person, he died during an epidemic on January 10, 681 (one source says he was 107 years old), and was buried in St. Peter's. He came to be venerated in the East and the West alike. Feast day: January 10.

80 LEO II, ST.

August 17, 682–July 3, 683

A Sicilian, Leo II was the pope who formally approved the acts of the Third Council of Constantinople (680–81), which condemned Monothelitism (a heresy that held that in Jesus Christ there is only one divine will rather than a human and a divine will) and which also included an explicit condemnation of a previous pope, Honorius I (625–38), for doctrinal deviation.

Elected in January 681, the new pope had to wait eighteen months before receiving imperial approval for his consecration. The emperor Constantine IV showed his approval of the newly elected pope's cooperation by inviting him to send a resident papal nuncio to the imperial court in Constantinople and by lowering the taxes on the papal patrimonies in Sicily and Calabria as well as the corn requisition for the army.

A well-trained singer in the papal choir school prior to his election to the papacy, Leo II was deeply concerned with the promotion of church music. He was also celebrated for his devotion to the poor and his efforts to improve their condition. He died on July 3, 683, and was buried in St. Peter's. In 1607 Paul V had the remains moved to a place under the altar in the basilica's Chapel of the Madonna della Colonna, where three other popes are buried: Leo III, Leo IV, and Leo XII. Feast day: July 3.

81 BENEDICT II, ST.

June 26, 684–May 8, 685

Serving less than a year as pope, Benedict II was known primarily for his humility, gentleness, and love for the poor. He had to wait nearly a year from the time of his election by the Roman clergy in early July 683 until the emperor sent formal approval of his consecration.

Benedict II confirmed his predecessor's support of the Third Council of Constantinople (680–81) and sent a delegate to Spain with copies of the acts of the council and Leo II's letters. But the strongly independent Visigothic church of Spain did not approve the acts of the council without subjecting them first to an exhaustively analytical examination at the Fourteenth

Council of Toledo (684). When the archbishop of Toledo learned that the pope had been verbally critical of some passages in a profession of faith that he had sent to him following the council, he sent the pope a blistering protest. The pope also carried out restorations of various Roman churches, including St. Peter's, where he was buried after his death on May 8, 685. Feast day: May 7.

82 JOHN V

Syrian, July 23, 685–August 2, 686

Because his short pontificate was marked by illness, John V established practically no record at all. Like Leo II (682–83), he was consecrated by the bishops of Ostia, Porto, and Velletri, three of Rome's neighboring (or suburbicarian) dioceses. John V suspended a bishop in Sardinia for having consecrated another bishop in his province without permission from Rome, and he was also generous in his will to his clergy, the charitable monasteries of Rome, and the lay sacristans of churches. He was buried in St. Peter's.

83 CONON

Thracian, October 21, 686–September 21, 687

A compromise candidate elected in old age, Conon had a short, but unfortunate, pontificate. He nominated a deacon of the church of Syracuse as rector

of the papal patrimony in Sicily, a lucrative post traditionally reserved for a member of the Roman clergy,
and allowed him the use of ceremonial saddlecloths
that were also reserved for members of the Roman
clergy. Moreover, his appointee proved to be an ex-
tortionist. The papal tenants revolted, and the rector
was arrested and deported by the governor of Sicily.
J. N. D. Kelly describes this pope as "unworldly and
of saintly appearance, . . . simple-minded and continu-
ously ill." His election and performance in office left
the Roman church deeply divided. Conon was buried
in St. Peter's.

84 SERGIUS I, ST.

Syrian, December 15, 687–September 8, 701

A strong pope, Sergius I asserted the authority of the
Bishop of Rome in the West and resisted the efforts
of the emperor Justinian II in the East to make the
pope bow to his will. Thus, he consecrated Damian
as the new archbishop of Ravenna in Rome (the first
such papal consecration since 666, when Ravenna
was declared autonomous), baptized Caedwalla, the
young king of the West Saxons, and received the see
of Aquileia back into communion with Rome, ending a schism begun in 553. And when the emperor demanded that the pope approve the acts of a council he
called in 692, ostensibly to complete the work of the
Second and Third Councils of Constantinople (553 and
680–81, respectively), Sergius I refused.

The council (known as the Trullan Council because it met in the domed room ["trullus"] of the imperial palace) had not included any Western bishops, ignored Western canon law, banned certain practices observed in the West (such as clerical celibacy and the Saturday fast in Lent), and expressly renewed the twenty-eighth canon of the Council of Chalcedon (451), granting Constantinople equivalent status to Rome. When the emperor learned of the pope's response, he sent the commander of the imperial bodyguard to force the pope to sign or to arrest him and bring him to Constantinople. But the imperial troops in Ravenna and elsewhere rallied to the pope's support, forced their way into Rome, and hunted down the imperial commander. Only the pope's pleas saved the man's life. The humiliated emperor was overthrown and exiled in 695.

An accomplished singer, Sergius I introduced the singing of the Agnus Dei ("Lamb of God") at Mass and processions on the four principal feasts of the Blessed Virgin Mary. He was buried in St. Peter's, and there is some indication that a cult developed soon after his death. Feast day: September 8.

85 JOHN VI

Greek, October 30, 701–January 11, 705

Very little of enduring importance or interest seems to have occurred during John VI's pontificate. Elected and consecrated on the same day, he did spend large sums of money ransoming prisoners taken during battles in defense of papal territories under attack from the duke of Benevento. He was also instrumental in saving the life of the imperial exarch Theophylact when he was threatened by mutinous members of the Italian militia. John VI died on January 11, 705, and was buried in St. Peter's.

86 JOHN VII

Greek, March 1, 705–October 18, 707

John VII was the first pope who was the son of an imperial official, an individual responsible for the maintenance of the imperial palace on the Palatine. Elected and consecrated on the same day, the new pope enjoyed good relations with the Lombards, whose king returned valuable estates in the Cottian Alps that had been taken from the papacy in previous military actions. In 706, however, the ruthless emperor Justinian II, who had been overthrown in 695, returned to power and sent two bishops to Rome with copies of the canons of the Trullan Council (692). Pope Sergius I had firmly refused to sign these documents. John VII was less forthright. He simply returned the documents unsigned without expressing assent or dissent. A patron of the arts and a builder, he constructed a new papal residence at the foot of the Palatine and restored a number of churches, adorning them with mosaics and frescoes, some of which included representations of himself. John VII died on October 18, 707, and was buried in the Chapel of the Blessed Virgin Mary, which he had added to St. Peter's Basilica.

87 SISINNIUS

Syrian, January 15–February 4, 708

Although greatly respected for his high moral character and pastoral sensitivity, the aged Sisinnius was so crippled with gout at the time of his election and consecration on January 15, 708, that he could not even use his hands to feed himself. His only recorded ecclesiastical act was the consecration of the bishop of Corsica. He also ordered the walls of Rome to be reinforced, but he died before the job could be undertaken—only twenty days after his election. He was buried in St. Peter's.

88 CONSTANTINE

Syrian, March 25, 708–April 9, 715

The key event in Constantine's pontificate was his yearlong trip to Constantinople at the request of the emperor Justinian II and in the hope of normalizing relations between Rome and Constantinople. The pope was received enthusiastically everywhere along the journey, and upon his arrival in Constantinople was greeted by the emperor himself, who kissed the pope's feet and received absolution and Holy Communion from him. Successful negotiations were held between papal and imperial sides, and the emperor was so pleased with the results that he published a decree confirming the privileges of the Roman church.

Pope Constantine returned to Rome on October 24, 711. Less than two weeks later the emperor was murdered by mutinous troops and succeeded by Philippicus Bardanes, a fanatical Monothelite (a heretic who held that in Jesus Christ there is only one divine will, rather than a divine and a human will). The new emperor sent the pope his own Monothelite profession of faith and demanded that the pope accept it. Pope Constantine refused. When the imperial exarch, headquartered in Ravenna, tried to enforce the emperor's demand, the Roman citizenry rebelled and there were bloody battles in the streets. Happily, the emperor was overthrown, and his successor promptly assured the pope of his own orthodoxy and his acceptance of the teaching of the Third Council of Constantinople on the two wills of Christ (680–81). Pope Constantine died on April 9, 715, and was buried in St. Peter's.

89 GREGORY II, ST.

ca. 669–731, pope May 19, 715–February 11, 731

The first Roman to be elected pope after seven consecutive popes of Greek, Syrian, or Thracian background, Gregory II was perhaps the outstanding pope of the eighth century. He persuaded the Lombard king to return valuable papal properties, led the resistance of the Italian people to the new, heavy taxes imposed by the emperor Leo III, and saved the city of Rome from a siege mounted by the Lombard king and the imperial exarch. He also firmly resisted the emperor's efforts to ban the use and veneration of sacred images (known as iconoclasm) out of concern, the emperor insisted, that such practices were an obstacle to the conversion of Jews and Muslims. The pope formally rebuked the emperor at a Roman synod in 727.

Because of Gregory II's support of the mission of Boniface (d. 754) to evangelize the Germans, Roman liturgical practice was adopted everywhere in the emerging German church. At home, the pope repaired the walls of the city and many churches and promoted monasticism by rebuilding and repopulating monasteries. He was also liturgically active, introducing a Mass for the Thursdays of Lent. Evidence of his cult first appeared in the ninth-century martyrology of Ado. Gregory II died on February 11, 731, and was buried in St. Peter's. Feast day: February 11.

90 GREGORY III, ST.

Syrian, March 18, 731–November 28, 741
(The Vatican's official list gives only the month
of November as the end of his pontificate.)

Gregory III, a Syrian by birth, was seized by cheering crowds at the funeral of Gregory II, brought to the Lateran, and elected pope by popular acclaim. He was consecrated five weeks later after obtaining official approval from the imperial exarch in Ravenna. He was the last pope to seek such approval. His pontificate was marked by growing tensions over iconoclasm (the emperor's policy of forbidding the display and use of sacred images). The new pope urged the emperor, Leo III, to back away from the policy, but when he received

no reply, he called a synod, which condemned iconoclasm and declared excommunicated anyone who destroyed sacred images. That would have included the
emperor himself and the patriarch of Constantinople.
In retaliation, the emperor dispatched an armed fleet
to Italy, which was lost in a shipwreck, seized papal
properties in Calabria and Sicily, and declared the ecclesiastical provinces of Illyricum and Sicily to be under the jurisdiction of the patriarch of Constantinople
rather than the pope. And yet Gregory III remained
loyal to the empire, viewing it as the only legitimate
political authority. Indeed, the pope's support of the
empire was crucial to the recapture of Ravenna from
the Lombards in 733. Both the emperor and the exarch showed their gratitude, respectively, by making a
truce with the pope and by donating six onyx columns
that were placed in front of the tomb of St. Peter in
the basilica.

In church matters, the pope gave his full support to
the missionary efforts of Boniface (d. 754) in Germany.
The pope also strengthened relations with the English
church, bestowing the pallium (the woolen vestment
worn around the neck as a sign of pastoral authority)
on Egbert of York and Tatwine of Canterbury and
appointing the latter papal vicar for all of England.
Gregory III died November 28, 741, and was buried in
St. Peter's in the oratory he had built. The first evidence of his cult, like that of his predecessor, appears
in the ninth-century martyrology of Ado. Feast day:
November 28.

91 ZACHARIAS [ZACHARY], ST.

Greek, December 10, 741–March 22, 752

Zacharias was the last of the Greek popes and also the last pope to send official notification of his election to the imperial court and patriarch in Constantinople. Through personal diplomacy, he reestablished peaceful relations with the Lombards in northern Italy, although eight years later a new Lombard king revived the old expansionist policies, capturing Ravenna in 751 and then turning his attention toward Rome itself. Relations with Constantinople were also improved.

Like his two predecessors, Gregory II and Gregory III, Zacharias gave his full support to the missionary efforts of Boniface in Germany and through Boniface forged even closer relations between Rome and the Frankish church and kingdom. When Pepin III, son of the deceased Charles Martel (d. 741), sought a ruling from the pope on the status of his royal title, the pope decreed that it was better for the title to belong to one who exercised effective authority than to one who had none. Subsequently, the last king of the Merovingian line was deposed (with papal approval) and Pepin, of the Carolingian line, was elected. The pope's support for this transfer of power would have extraordinary significance later on in relations between the pope and the emperor. Zacharias died on March 22, 752, and was buried in St. Peter's. Feast day: March 15 (in the West); September 5 (in the East).

92 STEPHEN II (III)

March 26, 752–April 26, 757

Stephen II (III) established the independence of the papacy from the Byzantine Empire and placed it under the protection of the Frankish kingdom, thereby shifting the sphere of influence over the papacy from the East to the West. Stephen II (III) also formed the Papal States.

The confusion over whether he was the second or third Stephen in the papal line stems from the fact that an elderly Roman priest, who would have been Stephen II, was elected pope on March 22 or 23, 752, and was duly installed in the Lateran, but had a stroke three days later and died before being consecrated. In those years (as again today) consecration as a bishop (as well as the acceptance of one's valid election) was the essential canonical requirement, because the pope is the Bishop of Rome. The *Annuario Pontificio* (the official Vatican directory) included the original Stephen II in its official list of popes until 1960, but suppressed his name in 1961, giving all subsequent popes called Stephen a dual numbering. This Stephen was a Roman priest who was unanimously elected pope in St. Mary Major Basilica immediately after the death of the elderly priest of the same name who had just been elected to succeed Zacharias.

Soon after the consecration of Stephen II (III), Rome faced a new threat from the Lombard king Aistulf, fresh from his conquest of Ravenna. The king obviously now regarded the duchy of Rome as his fief and imposed an annual tax on all of its inhabitants. He also rebuffed every effort to achieve a fair and peaceful settlement of disputes over expropriated imperial territories, in spite of pleas from the pope. When the pope's appeal to the emperor Constantine V for military assistance went unanswered, Stephen II (III) turned to Pepin III, king of the Franks. After Stephen journeyed across the Alps to meet with Pepin (he was the first pope to make that journey), Pepin agreed to save the Roman people from the Lombards.

Pepin tried peaceful means at first with the Lombards, but when they failed, he attacked and defeated them quickly in August 754, forcing them to hand over expropriated territories to the pope. Once the Franks had recrossed the Alps, however, Aistulf broke the peace and laid siege to Rome. Pepin once again invaded Italy, crushed the Lombard king, and forced upon him even harsher terms of peace in June 756. The formerly imperial lands taken by Aistulf but now ceded to the pope formed the basis of the Papal States; thus began the pope's role as temporal sovereign—a mixed blessing indeed. Stephen II (III) died on April 26, 757, and was buried in St. Peter's.

93 PAUL I, ST.

May 29, 757–June 28, 767

Paul I was the first pope to succeed his older brother to the papacy. He had been ordained a deacon by Pope Zacharias (741–52) and served his brother Stephen II

(III) as a close adviser and negotiator. Paul I's pontificate was marked by persistent efforts to consolidate
the papacy's control over the newly created Papal
States, which were threatened by a new Lombard
king, Desiderius, who repudiated the peace treaty that
had been carefully forged between Pepin, king of the
Franks, and the Lombard king Aistulf.

In the meantime, the iconoclast controversy (regarding the use and veneration of sacred images)
began heating up once again. A council held by the
emperor Constantine V at Hiereia (754) denounced
images and their veneration. Fortunately for the pope,
Pepin rebuffed the emperor's efforts to win his support for the iconoclastic policy. At a synod held at
Gentilly in 767, at which Franks and Greeks debated
iconoclasm and trinitarian doctrine, the papal view
prevailed. Paul I died shortly thereafter, on June 28,
767, in St. Paul's Basilica. He was buried in St. Peter's.
Feast day: June 28.

94 STEPHEN III (IV)

August 7, 768–January 24, 772

The unhappy pontificate of Stephen III (IV), a Sicilian raised in Rome, began under a cloud and ended in
disaster. (For an explanation of the dual numbering,
see Stephen II [III], number 92.) Because of the severe
administrative style of Stephen's predecessor, Paul I,
the lay aristocracy of Rome had become so alienated
that they even contemplated the pope's murder. They

decided against that course of action, however, and placed their hopes in electing a successor sympathetic to their interests. As it turned out, one of their number violated the oath not to circumvent normal canonical procedures and had his brother Constantine, a layperson, acclaimed pope by a mob of soldiers. However, Constantine's brother and chief supporter was killed in street fighting with Lombard troops, and Constantine fled to the Lateran oratory, where he was soon arrested and later imprisoned in a monastery. The powerful chief notary of the Holy See, Christopher, saw to it that Stephen was canonically elected to replace Constantine the following year, on August 1, 768. He was consecrated as Bishop of Rome on August 7.

Dominated from the start by Christopher, the one who had engineered Stephen's election, Stephen's pontificate was marked by vacillation, intrigue, and stupendous blunders. When the pope finally tried to break free of Christopher's influence, he entered into a disastrous alliance with Desiderius, king of the Lombards, who arranged the murders of both Christopher and his son Sergius. Desiderius, however, broke all of his promises to the pope and, for all practical purposes, reduced him to a state of complete subservience. In 771 Charles (Charlemagne), now sole ruler of the Franks, repudiated his marriage to the daughter of Desiderius and thus became the Lombard king's mortal foe. Stephen's pontificate ended in total failure. Stephen III (IV) died on January 24, 772, and was buried in St. Peter's.

95 HADRIAN [ADRIAN] I

February 9, 772–December 25, 795

During Hadrian I's lengthy pontificate (the fifth longest in history, after Pius IX [1846–78], Leo XIII [1878–1903], Pius VI [1775–99], and John Paul II [1978–2005]), Charlemagne, king of the Franks, conquered the Lombards (774), deposing the antipapal king Desiderius, and confirmed the transfer to the Holy See of territories that together constituted the Papal States (because of which Hadrian I is sometimes called the second founder of the Papal States, after Pope Stephen II [III]). Ordained a deacon by Stephen III (IV), Hadrian was unanimously elected on February 1 and was consecrated as Bishop of Rome on February 9.

It required three separate visits of Charlemagne to Rome (in 774, 781, and 787) before the boundaries of the Papal States were finally fixed. They were to remain in that essential form until their final dissolution in 1870. The Second Council of Nicaea was also held during Hadrian I's pontificate (787). The pope, of course, gave the council his full support for its teaching against iconoclasm (the Eastern prohibition against the use and veneration of sacred images). Charlemagne is said to have grieved at the pope's death on Christmas, 795, "as if he had lost a brother or a child," and had a magnificent marble slab inscribed with memorial verses that can be seen in the portico, or porch, of St. Peter's. Hadrian I was buried in the crypt of the basilica.

96 LEO III, ST.

> *December 27, 795–June 12, 816 (The Vatican's official
> list begins his pontificate on December 26, the day of
> his election, rather than the day of his consecration
> as Bishop of Rome, December 27.)*

Leo III is best known for his crowning of Charlemagne,
king of the Franks, as the first Carolingian emperor
(the Carolingian empire was the precursor of the
Holy Roman Empire) in St. Peter's on Christmas day,
800. He is also the first and only pope to offer obei-
sance to a Western emperor.

Leo III's election to the papacy on December 26,
795, although unanimous, was opposed by aristocratic
relatives of Leo's predecessor, Hadrian I. On April 25,
799, he was violently attacked while in procession to
Mass and an unsuccessful attempt was made to cut
out his tongue and blind him. He was then formally
deposed and sent off to a monastery, from which he
later escaped with the help of friends. He made his
way to Charlemagne's court at Paderborn and was received with all due pomp.

A year later Charles himself arrived in Rome and
was greeted in a manner appropriate for a visiting emperor. On December 1, 800, the king held a council in
St. Peter's to examine charges of perjury and adultery
against Leo, but the assembly refused to sit in judgment of the pope. On December 23 Leo declared himself ready to be purged of these "false charges" and
thereupon took an oath of purgation, swearing to his
innocence. His opponents were condemned to death,

but the pope had their sentences commuted to exile. Two days later, as Christmas Mass was beginning, Charles rose from his prayers in front of St. Peter's tomb, and the pope placed an imperial crown on his head. The congregation hailed him as "Emperor of the Romans," and Leo knelt in homage before him.

Although now rehabilitated and enjoying the full support of the new emperor, Leo III found himself overshadowed by Charlemagne, who interfered in the business of the Roman church and in the management of the Papal States. When Charlemagne died (January 28, 814), Leo began to act more independently, but unfortunately not more wisely. When another conspiracy against him came to light, he personally tried the conspirators on charges of treason and condemned scores of them to death (815). In spite of his severe, divisive, and morally dubious pontificate, Leo III was included in a catalogue of saints in 1673. He died on June 12, 816, and was buried in St. Peter's. Feast day: June 12.

97 STEPHEN IV (V)

June 22, 816–January 24, 817

Stephen IV (V) was the first pope to anoint an emperor, suggesting thereby that papal approval was necessary for the exercise of full imperial authority—a remarkable reversal of the centuries-old practice by which the Byzantine emperor's approval was necessary for the validity of a papal election. Conciliatory by nature, Stephen had been a widely popular choice for pope. (For an explanation of the dual numbering, see Stephen II [III], number 92.)

Immediately after his election, Stephen sought a meeting with Charlemagne's successor, Louis the Pious. It took place at Rheims in October 816. After an elaborate welcome by the emperor, Stephen anointed and crowned Louis and his consort, Irmengard, in the cathedral, using an alleged "crown of Constantine" he had brought with him from Rome. Extensive discussions reaffirmed the pact between the Frankish crown and the papacy, including the autonomy of the Papal States and the freedom of papal elections, and Stephen returned to Rome with many gifts. But he died three months afterwards, on January 24, 817, and was buried in St. Peter's.

98 PASCHAL I, ST.

January 25, 817–February 11, 824

During Paschal I's pontificate the practice of crowning the emperor in Rome became established. However, this pope was so detested by the Roman people because of his harsh manner of governance that his body could not be buried in St. Peter's as almost every other pope had been. Abbot of St. Stephen's monastery when elected to the papacy on January 24, 817, Paschal was consecrated as Bishop of Rome the very next day.

Soon thereafter the emperor Louis the Pious confirmed the agreements he had reached with Paschal's predecessor, Stephen IV (V), at Rheims, reaffirming papal authority over the Papal States and pledging noninterference in papal elections and other internal ecclesiastical affairs unless explicitly invited to do so. The harmonious relationship with the emperor continued throughout Paschal's pontificate. When Louis's son Lothair, having already been crowned as coemperor in 817 with the pope's approval, came to Italy in 823, Paschal invited him to Rome and solemnly anointed him on Easter Sunday.

Lothair, however, proved more independent than his father. Exercising his royal rights, he held a court and rendered a judgment whereby the abbey of Farfa, just north of Rome, would be exempt from taxation by the Holy See. The pope's supporters disapproved, but his opponents did not. After Lothair left Rome, however, members of the papal household blinded and beheaded two leaders of the pro-Frankish group in the Lateran because of their loyalty to the emperor. Paschal denied any personal involvement, but the emperor sent an investigating team to Rome. The event convinced the Frankish court to exercise closer supervision over Rome, but Paschal died, on February 11, 824, before any change occurred. Paschal's name was included in the catalogue of saints in the late sixteenth century, but his feast (May 14) was suppressed in 1963.

99 EUGENIUS [EUGENE] II

May 11(?), 824–August 27 (?), 827
(May 824– August 827 in the Vatican's official list)

During Eugenius II's pontificate, the papacy came under more direct control of the emperor Louis the

Pious. The change was prompted by factionalism in Rome between the pro-Frankish nobility and the Roman clergy and by the emperor's concern about the chain of events in the previous pontificate, of Paschal I, leading to the murder and exile of leading pro-Frankish officials. Eugenius's election followed several months of disturbances in Rome in which the clergy and aristocracy proposed rival nominations.

Eugenius not only informed the imperial court of his election, but acknowledged its sovereignty in the Papal States and swore an oath of allegiance to Louis. After a meeting between the new pope and the coemperor Lothair in Rome, a "Roman Constitution" was published (November 1, 824), strengthening Frankish control over Rome and the papacy. At a Lateran synod called by Eugenius II in November 826, the terms of the constitution were ratified.

However, the synod also showed its independence from the Frankish court in matters ecclesiastical. It applied to the Frankish church a collection of disciplinary canons dealing with simony (the buying and selling of church offices), the qualifications and duties of bishops, Sunday observance, marriage, and other matters. And when Louis sent an envoy to urge the pope to accept a compromise in the iconoclastic controversy with the East, the pope insisted that the matter had been settled by the Second Council of Nicaea (787). Eugenius II died in late August 827 and was buried in St. Peter's.

100 VALENTINE

August–September 827

Upon the death of Eugenius II, Valentine was unanimously elected by the clergy, nobility, and people of Rome, in accordance with the terms of the new constitution promulgated by the emperor in 824. Valentine was properly consecrated, probably the next day, but he died a month to forty days later. There is no record of any official activities during his brief pontificate. He was probably buried in St. Peter's.

101 GREGORY IV

March 29, 828–January 25, 844
(827–January 844 in the Vatican's official list)

Although Gregory IV's pontificate lasted some sixteen years, it was generally undistinguished. He came from an aristocratic Roman family and was elected with the support of the lay nobility, whose voting rights in papal elections had been restored by the Frankish coemperor Lothair's "Roman Constitution," promulgated during the pontificate of Eugenius II (824).

When a dynastic dispute arose between the emperor Louis the Pious and his sons Lothair, Pepin, and Louis the German, Gregory IV supported Lothair. The Frankish bishops were angered by the display of partisanship, reminded the pope of his oath of loyalty to Louis, and threatened to excommunicate him. The pope held his ground, asserting that the authority of St. Peter's successor was greater than imperial

authority. As the armies of the sons were gathered
against the army of their father near Colmar in the
summer of 833, the brothers persuaded the pope to
go to Louis's camp to negotiate. When he returned
with what he thought to be a reasonable settlement,
the pope found that Lothair had deceived him. On the
night the pope returned, most of Louis's supporters
deserted him and the emperor was forced to surrender unconditionally and was subsequently deposed.
Gregory IV returned to Rome dejected. Little else is
known about Gregory IV's pontificate. He died on January 25, 844, and was buried in St. Peter's.

102 SERGIUS II

January 844–January 27, 847

The pontificate of Sergius II was one of the more
corrupt in the history of the papacy. The cardinal-
priest of the church of Santi Martino e Silvestro ai
Monti, he was elderly and gout-ridden when elected
in late January 844 by his fellow Roman aristocrats
in his titular church. The Roman people had earlier
elected John, a deacon, and had him enthroned in the
Lateran Palace, from which he was quickly expelled.
Given the unsettled situation, Sergius's consecration
as Bishop of Rome took place without awaiting formal approval from the Frankish court, as required
in the Roman Constitution of 824. The emperor Lothair reacted angrily to this breach of protocol. He
sent his son Louis, the new viceroy of Italy, to Rome
with an army.

When he reached Rome, Louis ordered a synod, held in St. Peter's, to investigate the circumstances of Sergius's election and consecration. Although Sergius II's election was ratified, he and the Roman citizenry had to swear allegiance to Lothair and accept the principle that a pope-elect could not be consecrated without imperial approval and in the presence of the emperor's representative.

Sergius proved to be an ambitious builder, including among his accomplishments the enlargement of the Lateran basilica. But he engaged in dubious methods of fund-raising to accomplish these construction projects, including simony. In August 846, Saracen pirates successfully plundered St. Peter's and St. Paul's—acts that many contemporaries viewed as divine retribution for papal corruption. Sergius II died on January 27, 847, and was buried in St. Peter's.

103 LEO IV, ST.

April 10, 847–July 17, 855 (The Vatican's official list begins his pontificate in January, the month of his election, but he was not consecrated as Bishop of Rome until April 10.)

Leo IV did much to repair the city of Rome after the Saracen attacks of 846. Besides giving his attention to the walls of Rome, Leo organized an alliance among several Greek cities in Italy and in 849 launched a successful sea attack against the Saracens just outside of Ostia, as they were preparing to attack Rome once again. The pope's prestige grew with each new initiative and success. However, his relations with the Frankish emperor were strained, since he acted independently of the imperial court most of the time. Leo's authoritarian style was also reflected in his denunciation of powerful Frankish prelates like Hincmar, archbishop of Rheims, and John, archbishop of Ravenna, for their excessive use of episcopal authority; his excommunication of Anastasius, cardinal-priest of San Marcello (and a later antipope); and his refusal of Lothair's request that he appoint Hincmar apostolic vicar.

Leo IV was generally a strict disciplinarian on internal church matters such as penitential practices. Like many of his predecessors, Leo IV rebuilt or restored several churches in Rome, and his portrait in fresco can still be seen in the lower basilica of San Clemente. He died on July 17, 855, and was buried in St. Peter's. His feast day, now suppressed, was July 17.

104 BENEDICT III

September 29, 855–April 17, 858

Little is known of Benedict III's brief pontificate. When Leo IV died, the first choice of the Roman clergy and laity was Hadrian, cardinal-priest of San Marco. When Hadrian refused election, Benedict, the pious and learned cardinal-priest of San Callisto, was chosen. But he too resisted and took refuge in his titular church of San Callisto. The crowds followed him and conducted him directly to the Lateran Palace, where he was installed on July 20, 855. However, some influential pro-imperialist individuals preferred

Anastasius (known as Anastasius Bibliothecarius), the cardinal-priest whom Leo IV had excommunicated because he had sought refuge with the emperor and refused to return to Rome when the pope ordered him back. The pro-imperial party brought Anastasius to Rome and installed him in the Lateran Palace, after having dragged Benedict from the throne and imprisoned him. But after three days of anarchy it became clear that Benedict had wide popular support, while Anastasius was reviled. Anastasius was stripped of his papal insignia and ejected from the Lateran. However, he would reemerge during the next three pontificates as an important counselor to popes and be named librarian of the Roman church. Benedict III died on April 17, 858, and was buried in St. Peter's.

105 NICHOLAS I, ST.

ca. 820–67, pope April 24, 858–November 13, 867

Like Leo the Great (440–61), Gelasius I (492–96), and Gregory the Great (590–604) before him, Nicholas I conceived of the pope as God's representative on earth with authority over the whole Church, East and West, including all of its bishops, and with the right to watch over and influence the state and to receive protection from it.

Nicholas's exalted view of the papacy shaped his whole pontificate. He excommunicated and deposed the archbishop of Ravenna and reinstated him only after he promised to subject himself to Rome in the future. When King Lothair of Lorraine's wife appealed to the pope after being abandoned by her husband for another woman, and after a synod at Aachen and another at Metz ratified the divorce and approved Lothair's second marriage, the pope deposed and ex-communicated the two archbishops (of Cologne and Trier) when they delivered the synodal decrees to him in Rome. The emperor Louis II sent troops to Rome, and Nicholas took refuge in St. Peter's. But eventually the emperor backed off, and Lothair returned to his wife, at least temporarily.

Nicholas I was equally assertive in his relations with the East. He revived the long dormant jurisdictional claims of Rome over Illyricum, and when the patri-arch of Constantinople, Ignatius, was forced to abdi-cate in favor of Photius, the pope refused to recognize Photius and excommunicated him at a synod held in the Lateran in 863. Photius, in turn, excommunicated Nicholas. The pope died on November 13, 867, but the mutual excommunications clearly laid the founda-tion for the East-West Schism of 1054—a schism that perdures to this very day. Nicholas was buried in St. Peter's. Feast day: November 13.

106 HADRIAN [ADRIAN] II

792–867, pope December 14, 867–December 14, 872

Married before ordination, Hadrian II, cardinal-priest of San Marco, was so widely respected that he twice declined election to the papacy (in 855 and 858) before finally accepting election in 867, and then only because the supporters and opponents of Nicholas I's hard-line style could not agree on a successor. Hadrian II's pontificate was marred from the start, when the duke of Spoleto attacked and plundered Rome. Then his own daughter was raped and murdered along with her mother, the pope's wife, by a brother of the former antipope Anastasius, whom Hadrian II had appointed papal archivist. Hadrian fired and excommunicated Anastasius, but less than a year later gave him another position in the chancery.

When he learned of the excommunication and deposition of his predecessor by the patriarch Photius, Hadrian convened a synod in 869 that condemned Photius and his associates. At the same time, he sent personal representatives to the Fourth Council of Constantinople (869–70). The council upheld the Roman synod's condemnation of Photius, but also listed the patriarchates in the order of precedence followed in the East: Rome, Constantinople, Alexandria, Antioch, and Jerusalem. Rome had always opposed the placement of Constantinople ahead of Alexandria, but it relented in this case, thereby restoring peace temporarily between East and West. The pope died on December 14, 872, and was buried in St. Peter's.

107 JOHN VIII

December 14, 872–December 16, 882

John VIII was the first pope (but not the last) to be assassinated. A close collaborator of Pope Nicholas I (858–67) and for twenty years archdeacon, he was unanimously elected pope and consecrated as Bishop of Rome on the same day his predecessor, Hadrian II, died. These were violent and chaotic times, and John VIII's pontificate was faced with one major problem after another. He personally took charge of the defensive efforts against the attacks of the Saracens from the south, working diligently to forge a military alliance among the states of southern Italy. But the alliance soon fell apart when some of the states made their own separate "peace" with the invaders. The pope himself was reduced to bribing them as well.

John VIII turned eastward for help against the Saracens. Photius by now had been reinstated as patriarch of Constantinople, and there was still much bad blood between him and Rome. But the pope was willing to compromise to secure military aid. With Photius presiding, a council was held in the Hagia Sophia in Constantinople in November 879, at which the Second Council of Nicaea (787) was recognized. The council also annulled the synods that had anathematized Photius and forbade any additions to the creed of Constantinople (381). John VIII ratified the council's decisions so long as they did not contradict any of the instructions he had given his legates, and he recognized Photius as patriarch.

John VIII was poisoned by some of his associates, perhaps even by his own relatives, and then clubbed to death on December 16, 882. None of the sources indicates a reason for his murder. He was buried in St. Peter's.

108 MARINUS I

December 16, 882–May 15, 884

Marinus I was the first bishop of another diocese (Caere, now Cerveteri) to be elected Bishop of Rome, in violation of canon 15 of the First Council of Nicaea (325). The son of a priest, he entered the service of the Roman church at the age of twelve, was ordained a deacon by Nicholas I (858–67), and served as one of three papal legates to the Fourth Council of Constantinople (869–70). He later served as archdeacon and treasurer of the Roman church and then bishop of Caere in Etruria. Sometimes mistakenly listed as Martin II, he was elected and consecrated as Bishop of Rome on December 16, 882, without consulting the emperor, Charles III. However, when Charles III visited Italy, he gave his recognition to the new pope and had constructive discussions with him. Marinus tried his best to maintain good relations with Photius, the patriarch of Constantinople. Marinus I died on May 15, 884, and was buried in the portico, or porch, of St. Peter's.

109 HADRIAN [ADRIAN] III, ST.

May 17, 884–September 885

Almost nothing is known of Hadrian III's brief pontificate, but he may have been one of the few popes in history to have been assassinated. His election to the papacy, two days after the death of Marinus I, is shrouded in obscurity. He was consecrated the same day, May 17, 884. He seems to have been a supporter of the policies of Pope John VIII (872–82) rather than of his immediate predecessor, Marinus I, thus underscoring the point that popes are not usually succeeded by carbon copies of themselves. One of his few recorded acts was the blinding of a high official of the Lateran Palace, an enemy of Pope John VIII whom Pope Marinus had permitted to return from exile. There is also a report that Hadrian III had a noblewoman whipped naked through the streets of Rome. According to J. N. D. Kelly, these acts suggest that the bloody vendettas that erupted after Pope John VIII's assassination in 882 were continuing.

At the request of the emperor Charles III, the pope set out from Rome in the summer of 885 to attend the imperial Diet of Worms (in Germany). However, he seems to have met with foul play during his journey near Modena (in Italy). His body was buried in the abbey of Nonantola. In spite of his crude punishment of the palace official and the noblewoman, Hadrian III was regarded as a saint in Rome, and his name was officially added to the list of saints in 1891. Feast day: July 8 (or 9).

110 STEPHEN V (VI)

September 885–September 14, 891

Stephen V (VI) is largely responsible for pushing the Slavs away from Rome and eventually into the arms of Orthodoxy when, after the death of St. Methodius

(885), one of the apostles to the Slavs, he forbade the Old Slavonic liturgy. (For an explanation of the dual numbering, see Stephen II [III], number 92.) A priest of the church of Santi Quattro Coronati, Stephen was unanimously elected sometime toward the end of September 885 and was consecrated as Bishop of Rome by Bishop Formosus of Porto (who become pope himself in 891) in a ceremony witnessed by the imperial legate.

Stephen faced problems on two fronts: continued factional conflict in Rome and increasing Saracen raids. The emperor Charles III could be of no assistance to the pope because he had troubles of his own in France; in 887 he himself was deposed. The Carolingian empire had ended. When no one stepped in to fill the power vacuum, the pope turned in desperation to Guido III, the duke of Spoleto, who had seized the throne of Italy. The pope crowned him emperor in St. Peter's in 891. The duke thereupon asserted his own supremacy over the Papal States. Stephen V (VI) maintained friendly relations with Constantinople, with the hope that the Byzantine emperor could provide military aid against the Saracens.

When Methodius died on April 6, 885, at the prodding of the German clergy the pope informed Methodius's successor, Godarz, that the Moravian church could not use the Old Slavonic liturgy. Methodius's disciples then fled to Bulgaria, where they reverted to the Byzantine rite in the Slavonic language. Eventually this Slavonic-speaking church would spread into other countries, including especially Russia. Stephen V (VI) died September 14, 891, and was buried in the portico, or porch, of St. Peter's.

111 FORMOSUS

ca. 815–96,
pope October 6, 891–April 4, 896.

Formosus is most famous (or infamous) for what happened to him after his death. His body was exhumed, propped up on a throne in full pontifical vestments, and subjected to a mock trial, the so-called Cadaver Synod, in which the dead pope was found guilty of perjury and of coveting the papacy. His body was mutilated and thrown into the Tiber River (although subsequently reburied). The Cadaver Synod divided the Italian church in two and affected several subsequent papal elections.

Already about seventy-six when elected pope, Formosus was a man of exceptional intelligence, ability, and even sanctity. As pope, he strengthened and promoted Christianity in England and northern Germany and maintained friendly relations with Constantinople. However, he made some bitter political enemies because of his support for Arnuf, king of the Franks, who eventually invaded Italy. These included one of his own successors, Stephen VI (VII), who ordered Formosus's body exhumed nine months after his death at age eighty and put on trial, over which Stephen himself presided. It is perhaps little wonder that there has never been a Pope Formosus II.

112 BONIFACE VI

April 896

Boniface VI was the only man elected to the papacy after having been defrocked twice (by Pope John VIII, no less) for immorality, once from the subdiaconate and the other time from the ordained priesthood, or presbyterate. The son of a bishop, Boniface was elected almost immediately after the death of Formosus, probably on April 4 or 11, under pressure from rioting mobs. He was consecrated as Bishop of Rome on the Sunday following his election. The Roman people's action may have reflected their hostility toward the absent German emperor, Arnulf, and his resident governor. Boniface's was probably the second shortest pontificate in history, after Urban VII (twelve days in 1590). He died after only about fifteen days in office, the victim of a severe case of gout. He was buried in the portico, or porch, of St. Peter's.

113 STEPHEN VI (VII)

May 896–August 897

The name of Stephen VI (VII) belongs among the infamous popes for having ordered the exhumation of Pope Formosus's body and then for presiding over a mock trial (the so-called Cadaver Synod) of the deceased pope in January 897. (For an explanation of the dual numbering, see Stephen II [III], number 92.) The trial of Formosus (see Formosus, number 111) was surely inspired by fanatical hatred, but perhaps also by canonical calculation. Formosus, after all, had appointed Stephen as bishop of Anagni. If Formosus's papal acts and ordinations were declared invalid (which the Cadaver Synod did do), then Stephen's appointment and ordination as bishop of Anagni were invalid. In that case, his own election as Bishop of Rome could not be challenged canonically on the grounds that he was already the bishop of another diocese.

Following the mock trial Stephen VI (VII) required clergy ordained by Formosus to submit letters renouncing their ordinations as invalid. A few months later, however, an outraged populace, including many of Formosus's supporters, rebelled. Stephen was deposed, imprisoned, and strangled to death. He was buried in St. Peter's.

114 ROMANUS

Date of death unknown, pope August–November 897

Little or nothing is known of the pontificate of Romanus. After the deposition, imprisonment, and murder of Stephen VI (VII), Romanus was elected and consecrated as Bishop of Rome sometime in August 897. We do know that Romanus was a member of the pro-Formosan faction, which shows again how often popes are succeeded by men different from themselves in outlook and loyalties. He seems to have become a monk after his brief period on the papal throne. If so, he was probably deposed by the same pro-Formosan faction that elected him in the hope of replacing him with a more vigorous and effective defender of their hero's memory. In any case, the precise date of his death is unknown. Nor do we know where he was buried.

115 THEODORE II

November/December 897
(December 897 in the Vatican's official list)

Although he was in office only twenty days (the exact dates are unknown), Theodore II held a synod invalidating the so-called Cadaver Synod of 897, which had placed the corpse of Pope Formosus on trial (see Formosus, number 111). Theodore II rehabilitated Formosus, recognized the validity of his ordinations and papal acts, and ordered burned all the letters solicited by Pope Stephen VI (VII) from the clergy renouncing their ordinations. Theodore then ordered the body of Formosus to be exhumed from the private grave in which it had been placed after being flung into the Tiber River, reclothed in pontifical vestments, and reburied with honors in its original grave in St. Peter's. The circumstances of Theodore II's own death are unknown, but one historian believes that the pope's courageous acts cost him his life. Given the highly charged atmosphere at the time, such speculation is probably not without foundation. He was buried in St. Peter's.

116 JOHN IX

January 898–January 900

John IX also convened a Roman synod to continue the annulment of the so-called Cadaver Synod of 897, which had placed the deceased Pope Formosus on trial (see Formosus, number 111). John moved quickly to complete his predecessor's efforts in rehabilitating Pope Formosus. The synod also prohibited trials of deceased persons and decreed that, although the pope should be elected by bishops and clergy at the request of the senate and people of Rome, his consecration should take place in the presence of imperial representatives. However, the death of the young emperor in a hunting accident and the irregularity of the imperial succession prevented the matter pertaining to papal elections from being enforced. Total chaos would follow John's pontificate. He died in January 900 and was buried in St. Peter's. However, no monument honors his memory.

117 BENEDICT IV

February 900–July 903

Very little is known of Benedict IV's pontificate except that Rome continued to be torn apart by partisan conflict between the supporters and enemies of the late Pope Formosus (891–96). Because of the political and social chaos, few reliable records remain from this period—which explains why the circumstances and date of Benedict IV's election and consecration as Bishop of Rome are uncertain. We do know that he held a synod at the Lateran (the papal palace) on August 31, 900, which confirmed Arginus as bishop of Langres (France) and ratified Pope Formosus's granting of the pallium (the woolen vestment worn around the neck as a sign of pastoral authority) to him.

With the accidental death of the young Lambert of Spoleto, who left no male heir, Italy was thrown into political chaos. Berengar of Friuli, king of Italy since 888, might have filled the void, but he was defeated by the Magyars in 899 and his supremacy in Italy was subsequently challenged by the young king Louis "the Blind" of Provence, grandson of the emperor Louis II. The pope crowned Louis emperor in February 901, but soon thereafter Berengar regained his political and military strength and defeated Louis in August 902, driving him permanently out of Italy. Without an imperial protector, Rome once again fell into political and social anarchy. Benedict IV is believed by some to have been murdered by agents of Berengar, probably in July 903. He was buried in St. Peter's.

118 LEO V

d. early 904 or October 905,
pope July/August–September 903

After less than two months in office, Leo V was overthrown by an antipope, Christopher, imprisoned, and murdered. At the time of his election, Leo was a priest in a town about twenty miles southwest of Rome. Historians do not know how a man who was not a member of the Roman clergy could have been elected pope in this period. But perhaps because he was an outsider, he was overthrown in a palace revolution by

Christopher, cardinal-priest of San Damaso, who declared himself pope and had Leo thrown into prison.
But Christopher was, in turn, overthrown by Sergius
(later Pope Sergius III) and sent to prison with Leo. After enduring several weeks of misery, both were murdered. Leo V may have been buried in St. Peter's or in
the Lateran.

119 SERGIUS III

January 29, 904–April 14, 911

Although conventional wisdom makes Alexander VI
(1492–1503) the historic symbol of papal corruption,
few other popes in history can vie with the murderous
Sergius III, who was responsible for the deaths of his
predecessor and his predecessor's rival, the antipope
Christopher. Subsequently, he held a synod that reaffirmed the infamous Cadaver Synod of 897, which had
placed the corpse of Pope Formosus on trial.

Gripped by hatred of Formosus, Sergius was originally elected pope to succeed Theodore II in 897 and
was even installed in the Lateran Palace, but was
quickly ejected in favor of the pro-Formosan John
IX, who had the support of the emperor Lambert of
Spoleto. Sergius was deposed and driven into exile,
but found himself with a second chance when, seven
years later, the antipope Christopher overthrew Leo V.
Sergius marched on Rome with an armed force, threw
Christopher into prison, was acclaimed pope, and was
consecrated on January 29, 904. Soon afterward, he

had both Leo and Christopher strangled to death in prison.

Sergius dated his own reign from December 897, when he was first "elected," and he regarded all subsequent popes as intruders. He forced the clergy under threat of violence to attend a synod that reaffirmed the Cadaver Synod and declared Formosus's papal acts and ordinations invalid. Since Formosus had created many bishops and they, in turn, had ordained many priests, there was complete confusion in the Church. Sergius ordered, again under threat, that all those ordinations be repeated. Public opposition was impossible. Sergius had the support of the noble families, particularly that of Theophylact, a powerful official who commanded the local militia. Sergius III died on April 15, 911, and was buried in the Lateran Basilica. His tomb has not been preserved.

120 ANASTASIUS III

ca. June 911–ca. August 913 (April 911–June 913 in the Vatican's official list; September 911– October 913 in Levillain's Dictionnaire historique de la papauté)

The pontificate of Anastasius III was completely dominated by the Theophylact family, specifically by its powerful head (consul, senator, financial director of the Holy See) and his ambitious wife. No records survive of Anastasius's election and consecration as Bishop of Rome, and little of his pontificate. He did receive a lengthy letter from Nicholas, the reinstated

patriarch of Constantinople, that deplored Pope
Sergius III's approval of the emperor Leo VI's fourth
marriage in 906 and the behavior of the papal legates.
There is no record of the pope's reply, but it probably was unsatisfactory, because Nicholas removed
the pope's name from the list of those to be prayed
for at Mass and once again relations between Rome
and Constantinople soured. After a pontificate of just
over two years, Anastasius III died and was buried in
St. Peter's.

121 LANDO [LANDUS]

*ca. August 913–ca. March 914 (July 913–February 914
in the Vatican's official list; November 913–March 914
in Levillain's Dictionnaire historique de la papauté)*

Historians do not agree on the date of Lando's election and consecration as Bishop of Rome. It is likely
that his candidacy had been approved by the powerful
Theophylact family in Rome. His brief pontificate of
about six months was undistinguished. Indeed, nothing is recorded of his reign except a donation, given
in memory of his father, to the cathedral church in
his home territory of Sabina. He was buried in St.
Peter's.

122 JOHN X

*March/April 914–May 928 (March 914–May 928 in
the Vatican's official list; Levillain's* Dictionnaire
historique de la papauté *begins his pontificate in
early April and places his death in 929.)*

John X had been archbishop of Ravenna for nine years
when, at the instigation of the Roman nobility and especially of the Theophylact family, he was elected to
the papacy. Perhaps the Roman nobles' real motive for
summoning John X from Ravenna to Rome was his
reputation for leadership; at the time their grand estates were being threatened by the continued Saracen
raids on central Italy. John X immediately organized
a coalition of Italian princes and persuaded the Byzantine emperor, Constantine VII, to help defeat the
Saracens.

During his fourteen-year pontificate, John X approved the monastic rule of the abbey of Cluny (910),
promoted the conversion of the Normans, settled disputes over episcopal succession, and worked to bring
Croatia and Dalmatia back into communion with
Rome and to restore unity with the Eastern Church.
What led to the pope's downfall were his deliberate
efforts to mark a course independently of Rome's
powerful noble families. John X's pact with the new
king of Italy, Hugh of Provence, alarmed the powerful Theophylact family, who organized a revolt against
John X and his brother Peter, whom the pope had
come increasingly to rely upon. Peter was killed in the
Lateran before John X's eyes, and a half year later the

pope himself was deposed and imprisoned at Castel Sant'Angelo. He died after several months (probably in early 929), almost certainly by suffocation. He was buried in the Lateran Basilica.

123 LEO VI

May–December 928

The brief pontificate of Leo VI, an elderly priest (in the title of Santa Susanna) elected in order to keep the papal throne warm for a son of the powerful Theophylact family, has left no significant historical trace. It is canonically significant, however, that he was elected and consecrated as Bishop of Rome while his predecessor, John X, was still alive and in prison. Had John's deposition from office been canonically valid? If not, Leo VI's election was invalid and he does not belong on the official list of popes. Leo VI died before his predecessor, John X, was murdered in prison. Leo VI was buried in St. Peter's.

124 STEPHEN VII (VIII)

December 928–February 931

Stephen VII (VIII; for an explanation of the dual numbering, see Stephen II [III], number 92) was elected to succeed Leo VI while Leo's predecessor, John X, was still alive and in prison. The same canonical question that can be raised about the validity of Leo VI's election to the papacy can be raised about Stephen's. Had

John's deposition from office been canonically valid? If not, Stephen's election was invalid and he, like Leo VI, does not belong on the official list of popes. Like Leo VI, Stephen VII (VIII) was a stopgap appointment, manipulated by the powerful Theophylact family, and particularly by Marozia, who wanted to ensure that her son John would someday be pope. Because of the absence of written records from this turbulent and chaotic period of papal history, Stephen's only recorded actions concern the confirmation or extension of privileges granted to certain monasteries and religious houses in Italy and France. He was buried in the crypt of St. Peter's.

125 JOHN XI

March 931–December 935 or January 936 (March 931–December 935 in the Vatican's official list)

Elected and consecrated as Bishop of Rome while still in his early twenties, Pope John XI was the illegitimate son of Pope Sergius III (904–11) and Marozia, the head of the powerful Theophylact family. This is the only recorded instance of an illegitimate son of a previous pope succeeding to the papacy himself.

Among John XI's first official acts was to confirm that the new reformist abbey of Cluny (founded in 909) was under the protection of the Holy See and that its abbots were to be freely elected. The summer of 932 John XI officiated at the wedding of the widowed Marozia and Hugh of Provence, king of Italy. The wedding and the pope's participation in it were highly controversial because Hugh was Marozia's brother-in-law. A revolt was incited by Alberic II, Marozia's son from her first marriage, whom Hugh had insulted at the wedding banquet. In December an armed mob stormed Castel Sant'Angelo, where the couple were residing. Hugh escaped, but Alberic imprisoned his mother and his half brother, the pope, and proclaimed himself prince of Rome, senator of all the Romans, count, and patrician. John XI was later released from prison and placed under house arrest in the Lateran, where Alberic treated him as his personal slave. He was buried in the basilica of St. John Lateran.

126 LEO VII

January 3, 936–July 13, 939

Elected through the direct influence of Alberic II, the absolute ruler of Rome at this time, Leo VII was consecrated as Bishop of Rome on January 3, 936, and restricted thereafter to purely ecclesiastical functions during his pontificate. Probably of Benedictine background himself, Leo VII promoted the revival of monasticism. A serious moral blot on his record occurred in 937 or thereabouts when he encouraged his newly appointed archbishop of Mainz to expel Jews who refused to be baptized. He died on July 13, 939, of unknown causes and was buried in St. Peter's.

127 STEPHEN VIII (IX)

July 14, 939–October 942

Like his predecessor, Leo VII, Stephen VIII (IX) was elected (on the same day Leo VII died) through the direct influence of Alberic II, the absolute ruler of Rome at this time. (For an explanation of the dual numbering, see Stephen II [III], number 92.) He was consecrated as Bishop of Rome the next day, July 14. And like Leo VII, he was restricted by Alberic to purely ecclesiastical matters. He supported the new reformist monastery in Cluny and the reform of monasteries in Rome and central Italy. He also supported Louis IV as king of France and ordered the people of France and Burgundy to do so under pain of excommunication. In the last months of his life, Stephen VIII (IX) fell out of favor with Alberic, perhaps because he became involved in a conspiracy against him. The pope was imprisoned, mutilated, and died of his wounds sometime in late October 942. He was buried in St. Peter's.

128 MARINUS II

October 30, 942–May 946

Like his two immediate predecessors, Marinus II was the creature of Alberic II, the absolute ruler of Rome, and was allowed to do little during his pontificate. Elected and consecrated as Bishop of Rome a few days after the death of Stephen VIII (IX), Marinus II left little or no historical trace. Among his recorded acts were his defense of the privileges and properties of the abbey of Monte Cassino against the avaricious bishop of Capua and his appointing its abbot as head of the monastery attached to the Roman basilica of St. Paul's Outside the Walls. Marinus II is sometimes mistakenly listed as Martin III (just as the first Pope Marinus [882–84] was mistakenly listed as Martin II). He died sometime during the month of May 946 and was buried in St. Peter's.

129 AGAPITUS II

May 10, 946–December 955

Like his three immediate predecessors, Agapitus II had been elected through the direct influence of Alberic, the absolute ruler of Rome. He was consecrated as Bishop of Rome on May 10, 946. With King Otto I of Germany and King Louis IV of France, the papal delegate of Agapitus II presided over a synod at Ingelheim, which resolved the dispute over episcopal succession in the diocese of Rheims and ordered Louis's rival in France to submit to Louis under pain of excommunication. The pope ratified these decisions at a Roman synod in 949.

As Alberic lay dying, he summoned the clergy and nobility to St. Peter's, where he compelled them, in the presence of the pope and in direct violation of the decree of Pope Symmachus in 499, to take an oath that his illegitimate son Octavian would be elected to succeed Agapitus II. The pope died a year later and was buried in the apse of the basilica of St. John Lateran.

130 JOHN XII

December 16, 955–May 14, 964

John XII was elected (at age eighteen) because of the oath exacted illegally from the clergy and nobility by his dying father, Alberic II, absolute ruler of Rome. He is known for establishing the Holy Roman Empire and for the gross immorality of his private life.

John XII engaged in a disastrous attempt to enlarge the Papal States by military force against Capua and Benevento, while the northern regions of the papal territories were being plundered by the king of Italy. The pope dispatched two envoys to the king of Germany, Otto I, to ask for his help and to offer the imperial crown in return. Otto restored papal sovereignty in the north of Italy and entered Rome on January 31, 962. On February 2 the pope anointed and crowned him emperor. This act established the Holy Roman Empire, which was to last until 1806.

Otto added substantial territories to the Papal States, but also subjected papal elections once again to imperial approval and made popes swear allegiance to the emperor and recognize him as overlord of the Papal States. Resentful, the pope began intriguing against the emperor as soon as he left Rome. In November 963, the emperor returned, and John XII fled with the papal treasury to Tivoli. In his absence, he was deposed by a Roman synod presided over by Otto, who then proposed the name of Leo, a layman, as a worthy successor. Leo was elected on December 4, 963, and consecrated as Bishop of Rome two days later, after receiving all the requisite Holy Orders in sequence. Did the synod have the right to judge the pope and to depose him? If not, are Leo VIII's election and consecration valid?

Leo's own behavior in office disturbed the Roman people, who rallied to John's support after the emperor left the city once more. Leo VIII fled, and John XII exacted severe reprisals against the imperial partisans. At a synod on February 26, 964, the previous imperial synod was nullified, Leo VIII was deposed, and his ordinations were declared invalid. But soon thereafter Otto marched back into Rome and John retreated from the city once again. In early May he suffered a stroke (it is said, while in bed with a married woman) and died a week later, still in his middle twenties. He was buried in the Lateran Basilica.

131 LEO VIII

December 6, 963–March 1, 965

Leo VIII's pontificate overlapped with two others: John XII's (between December 4, 963, and John's death on May 14, 964) and Benedict V's (between May 22 and June 23, 964). The legitimacy of Leo's own election in 963 has been a matter of canonical debate because of the questionable nature of John XII's deposition by a Roman synod presided over by the German emperor on December 4, 863. Significantly, the official list of popes in the Vatican's *Annuario Pontificio* accepts the overlapping without resolving the canonical question.

Leo VIII had been a skilled Lateran official of good reputation. Leo's election, however, proved unpopular with the Roman people. They were encouraged in their dissatisfaction by the deposed John XII from his refuge in Tivoli. As soon as the emperor and his troops left Rome in mid-January, widespread disturbances erupted in the city, and Leo VIII was forced to seek asylum in the imperial court, thereby allowing John XII to regain the papal throne. When John XII died, the Romans ignored Leo VIII and urged the emperor to elect the cardinal-deacon Benedict. The emperor refused because he had personally arranged Leo's election. But the Romans ignored the emperor's wishes and proceeded to elect and enthrone Benedict as Benedict V on May 22. The emperor reentered the city on June 23 and reinstated Leo VIII as pope. A few days later Leo convened yet another synod, which deposed and ecclesiastically degraded Benedict V, who was later deported to Hamburg in 865. Nothing else is known of Leo VIII's brief and canonically dubious pontificate. He was buried in St. Peter's.

132 BENEDICT V

   d. July 4, 966, pope May 22–June 23, 964

Benedict V's one-month-long pontificate was canonically dubious because another claimant to the papacy, Leo VIII, was still alive. When the licentious John XII died on May 14, 964, the Roman people and many of the clergy ignored the wishes of the emperor Otto I to reinstate Leo VIII (whom John XII had deposed as a usurper). Instead, on May 22 they acclaimed Benedict, a learned, reformist cardinal-deacon, as pope, had him consecrated as Bishop of Rome, and enthroned him in the Lateran Palace.

The emperor laid siege to the city of Rome, threatening to starve the people into submission. The people soon yielded and handed over Benedict to the emperor on June 23. A synod presided over jointly by Leo VIII and the emperor Otto I condemned Benedict as a usurper. Benedict retained the rank of deacon but was deported to Hamburg, where the local bishop treated him with courtesy and dignity. When Leo VIII died on March 1, 965, some called for Benedict V's restoration, but there was no general interest in him. Twenty years after his death in Hamburg (July 4, 966), Benedict's body was returned to Rome. His place of burial in Rome, however, is unknown.

133 JOHN XIII

October 1, 965–September 6, 972

John XIII's pontificate was largely in the service of the ecclesiastical and political agenda of the German emperor Otto I, who had directly influenced John's election. The Roman people resented John XIII's dependence on a foreign sovereign and hated him for his authoritarian style of governance. In the midst of a popular revolt less than three months after his election, John was assaulted, imprisoned, and exiled to the Campagna. He escaped and made contact with the emperor. The Romans eventually repented of their actions and, on November 14 of the following year, welcomed John XIII back to the city.

At Christmas, 967, John crowned Otto's twelve-year-old son Otto II as coemperor. Less than five years later, in the hope that relations between East and West could be improved, John XIII officiated at the marriage of Otto II and a Greek princess, a niece of the Byzantine emperor John I, and crowned her as empress. But tensions deepened, especially when the pope elevated Capua and Benevento to metropolitan archdioceses, even though they fell within provinces under Byzantine control. After his death on September 6, 972, John XIII was buried in the basilica of St. Paul's Outside the Walls.

134 BENEDICT VI

January 19, 973–July 974 (January 19, 973–June 974 in the Vatican's official list)

The circumstances of Benedict VI's election remain obscure. He seems to have had the support of both the pro-imperial party and the reformers, but not the Roman aristocracy. His early decisions were consistent with the emperor's interests as well as the reformers', but when Otto died on May 7, the pope lost his pillar of support. The new emperor, Otto II, preoccupied with his own troubles in Germany, could provide no help when a nationalist faction, led by the head of the Crescentii family, mounted a revolt against Benedict VI. In June 974 the pope was seized and imprisoned in Castel Sant'Angelo. A cardinal-deacon named Franco, the candidate originally favored by the Crescentii family to succeed John XIII, was quickly elected and consecrated as pope, taking the name Boniface VII. The imperial representative hurried to Rome the next month to demand Benedict's release, but Boniface, the antipope, had Benedict strangled to death in order to strengthen his own claim on the papacy.

Remarkably, the antipope Boniface VII remained in office for some eleven months without significant imperial or popular protest. He died suddenly on July 20, 985, giving rise to suspicions that he had been murdered. Until 1904 Boniface VII was classified as a legitimate pope, and the next pope to assume the name Boniface took the number VIII. Some have argued that Boniface VII was a legitimate pope from the date of John XIV's death in August 984. The legitimate pope, Benedict VI, had died by strangulation in June 974 and was buried in St. Peter's.

135 BENEDICT VII

October 974–July 10, 983

After Benedict VI was murdered by the antipope Boniface VII, Benedict VII, then bishop of Sutri, near Viterbo, was elected pope with the support of the emperor Otto II and the pro-imperial party and aristocratic families of Rome. The new pope immediately convened a synod at which the antipope Boniface VII was excommunicated. However, Boniface mounted a revolt against Benedict VII in the summer of 980, forcing the pope to leave the city. The pope appealed to the emperor, but it took until the following March to be restored.

Benedict VII was primarily a spiritual rather than a political pope. He promoted monasticism and monastic reform in France, Germany, and Italy and prohibited simony (the buying and selling of church offices and spiritual benefits). But in other ecclesiastical matters, he was little more than a tool of the emperor. For example, he suppressed and divided the diocese of Merseburg in Germany so that its bishop, a favorite of the emperor, could be promoted to the more prestigious diocese of Magdeburg. After his death on July 10, 983, Benedict VII was buried in Santa Croce in Gerusalemme, one of the seven ancient basilicas of Rome.

136 JOHN XIV

December 983–August 20, 984

John XIV was not the first pope to change his name upon election to the papacy (John II had done so in 533, John III in 561, and John XII in 955), but he is the first one to have done so because his baptismal name was Peter. He did not wish to take the papal name of the Blessed Apostle himself.

No sooner had John XIV been installed when Otto II was stricken with malaria and died in the pope's arms. The empress, Theophano, immediately left Rome for Germany to defend the claim of her three-year-old son, Otto III. John XIV was now completely defenseless against his enemies. The antipope Boniface VII returned from exile in Constantinople in April 984. John was arrested, beaten, deposed from office, and imprisoned at Castel Sant'Angelo. He died four months later of starvation. Some reports indicate that he was poisoned. John XIV was buried in St. Peter's.

137 JOHN XV

August 985–March 996

John XV was the first pope formally to canonize a saint: Ulric, bishop of Augsburg, in 993. Cardinal-priest of the church of San Vitale when elected with the support of the powerful Crescentii family, John XV, it should be noted, was regarded as the successor of the antipope Boniface VII, who died on July 20, 985, rather than of Pope John XIV, who died of starvation or poisoning on August 20, 984, after having been deposed and imprisoned by Boniface. Indeed, Boniface VII has only been considered an antipope since 1904. Before that, he was included on the ancient lists of popes, even though usually described as an intruder. Moreover, the next pope to take the name Boniface took the number VIII, not VII. Thus can the Holy Spirit cross the canonical wires!

Immediately after his election, John XV allied himself with the Roman nobility and alienated his clergy in the process. His greed also fueled their contempt for him. Nevertheless, the new pope attended to (mostly) political business. He mediated a dispute between the king of England and the duke of Normandy in 991. The following year he accepted Poland from Duke Mieszko as a papal fief, with responsibility for protecting Poland from Germany and Bohemia. Even his historic canonization of Ulric of Augsburg in 993 advanced imperial interests.

In March 995, facing the contempt of his own clergy for his avariciousness and nepotism and suffering under the harsh thumb of the powerful Crescentii family, who controlled the Papal States, John XV sought asylum in Sutri, from which he sent envoys to the young emperor Otto III to seek help against his enemies. Otto III set out from Regensburg in February 996, but the pope died of fever before the emperor reached Rome. John XV was buried in St. Peter's.

138 GREGORY V

Saxon, 972–99, pope May 3, 996–February 18, 999

Gregory V was the first German pope. He was only twenty-four years old when chosen by his father's cousin, the emperor Otto III, whom he served as chaplain. The pope-designate, Bruno by name and the great-grandson of the emperor Otto I, was accompanied to Rome by two German bishops and was formally elected and consecrated on May 3, 996, taking the name Gregory V out of respect for Pope Gregory the Great (590–604).

On the feast of the Ascension, a little more than two weeks later, Gregory V crowned Otto as emperor and patrician in St. Peter's and named him protector of the Church. After the emperor left Rome in June 996 for Germany, local resentment toward the foreign pope boiled over, and the pope was driven out of Rome by the powerful Crescentii family. Gregory V sought refuge in Spoleto, from which he made two armed attempts to recover Rome. Both attempts failed. He moved to Lombardy in January 997 and early the next month excommunicated Crescentius, the head of the Crescentii family. Later that month the now excommunicated Crescentius in effect declared the papal office vacant and, with the connivance of the Byzantine envoy, had John Philagathos, archbishop of Piacenza, elected and consecrated as John XVI. The new antipope was soon excommunicated by the Western bishops, and Gregory V returned to Rome in the company of the emperor, where he presided over a synod that deposed the antipope John XVI. Crescentius was beheaded. Gregory V died of malaria in February 999, not yet thirty. He was buried in St. Peter's.

139 SYLVESTER [SILVESTER] II

French, ca. 945–1003,
pope April 2, 999–May 12, 1003

Sylvester II was the first French pope. His choice of the name Sylvester represented a conscious decision to associate himself with Pope Sylvester I (314–35), who had long been considered a model of papal cooperation with the emperor. Well-educated in literature, music, mathematics, philosophy, logic, and astronomy, Sylvester made an about-turn after his election to the papacy. A strong supporter of the rights of the French bishops and an equally strong critic of the papacy in the midst of the dispute over the archdiocese of Rheims (991–95), he became a tenacious advocate of papal rights, acting in an authoritarian manner toward various bishops who incurred his displeasure.

But in February 1001, the Romans revolted once again against foreign domination. The emperor and pope were forced to leave the city. Otto died the following year before he could reestablish his authority in Rome. The new head of the Crescentii family, John II Crescentius, allowed the pope to return, but on condition that he limit himself to spiritual functions. The pope died less than a year later, on May 12, 1003, and was buried in the Lateran Basilica.

140 JOHN XVII

May 16–November 6, 1003 (June–December 1003 in the Vatican's official list; but J. N. D. Kelly and Levillain's Dictionnaire historique de la papauté *give the May–November dates.)*

John XVII's short pontificate left little or no trace in the history of the papacy. He took the number XVII because there was an antipope named John XVI between John XV and himself. John XVII was probably a relative of the dominant Crescentii family in Rome, and his election was undoubtedly engineered by the family's leader, John II Crescentius. The pope's only notable recorded papal act was his authorizing of Polish missionaries to work among the Slavs. It is not known how he died or how old he was when he died. He was probably buried in the Lateran Basilica.

141 JOHN XVIII

December 25, 1003–June/July 1009 (January 1004–July 1009 in the Vatican's official list; J. N. D. Kelly gives June/July as the end of this pontificate; Levillain's Dictionnaire historique de la papauté *gives late June.)*

Little is known of John XVIII's pontificate, but he may have abdicated shortly before his death and become a monk at the basilica of St. Paul's Outside the Walls. He was cardinal-priest of St. Peter's when elected to the papacy through the decisive influence of the head of the powerful Crescentii family, who ruled Rome from 1003 to 1012. In 1004 he did restore the diocese of Merseburg, which Pope Benedict VII had suppressed and divided in 981 and also approved in 1007 the establishment of the diocese of Bamberg in Bavaria. There is evidence that relations between Rome and Constantinople improved during this pontificate, perhaps because of the pro-Byzantine sympathies of the Crescentii family head. If John XVIII did abdicate before his death in late June or early July 1009, it is probable that he was forced to do so. He was buried in the basilica of St. Paul's Outside the Walls.

142 SERGIUS IV

July 31, 1009–May 12, 1012

Sergius IV was the second pope to have changed his name upon election to the papacy because his baptismal name was Peter. He did not want to take the name

of the Blessed Apostle Peter. Like that of his immediate predecessors, his elevation to the papacy was the
product of the powerful Crescentii family of Rome.
Very little is known of this pontificate. Sergius IV did
send representatives to the consecration of the Bamberg cathedral and ratified the privileges bestowed on
it by Pope John XVIII. In May 1012 there was a violent revolt in Rome. Both the pope and the head of
the Crescentii family, John II Crescentius, disappeared
within a week of one another, and a new pope was
elected under the influence of the rival Tusculan family. These circumstances have given rise to the not im-
probable belief that both Pope Sergius IV and John II
Crescentius were murdered. The pope was buried in
the basilica of St. John Lateran.

143 BENEDICT VIII

*ca. 980–1024, pope May 18, 1012–April 9, 1024 (J. N. D.
Kelly begins the pontificate on May 17, and Levillain's*
Dictionnaire historique de la papauté *identifies the
date of consecration as May 21.)*

The first in a series of three laymen elected consecu-
tively to the papacy, Benedict VIII (born Theophylact)
established himself from the outset as a political and
even military pope. Elected on May 17, 1012, he was
given minor and major sacramental Orders and consecrated as Bishop of Rome on May 18 (or possibly May
21). A product of the newly ascendant Tusculan family,
he used armed force to crush the rival Crescentii family while his brother Romanus (later Pope John XIX)

assumed the reins of civil government in Rome. Benedict VIII restored good relations with the German emperor, inviting Henry II to Rome and crowning him in St. Peter's in February 1014. The pope spent most of the next six years in military campaigns designed to solidify the political power of Rome throughout central Italy.

Later, at a synod in Pavia (1022), the emperor Henry and the pope together pushed through legislation prohibiting clerical marriage, including those at the rank of subdeacon, and reducing to serfdom the children of clerical unions. The emperor was principally behind the reforms and immediately incorporated them into the imperial code. The pope, on the other hand, was more concerned with the loss of church properties to the children of clerical unions. Benedict VIII died on April 9, 1024, and was buried in St. Peter's.

144 JOHN XIX

April 19, 1024–October 20, 1032 (May 1024–1032 in the Vatican's official list; J. N. D. Kelly and Levillain's Dictionnaire historique de la papauté *agree with our dates rather than those in the* Annuario Pontificio.*)*

John XIX was the second pope to succeed his older brother to the papacy (the first was Paul I [757–67]). Like his older brother, he was still a layman (born Romanus) when "elected" (quotation marks are necessary because he actually bought the election through bribery). John's bribery and his canonically illicit passage from lay status to the papacy in a single day shocked and infuriated many Romans. Early in 1027 John XIX crowned Conrad II emperor in St. Peter's, but Conrad did not renew the traditional imperial privileges granted to the Holy See, nor did he promise to be its protector, as previous emperors had done. Indeed, the emperor treated the pope with little respect and ordered him around at will. Perhaps because of the unseemly manner in which he ascended to the papacy, a moral cloud hung over John XIX's head throughout his pontificate. He died on October 20, 1032, and was buried in St. Peter's.

145 BENEDICT IX

d. ca. November/December 1055, pope October 21, 1032–September 1044; March 10–May 1, 1045; November 8, 1047–July 16, 1048 (The Vatican's official list of popes gives the three sets of dates as 1032–1044, April 10– May 1, 1045, and November 8, 1047–July 17, 1048; J. N. D. Kelly and Levillain's Dictionnaire historique de la papauté *agree with our dates rather than those in the* Annuario Pontificio.)

Benedict IX (born Theophylact) was the third consecutive layman to assume the papal office and the only pope in history to have held the office for three separate periods of time (depending on how one assesses the legality of his two depositions from office and his abdication). In any case, his was one of the most canonically confusing pontificates in all of papal history.

Upon the death of John XIX, Alberic III, the new head of the ruling Tuscular family in Rome and John XIX's brother, arranged through bribery to have his own son Theophylact, the nephew of the previous two popes, elected and enthroned as Benedict IX. Generally speaking, the new pope put the interests of himself and his family ahead of the spiritual concerns of the Church. Nevertheless, he did manage to have a relatively active pontificate. In September 1044, however, there was another revolt in Rome, mostly in reaction to the pope's immoral life and the dominance of the Tuscular family over Church and state alike. Benedict IX fled the city.

The following January (1045) even though Benedict had never been formally deposed, a branch of the rival Crescentii family installed John, bishop of Sabina, as pope (Sylvester III). Benedict promptly excommunicated him and on March 10 expelled him from Rome and reclaimed the papal throne. Two months later, however, for reasons that are not clear (perhaps it was the money he would earn from the sale of his office), he abdicated in favor of his godfather, John Gratian (Gregory VI). In the fall of 1046 the emperor Henry III came to Italy to be formally crowned by the pope. He had all three claimants—Benedict IX (who had withdrawn to his family estate outside of Rome), Sylvester III, and Gregory VI—deposed. The emperor then named Suidger of Bamberg as pope (Clement II). Clement died suddenly eight months later, and the people, perhaps encouraged by bribes, demanded that Benedict IX be restored to office.

Benedict IX was reinstated on November 8, 1047, and remained in office until July 16, 1048, when he was forced from the papal throne by order of the emperor. Poppo of Brixen was installed as Damasus II. Benedict retreated to his Tusculan homeland, continuing to regard himself as the lawful pope against the intruder Damasus and, later, against Damasus's successor, Leo IX. Benedict IX lived at least another seven and a half years, died sometime between mid-September 1055 and early January 1056, and was buried in the abbey church of Grottaferrata in the Alban hills.

146 SYLVESTER [SILVESTER] III

d. 1063, pope (or antipope?) January 20–March 10, 1045 (January 20–February 10, 1045, in the Vatican's official list; J. N. D. Kelly gives our dates, and Levillain's Dictionnaire historique de la papauté gives January 13 or 20–March 1046.)

The legitimacy of Sylvester III's pontificate is open to question. If his election was not valid, he belongs on the list of antipopes. After Benedict IX was expelled from Rome, Sylvester was elected as the candidate of the Crescentii family, which had dominated Roman politics until displaced by the newly powerful Tusculan family. As soon as Benedict IX heard of Sylvester's election, he excommunicated him. Two months later Benedict returned to Rome and had Sylvester removed from the papal throne. Sylvester thereupon resumed his duties as bishop of Sabina, a post he had never relinquished. Eighteen months later, on December 20, 1046,

Henry III, king of Germany, had Sylvester III condemned at the synod of Sutri, confined to a monastery,
and stripped of his Holy Orders. The sentence must
have been suspended, however, because Sylvester continued to function in Sabina until 1062, when a successor was named. He is probably buried in Sabina.

147 GREGORY VI

d. late 1047, pope May 5, 1045–December 20, 1046

Born John Gratian, Gregory VI was archpriest of San
Giovanni a Porta Latina (St. John at the Latin Gate)
when his godson Benedict IX abdicated in his favor
on May 1, 1045—and for a great sum of money. Many
church reformers greeted his election with enthusiasm (they were not aware as yet of the financial ar-
rangements). Henry III came down from Germany
with the hope of being crowned emperor by the pope,
but there were at least three possibilities from which
to choose: Benedict IX, Sylvester III, and Gregory VI.
At a synod in Sutri on December 20, 1046, the king and
the synod pronounced Gregory guilty of simony and
deposed him from office. He died toward the end of
that same year. His burial place is unknown.

148 CLEMENT II

Saxon, December 25, 1046–October 9, 1047

Clement II (Suidger) was the first pope to remain bishop
of another diocese (Bamberg) while serving as Bishop
of Rome. He was also the first of four German popes

imposed upon the Church by King Henry III of Germany in order not only to rescue the papacy from the power of feuding Roman families, but also to ensure German control over it. In fact, Clement II crowned Henry and his wife emperor and empress on the same day (Christmas) he himself was enthroned as pope.

At the time of Clement's selection by Henry, there were three possible claimants to the papal throne: Benedict IX, who had abdicated in favor of his godfather, Gregory VI, and Sylvester III, who was elected after Benedict was expelled from Rome in January 1045. At two successive synods (at Sutri and Rome), the three were formally deposed, and the emperor nominated Suidger, bishop of Bamberg. Because he suddenly fell ill and died in an abbey near Pesaro in early October 1047, rumors circulated that he had been poisoned by Benedict IX. An exhaustive examination of his remains in 1942 disclosed that Clement II had probably died of lead poisoning. He was buried in the Bamberg cathedral.

149 DAMASUS II

Bavarian, July 17–August 9, 1048

The pontificate of Damasus II, the second of the four German popes imposed by King Henry III, was brief and uneventful. Like his predecessor, he retained his diocese of Brixen after election and was only the second pope in history to do so. Upon the sudden death of Clement II in October 1047, the emperor, in his capacity as patrician (with the authority to appoint the pope), nominated Poppo, bishop of Brixen, on Christmas day. In the meantime, however, the deposed Benedict IX returned to Rome to reclaim the papal throne with the support of the powerful count of Tuscany, who prevented Poppo from reaching Rome. When Poppo returned to Germany and informed the emperor, Henry III threatened to come to Rome himself and place a new pope on the throne. The count relented and had Benedict IX expelled from Rome on July 16, 1048. The next day Poppo was consecrated and enthroned. Twenty-three days later, however, he died at Palestrina, where he had retreated to escape the Roman heat.

150 LEO IX, ST.

Alsatian, 1002–54, pope February 12, 1049–April 19, 1054

The third and best of the German popes imposed on the Church by the emperor Henry III, Leo IX (Bruno of Egisheim), like his two immediate predecessors, retained his diocese of Toul (until 1051) while serving as Bishop of Rome. When he reached Rome, dressed in the simple garb of a pilgrim, he was greeted with acclaim and crowned on February 12, taking the name Leo to recall the ancient, still uncorrupted Church. Called the "Apostolic Pilgrim," Leo promoted his reforms against simony and violations of clerical chastity by traveling extensively throughout Europe—in Italy, Germany, France, and even Hungary—holding a dozen synods in Rome, Bari, Mainz, Pavia, Rheims, and Rome.

In 1053 Leo IX led a disastrous military expedition against the Normans in southern Italy in defense of the Papal States; he himself was captured and held for nine months. Meanwhile, the anti-Latin patriarch of Constantinople, Michael Cerularius (d. 1058), closed down the Latin churches in Constantinople and vehemently attacked various Latin practices, including the use of unleavened bread in the Eucharist. In January 1054, while still a prisoner, Leo IX sent a delegation to Constantinople led by Humbert of Silva Candida. The mission was a spectacular failure because of the intransigence of both sides. On July 16, 1054, Humbert issued a bull excommunicating the patriarch and his supporters. Cerularius countered with his own condemnations on July 24. The East-West Schism, which has lasted to this very day, is conventionally dated from this tragic series of events. Leo's last days were marred by illness and deep regret, but soon thereafter he came to be regarded as a saint. He is buried in St. Peter's. Feast day: April 19.

151 VICTOR II

Swabian, ca. 1018–57, pope April 13, 1055–July 28, 1057 (April 16, 1055, in the Vatican's official list; J. N. D. Kelly and Levillain's Dictionnaire historique de la papauté *both agree on April 13.)*

The fourth and last of the German popes nominated by the German king Henry III, Pope Victor II (Gebhard), like his three predecessors, continued as bishop of his diocese (Eichstätt) after being elected to the papacy. As an expression of confidence in Victor II, the emperor appointed him duke of Spoleto and count of Fermo, making the pope in effect an imperial officer. After a brief illness in October 1056, Henry III died, having personally entrusted the care of the empire and of his five-year-old son to the pope, who was in Germany at the time seeking military assistance against the Normans in southern Italy. Victor II adroitly ensured the succession of the boy (Henry IV), crowning him at Aachen, with his mother, Agnes, as regent.

The pope returned to Italy in mid-February 1057. But six days after holding a local synod at Arezzo on July 23, the pope died of fever. His German staff wanted to take his body back to Eichstätt, but the people of Ravenna seized the body and it was buried in Santa Maria Rotonda (the mausoleum of Theodoric the Great [d. 526]), just outside the walls of the city.

152 STEPHEN IX (X)

French, ca. 1000–1058, pope August 2, 1057–March 29, 1058 (The Vatican's official list begins his pontificate on August 3, 1057, the day of his enthronement, rather than August 2, the day of his election and consecration.)

Born Frederick (of Lorraine), Stephen IX (X) was abbot of Monte Cassino when elected and consecrated on the same day, August 2, 1057. (For an explanation of the dual numbering, see Stephen II [III], number 92.) He took the name Stephen because August 2 was St. Stephen I's feast day. No effort was made to contact the imperial court in Germany before proceeding to the election. The Romans were undoubtedly taking advantage of the fact that the new emperor, Henry IV, was a very young child.

Stephen IX (X) promoted the reformist activities of Peter Damian (d. 1072) by naming him cardinal-bishop of Ostia, and the reformers Humbert of Silva Candida and Hildebrand were among the pope's closest advisers. The pope died in Florence on March 29, 1058, while trying to arrange an alliance against the Normans in southern Italy and was buried in San Reparata.

153 NICHOLAS II

French, ca. 1010–61, pope December 6, 1058–July 27, 1061 (The Vatican's official list begins this pontificate on January 24, 1059, the day of enthronement, rather than the day of his acceptance of election.)

After the death of Stephen IX (X), an anti-reformist faction within the Roman aristocracy refused to honor Stephen's request that they wait for the reformer Hildebrand's return from Germany and elected an antipope, Benedict X. The reformist cardinals refused to recognize Benedict, left Rome, and elected Gerard, bishop of Florence, pope on December 6, 1058, in Siena. The new pope, Nicholas II, convened a synod, deposed the antipope, and traveled to Rome, where he was enthusiastically received and installed at the Lateran on January 24, 1059. Nicholas continued to serve as bishop of Florence after his election to the papacy. He may have been the first pope crowned with a tiara.

Like his predecessor, Nicholas II was greatly influenced by the leading reformers of the day: Humbert of Silva Candida (d. 1061), Hildebrand (the future Pope Gregory VII, d. 1085), and Peter Damian (d. 1072). At a Lateran synod on April 13, which declared Benedict X's election uncanonical, the pope promulgated a historic decree mandating that, in order to avoid the risk of simony (the buying and selling of church offices), papal elections should be conducted by the cardinal-bishops, with the subsequent assent of the Roman clergy and laity.

Politically Nicholas II reversed the policy of his immediate predecessors toward the Normans in southern Italy. Instead of fighting them, he entered into an alliance and thereby secured a political and economic foothold for the papacy in most of the south. However, the new alliance generated resentment in the imperial court and within the German hierarchy, led by the archbishop of Cologne. Before there were any repercussions in the Holy See, the pope died in Florence, his second diocese, on July 27, 1061, and was buried in San Reparata.

154 ALEXANDER II

September 30, 1061–April 21, 1073 (The Vatican's official list begins his pontificate on October 1, the day of enthronement, rather than September 30, the day of election.)

A reformer pope like his immediate predecessors, Alexander II (born Anselm) supported the liberation

of Christian lands from the Muslims as well as the vic-
torious Duke William of Normandy against Harold
of England in the battle of Hastings in 1066. He was
bishop of Lucca when elected Bishop of Rome on
September 30, 1061.

However, the cardinal-electors had not consulted
with the German imperial court, so the court nominated a rival pope, Honorius II (Cadalus, the wealthy
anti-reformist bishop of Parma), at an assembly in
Basel and with the support of the Roman aristocracy.
The antipope Honorius II defeated Alexander's armed
forces in April 1062 and installed himself in Rome. But
the powerful duke of Lorraine arrived the next month
with superior forces and persuaded both claimants to
withdraw until the German court settled the conflict.
After hearings in Augsburg and Rome, a judgment
was rendered in favor of Alexander II, although the
schism continued.

The pope sent banners and granted indulgences
to Norman soldiers and French knights fighting the
Muslims in Sicily and Spain, respectively. Indeed, the
reconquest of lands previously taken by the Muslims
was an important prelude to the Crusades. But in 1063
the pope also intervened in southern France and Spain
to defend Jews who had suffered in these military campaigns. He renewed the prohibition of Pope Gregory
the Great (590–604) against the mistreatment of Jews.

As the schism between the followers of Alexander
II and of Honorius II dragged on, Peter Damian persuaded the archbishop of Cologne to convene a synod
in Mantua in May 1064, to which both claimants would

be invited. Honorius refused to attend because he was denied the right to preside. Alexander did attend, presided, and took an oath of purgation, swearing that he had never been guilty of simony. As a consequence, Alexander II was acknowledged as pope and Honorius II was formally condemned. Alexander II died in April 1073 and was buried in the Lateran Basilica.

155 GREGORY VII, ST.

> *ca. 1020–85, pope June 30, 1073–May 25, 1085 (The Vatican's official list begins his pontificate on April 22, the day he was elected by popular acclaim, but he was not consecrated Bishop of Rome until June 30.)*

The pontificate of Gregory VII, one of the most important and influential popes in the entire history of the Church, marks a real watershed in the history of the papacy, from the first to the second Christian millennium. In the first Christian millennium the papacy functioned to a great extent as a mediator of ecclesiastical and political disputes. The Bishop of Rome was only one of several Western patriarchs. Gregory was the first pope effectively to claim universal jurisdiction over the whole Church—laity, religious, and clergy, princes and paupers alike.

Born Hildebrand, he served in numerous high offices under several popes. Upon the death of Alexander II, he was elected pope by acclamation and took the name Gregory, after both his patron, Gregory VI, and Gregory the Great (590–604). He did not inform or seek the approval of the German king, Henry IV.

Gregory made reform the centerpiece of his
pontificate. But in order to accomplish his reforms,
he inflated traditional papal claims over both spiritual and temporal spheres. In March 1075 he issued
his *Dictatus papae* ("Pronouncements of the Pope"),
containing twenty-seven propositions about the
powers of the pope, including such claims as: "he
alone can use imperial insignia"; "only the pope's
feet are to be kissed by all princes"; "no synod
ought to be called 'general' without his command";
and "he ought to be judged by no one." The norm
of Catholic fidelity was unquestioning obedience to
the Bishop of Rome, who exercised a universal rule
over the whole of Christendom, including kings
and emperors.

Gregory's prohibition of lay investiture (the interference of lay princes and other temporal rulers in the appointment and installation of bishops
and abbots) provoked strong opposition, this time
from the king of Germany himself, Henry IV. After defeating the Saxons in 1075, Henry nominated
his own men as archbishops, bishops, and abbots in
Germany and other parts of Italy, including Spoleto
and Fermo. When the pope rebuked the king, Henry
IV convened a synod of twenty-six German bishops
at Worms (January 24, 1076), which deposed the
pope. Gregory excommunicated Henry, suspended
him from the exercise of his royal powers, and released the king's subjects from all allegiance to him.
Gregory eventually forgave and absolved the king,
but three years later he again excommunicated and

deposed Henry, who thereupon called a council, deposed Gregory again, and selected an antipope, Clement III, to replace Gregory.

Henry was still open to compromise because he wanted to be crowned as emperor, but Gregory was inflexible. After Henry seized Rome in March 1084 following a two-year siege, the Roman clergy and laity elected Clement III pope, and he was enthroned in the Lateran Basilica on March 24, 1084. But both Henry and Clement left Rome when Robert Guiscard, duke of Apulia, marched on Rome with Norman troops and rescued Gregory. The violent behavior of Robert's troops infuriated the Roman people, and they turned on the pope who had invited them in. Gregory VII fled to Salerno, where he died on May 25, 1085. He was buried in Salerno's cathedral.

Although one of the great reformer popes in history, Gregory is the pope who, more than any other, shaped the development of the papacy in the West throughout the second Christian millennium—for good or for ill. He was beatified in 1584 and canonized by Pope Paul V in 1606. Feast day: May 25.

156 VICTOR III, BL.

ca. 1027–87, pope May 9–September 16, 1087 (The Vatican's official list begins his pontificate on May 24, 1086, the date of his first election—an election he did not formally accept—and almost a year before his consecration as Bishop of Rome on May 9, 1087.)

When the great reformer pope Gregory VII died in exile in Salerno, electors concluded that Desiderius, the influential abbot of Monte Cassino, might bring about a reconciliation with the emperor Henry IV. So, on May 24, 1086, they elected him pope in the diaconal church of Santa Lucia in Rome. After a long period of indecision, Desiderius finally accepted and was canonically elected at Capua on Palm Sunday, March 21, 1087, taking the name Victor III in honor of Pope Victor II.

Twice, discouraged by the civil disturbances and the bitter factional disputes between the Gregorians and the anti-Gregorians, Victor III put aside his papal insignia and returned to his monastery at Monte Cassino. He came back to Rome by sea in early June in response to pleas from the countess Matilda of Tuscany. On July 1, 1087, those loyal to him were able to retake the entire city. Then, just a couple of weeks later, with rumors circulating about the emperor Henry IV's impending arrival in Italy, the pope returned yet again to Monte Cassino, where he remained as abbot until three days before his death on September 16, 1087. In late August he did hold a local council at Benevento that reaffirmed Gregory VII's prohibition of lay investiture (the appointment and installation of bishops and abbots by lay rulers) and excommunicated the antipope Clement III. During the council, however, Victor III's health deteriorated. He returned immediately to Monte Cassino, where he died and was buried. Victor III was beatified by Pope Leo XIII in 1887, but he has never been canonized a saint. Feast day: September 16.

157 URBAN II, BL.

French, ca. 1042–99, pope March 12, 1088–July 29, 1099

During the pontificate of Urban II, the Roman Curia was established and the First Crusade (to liberate Jerusalem from the Muslims) was launched (1096–99). Baptized Oddone (di Châtillon), Urban II was former prior of the reformist abbey of Cluny in Burgundy and current cardinal-bishop of Ostia when Victor III died on September 16, 1087. Rome was once again under the control of forces loyal to the antipope Clement III. Accordingly, the election of a successor to Victor III had to be conducted in St. Peter's Cathedral in Terracina, south of Rome. The cardinals elected Cardinal Oddone unanimously on March 12, 1088, and he was consecrated the same day.

Urban II attempted from the outset to mark a more moderate course on church reform. He adopted a relatively benign approach to bishops who had been invested by their sovereigns but canonically elected and to the validity of Masses celebrated by schismatic priests who had been properly ordained. His conciliatory efforts did not mollify the emperor, Henry IV, who forced the pope in 1090 to surrender Rome to the antipope Clement III and to seek asylum with his Norman allies in southern Italy.

After the defection of Henry's son Conrad to the pope's side, however, Urban II managed to return to

Rome in late 1093 and, through bribery, to recover the Lateran Palace in 1094 and Castel Sant'Angelo in 1098. By 1095, even though the imperially supported schism supporting the antipope Clement III continued, Urban II's position was now secure enough for him to convene a number of synods—one, at Clermont in November 1095, issued a summons to the First Crusade (1096–99) to liberate Jerusalem from the Muslims. Urban II died on July 29, 1099, in Carcere. Two weeks before his death the Crusaders had reconquered Jerusalem, but the news of the victory did not reach the pope in time. He was buried in St. Peter's. A man of monastic piety and humility, he was beatified by Pope Leo XIII in 1881. Feast day: July 29.

158 PASCHAL II

August 14, 1099–January 21, 1118

Under pressure from the emperor Henry V, Paschal II reversed many of the reforms initiated by Pope Gregory VII (1073–85). Consequently, the papacy suffered a decline in prestige during Paschal's pontificate.

Born Raniero (Rainerius), he served as abbot of St. Paul's Outside the Walls (or the abbey of St. Lawrence) and as cardinal-priest of the church of San Clemente. Sixteen days after Urban II's death, Raniero was elected pope on August 13, 1099, consecrated the next day, and took the name Paschal. Why he did so is unknown. The first Pope Paschal was so detested by the people of Rome that, after his death, his body could not be buried in St. Peter's.

Paschal II's personality (timid and weak, but also stubborn and inflexible) did not aptly suit him to face the problems inherited from his predecessor: the lay investiture controversy (the appointment and installation of bishops and abbots by lay rulers) in Germany, France, and England; a hostile emperor (Henry IV); and a determined and durable antipope (Clement III). With the help of financial backing from the Normans, Paschal II had the antipope Clement III removed from Rome. But the investiture problem got worse, not better. Although Henry IV had no interest in supporting any of the three antipopes who arose after the death of Clement III in September 1100, he did want to continue lay investiture. But Paschal II renewed the prohibition of lay investiture at a synod in Rome in 1102. After Henry V successfully overthrew his father, it soon became obvious that he too wanted to continue the practice of lay investiture. The pope saw to it, however, that lay investiture was condemned and prohibited.

In spite of all this, Henry V still wanted to be crowned emperor in Rome. A short-lived compromise was worked out at Sutri on February 9, 1111. Henry would allow the free election of bishops and abbots, and in return the German churches would surrender all properties and privileges bestowed by the empire except for strictly ecclesiastical revenues. When the agreement, or concordat, was read aloud at the coronation ceremony in St. Peter's three days later (February 12), there were cries of protest, and the service had to be brought to an abrupt end. Henry withdrew his acceptance of the agreement and had the pope and the cardinals arrested. After two months of harsh imprisonment, the pope agreed to the emperor's terms, known as the Privilege of Ponte Mammolo, on April 12. Paschal II's abject surrender to the emperor's demands evoked a storm of protest, and he agreed to a nullification of the Privilege of Ponte Mammolo at a Lateran synod in 1112.

The last years of Paschal II's lengthy pontificate were not happy. In 1116 rioting in the city forced him to flee to Benevento. A few days after returning to the city in early 1118, the pope died at Castel Sant'Angelo on January 21 and was buried almost secretly in the Lateran Basilica because St. Peter's was under the control of the emperor's forces.

159 GELASIUS II

March 10, 1118–January 28, 1119 (The Vatican's official list begins his pontificate on January 24, the date of election, but he was not consecrated Bishop of Rome until March 10.)

Baptized Giovanni (John), Gelasius II was cardinal-deacon in the title of Santa Maria in Cosmedin and chancellor of the Holy Roman Church for some three decades under both Urban II and Paschal II, who also named him archdeacon and librarian. Upon his election on January 24, 1118, not at the Lateran but secretly in the monastery of Santa Maria in Pallara on the Palatine Hill because of the dangerous political and military situation in Rome, he was violently assaulted and imprisoned by Cencius Frangipani, head of a patrician family who detested Paschal II, to whom the new pope had been intensely loyal. At the urging of the other aristocratic families and the Roman people, Gelasius II was released, but he and the cardinals had to flee Rome almost at once because the emperor Henry V was on his way to the city.

Henry V demanded that the pope return to Rome to discuss the investiture controversy (the appointment and installation of bishops and abbots by lay rulers). When the pope refused to return, the emperor had the archbishop of Braga proclaimed Pope Gregory VIII. Gelasius excommunicated both the emperor and the antipope a month later at Capua (April 9). When Henry left Rome because of the approach of Robert of Capua's army, Gelasius II returned only to find the city under the control of the antipope Gregory VIII and other hostile forces. On July 21 he was once again attacked by the agents of Frangipani. Gelasius II fled to France. He held a synod at Vienne in southern France in early January 1119, but after falling ill, he retired to the abbey of Cluny, where, a few weeks later (January 28, possibly 29), he died and was buried near the main altar of the abbey church.

160 CALLISTUS [CALIXTUS] II

French, 1050–1124,
pope February 2, 1119–December 13, 1124

On February 2, 1119, at Cluny, the handful of cardinals who had accompanied Gelasius II to France (see

Gelasius II, number 159) unanimously elected Guido, the reform-minded archbishop of Vienne, as pope. Callistus II's election was ratified by the Roman clergy and laity on March 1. The new pope reaffirmed the ban on lay investiture and the excommunication of Henry V at a council in Rheims (October 29–30, 1119). He returned to Rome triumphally, where he deposed the antipope Gregory VIII and confined him to a monastery.

In the meantime, the German princes urged Henry to recognize the new pope and to negotiate with him over the lay investiture matter without harming the interests of the empire. After three weeks of hard bargaining, the historic Concordat of Worms was approved on September 23, 1122. Under the agreement the emperor renounced his putative right to invest bishops and abbots with ring and crozier (symbols of spiritual authority), and the free elections and consecrations of bishops and abbots were guaranteed. In return, the pope conceded to Henry the assurance that the elections of bishops and abbots in Germany would be held in his presence and that Henry would invest those elected with the symbol of temporal authority (the scepter). The long struggle between Church and state over lay investiture was finally over. In March 1123 the pope convened a general, or ecumenical, council at the Lateran, which solemnly ratified the Concordat of Worms. Callistus II died on December 13, 1124, in the Lateran and was buried there next to the tomb of Paschal II (1099–1118).

161 HONORIUS II

December 21, 1124–February 13, 1130

The most memorable aspect of this pontificate is the way in which Honorius II came into office. Upon the death of Callistus II, a majority of the cardinals, allied with the Pierleoni family of Rome, elected the elderly cardinal-priest Teobaldo pope on December 15, 1124, as Celestine II. Lamberto, cardinal-bishop of Ostia, was elected the same day by cardinals favorable to the Frangipani family. While Celestine II's installation was in progress on December 21, the Frangipani family, with the secret support of Aimeric, the chancellor of the Holy Roman Church, broke into the ceremony and at sword point had their nominee, Lamberto, acclaimed as pope. Celestine, who suffered severe wounds in the attack, thereupon resigned. (Because Celestine II had not been formally consecrated or enthroned, he is not included in the official list of popes but is classified as an antipope.) The city prefect and the Pierleoni family were bought off with substantial bribes, and Lamberto was then formally "reelected" by the assembled cardinals and enthroned as Honorius II.

Because of the peace with the emperor secured through the Concordat of Worms (1122) and the death of Henry V in 1125, Honorius II was able to move his reformist agenda forward. He promoted the moral and spiritual renewal of the Church, showing special favor toward the newer religious orders that combined the contemplative with the active life, such as the Premonstratensians (Norbertines, approved in 1126) and the Knights Templar (approved in 1128), protectors of Holy Land pilgrims.

When the pope fell ill in January 1130, his powerful chancellor Aimeric had him taken to the monastery of San Gregorio, protected by the Frangipani family. And after the pope died several weeks later, during the night of February 13/14, Aimeric had him temporarily buried in the monastery so that an election could be held immediately. Once his successor, Innocent II, had been elected, Honorius II's body was taken to the Lateran for final burial.

162 INNOCENT II

February 23, 1130–September 24, 1143 (The Vatican's official list begins his pontificate on February 14, the day of his election, but he was not consecrated Bishop of Rome until February 23.)

Gregorio Papareschi was cardinal-deacon of the church of San Angelo when elected to the papacy on the night of his predecessor's death in a clandestine meeting of a minority of (younger) cardinals in the fortified convent of San Andrea. He took the name Innocent II. When word of the election reached about twenty-four other, older cardinals, mostly old-line Gregorians, they met themselves later that same morning in the church of San Marco and elected Cardinal Pietro Pierleoni, who took the name Anacletus II. Both elections were canonically irregular.

The result was an eight-year schism. Anacletus's position was at first more secure than Innocent's, perhaps because he had better political connections in Rome and the support of the Norman king, Roger II. Innocent II fled to France, where he gradually won recognition as pope from everywhere except Scotland, Aquitaine, and southern Italy, perhaps because many preferred the spiritual emphasis in his reform agenda. The strife between Innocent II and Anacletus II ended only upon Anacletus's death on January 25, 1138.

In April 1139 Innocent II convened the Second Lateran Council, which annulled all the official acts (including ordinations) of Anacletus II and his allies and reaffirmed the reform legislation of previous decades. Innocent II died on September 24, 1143, and was buried in the Lateran Basilica. His remains were transferred to the church of Santa Maria Trastevere after the Lateran Basilica was destroyed by fire in 1308.

163 CELESTINE II

October 3, 1143–March 8, 1144 (The Vatican's official list begins his pontificate on September 26, the day of his election, but he was not consecrated Bishop of Rome until October 3.)

Because Cardinal Teobaldo Boccapecci is regarded officially, though unfairly, as an antipope, having taken the name Celestine II when elected to succeed Callistus II in 1124 (see Honorius II, number 161), this Pope Celestine took the number II rather than III when elected to succeed Innocent in 1143. Born Guido, he was cardinal-priest of the church of San Marco when unanimously elected pope two days after Innocent II's death.

Celestine II's first two official acts were reversals of positions taken by his predecessor, Innocent II. First, he lifted the interdict on all places sheltering King Louis VII of France (who had originally opposed Innocent II on the appointment of the duly elected archbishop of Bourges). Second, he refused to ratify the treaty that Innocent had been forced to accept while a prisoner of King Roger II of Sicily. The treaty called for the pope to recognize Roger's sovereignty over southern Italy as well as Sicily. But Celestine eventually had to soften his approach to Roger because of military pressure on the borders of the Papal States. Already elderly when elected, Celestine II served less than six months as pope. He died on March 8, 1144, and was buried in the Lateran.

164 LUCIUS II

March 12, 1144–February 15, 1145

The pontificate of Lucius II was marked by serious political strife in Rome. Born Gherardo Caccianemici, Lucius was cardinal-priest of the church of Santa Croce in Gerusalemme and chancellor and librarian of the Roman Church when elected pope on March 12, 1144. The details of his election are unknown. He was immediately consecrated as Bishop of Rome.

Lucius II was preoccupied with events in the city of Rome, where an independent senate was now functioning under the leadership of Giordano Pierleoni, the brother of the late antipope Anacletus II, and where many of the citizens were demanding that the clergy confine themselves to spiritual functions. The pope turned for help first to Roger II of Sicily and then to the new German king, Conrad III. Both efforts failed. The pope decided, in the end, to lead his own military force against the insurgents. He was injured by heavy stones during an attack upon the Capitol, where the senate met, and died shortly thereafter in the monastery of San Gregorio on February 15, 1145. He was buried in the Lateran.

165 EUGENIUS [EUGENE] III, BL.

February 18, 1145–July 8, 1153 (The Vatican's official list begins his pontificate on February 15, the day of his election, but he was not consecrated Bishop of Rome until February 18.)

A Cistercian, Eugenius III retained the habit and lifestyle of a monk while serving as pope and is regarded as the last of the reform popes of this particular historical period. Born Bernardo Paganelli (or Pignatelli), he was abbot of the Cistercian house of SS. Vincenzo and Anastasio outside of Rome when elected to the papacy on the very day (February 15, 1145) that his predecessor, Lucius II, died from wounds sustained while leading a military expedition against the Roman senate. Since Eugenius III refused to recognize the popular commune now governing Rome, he had to be consecrated three days later at Farfa, twenty-five miles north of the city, and to take up residence in Viterbo. The commune, however, soon accepted him as pope as well as his sovereignty, and he celebrated Christmas in Rome that year. But the agreement collapsed and he was back in Viterbo in January 1146; from there the following year he went to France.

On December 1, 1145, Eugenius III had proclaimed the Second Crusade after having learned of the Turks' capture of the Crusader outpost of Edessa, and he commissioned his fellow Cistercian, Bernard of Clairvaux (d. 1153), to preach on its behalf. At Bernard's urging, Eugenius III promoted clerical and monastic reform at such important synods as Paris (1147), Trier (1147–48), and Rheims (1148).

The pope reached an understanding with the Roman citizens with the help of the new German king, Frederick I Barbarossa, and was able to return to Rome in 1152. The pope promised the king the imperial crown, and the king promised not to make peace with the commune or the Normans without the pope's consent. Eugenius III, however, died of a violent fever at Tivoli on July 8, 1153, long before Frederick could come to Rome to be crowned. The pope's body was transported back to Rome and buried in St. Peter's next to Gregory VII (1073–85). Eugenius III was beatified by Pope Pius IX in 1872. Feast day: July 8.

166 ANASTASIUS IV

July 12, 1153–December 3, 1154

Peaceful relations were established between the papacy and the Roman commune during the brief pontificate of Anastasius IV. Born Corrado della Suburra, he was cardinal-bishop of Santa Sabina and papal vicar for

Rome during the absences from the city of Innocent II and Eugenius III. A very old man, he was unanimously elected pope on July 12, 1153, four days after his predecessor, Eugenius III, died, and was immediately installed in the Lateran. He seems to have enjoyed the confidence of the Roman senate, because he was not only enthroned in the Lateran, but he was allowed to remain in Rome afterwards without any resistance. He was also respected by the Roman people, having assisted them during a period of famine. Anastasius IV died on December 3, 1154, and was buried in the Lateran.

167 HADRIAN [ADRIAN] IV

English, December 4, 1154–September 1, 1159

Hadrian IV was the first and only English pope. Born Nicholas Breakspear, he had left England as a young man to study in France, where he entered an Augustinian monastery and eventually became abbot. When the community complained that Nicholas was too strict, Pope Eugenius III removed him and brought him to Italy as cardinal-bishop of Albano. He also served as a highly successful papal legate to Scandinavia, reorganizing the churches of Sweden and Norway, and after his return was unanimously elected pope upon the death of Anastasius IV.

Hadrian resumed the papacy's domestic battle with the Roman commune, arresting and executing in 1155 its leader, Arnold of Brescia, with the cooperation of the German king Frederick. The pope's personal relations with the king, however, were not positive. Frederick did not pay the pope proper courtesies, and when Hadrian finally crowned Frederick in St. Peter's on June 18, he altered the service to emphasize the emperor's subordination to the pope. Tensions between the pope and the emperor continued for several years and worsened when Frederick, at the Diet of Roncaglia (1158), made claims over northern Italy and Corsica. Hadrian, in turn, refused to approve the emperor's nominee as archbishop of Ravenna and threatened to excommunicate Frederick unless he annulled the decrees of Roncaglia within forty days. The pope died on September 1, 1159, before the deadline was reached. He was buried in the crypt of St. Peter's Basilica.

168 ALEXANDER III

ca. 1105–81, pope September 20, 1159–August 30, 1181 (The Vatican's official list begins his pontificate on September 7, the date of his election, but he was not consecrated Bishop of Rome until September 20.)

Alexander III was the first of many lawyers to become pope. Unfortunately, his election provoked a twenty-year schism between those loyal to him and those loyal to the three antipopes supported by the German emperor, Frederick Barbarossa. Born Orlando Bandinelli, he served as chancellor and papal legate under his predecessor, Hadrian IV, and was a cardinal-priest at the time of his own election to the papacy. Despite being assaulted by supporters of his rival, Cardinal Ottaviano of Monticelli, Alexander III was consecrated as Bishop of Rome on September 20 at Ninfa, southeast of Velletri. Ottaviano was consecrated as Victor IV at the imperial abbey of Farfa, northeast of Rome, on October 4.

Thereupon, the emperor convened a synod of German and Italian bishops at Pavia in February 1160, which endorsed the antipope Victor IV and excommunicated Alexander III. The pope had already excommunicated Victor, and on March 24 he condemned Frederick. With support from King Henry II of England and King Louis VII of France, Alexander III returned to Rome in November 1165 but could not prevent the recoronation of Frederick and the coronation of his wife as empress in 1167 by the antipope Paschal III (whose election had followed the death of the antipope Victor IV in 1164). A third antipope, Callistus III, was elected in 1168 and served until 1178, when he submitted to Alexander III.

Alexander III eventually moved to Benevento. After the Lombard League of northern Italian cities defeated Frederick at Legnano in 1176 with the pope's support, the emperor was ready to negotiate. At Venice he and the pope agreed that the excommunication would be lifted from Frederick in return for his acknowledgment of Alexander as pope.

From March 5 to March 19, 1179, Alexander III presided over the Third Lateran Council, which brought the schism to a definitive end; the council also decreed a two-thirds majority of cardinals for papal election, encouraged universities and cathedral schools, and provided for the punishment of heretics. (In September 1179 a fourth antipope, Innocent III, was installed and quickly disposed of.) Alexander spent the last two years in various parts of the Papal States and died on August 30, 1181, at Città Castellana, about thirty-five miles north of Rome. His body was taken back to Rome for burial in the Lateran, but the citizens desecrated it beforehand.

169 LUCIUS III

September 1, 1181–November 25, 1185 (The Vatican's official list gives his death as August 25, 1185, but the November 25 date appears in J. N. D. Kelly, Levillain's Dictionnaire historique de la papauté, *and* The New Catholic Encyclopedia.)

Born Ubaldo Allucingoli, Lucius III was a Cistercian monk early in his life and then cardinal-bishop of Ostia and Velletri when elected pope. Because of the hostility of the Roman people, however, the new pope's coronation was held in Velletri on September 6, 1181. Apart from the period November 1181–March 1182, Lucius III spent his pontificate outside of Rome, mostly in Velletri and Anagni. Early in his pontificate, there were attempts to mediate the disputes between the emperor Frederick and the papacy, but they were of little avail on secular issues. On some ecclesiastical matters there was agreement: a program for dealing with heretics (they were to be excommunicated by the Church and then handed over to the state for punishment) and preparations for a new crusade in the Holy

Land. Lucius died on November 25, 1185, before relations with the emperor broke down completely. He is buried in the Duomo (cathedral) in Verona.

170 URBAN III

November 25, 1185–October 20, 1187

So dedicated an opponent of the German emperor was Urban III that he remained archbishop of Milan during his pontificate so that the customary year's revenues from the archdiocese would not pass to the emperor after his resignation from the see.

Born Umberto Crivelli, he was unanimously elected to the papacy in Verona on the very day of Lucius III's death. He was crowned on December 1, 1185. The cardinal-electors were looking for a candidate less beholden to the emperor than Lucius III had been, but they got an even more independent-minded pope than they had expected. The pope refused to crown the emperor's son Henry VI as coemperor and suspended the patriarch of Aquileia for crowning the son as king of Italy. The emperor Frederick immediately ordered his son to invade and occupy the Papal States and to isolate the pope and the Curia in Verona, where they were under virtual house arrest. At the Diet of Gelmhausen in 1186, the emperor isolated the archbishop of Cologne, the leader of a rebellion, and retained the support of the German bishops. Although the pope capitulated, he soon reverted to type and was actually planning to excommunicate Frederick, that is, until the pro-imperial civil authorities of Verona learned of it and asked the pope and his party to leave the city. After setting out on horseback for Ferrara, Urban III fell ill on the road and died upon reaching the city on October 20, 1187. He was buried in the Duomo (cathedral) of Ferrara.

171 GREGORY VIII

ca. 1100–1187, pope October 25–December 17, 1187 (The Vatican's official list begins his pontificate on October 21, the day of his election, but he was not consecrated Bishop of Rome until October 25.)

Already about eighty-seven when elected pope in Ferrara the day after Urban III's death in that city, Gregory VIII served just under two months. Born Alberto de Morra (or Mora), he served for nine years as chancellor of the Holy Roman Church and was, since 1158, cardinal-deacon in the title of San Lorenzo in Lucina. In the election held after Urban III's death, the cardinals at first unanimously chose Enrico di Castel Marsiaco, monk of Chiaravalle and bishop of Albano, but he refused election and recommended Morra. Morra took the name Gregory VIII and was consecrated as Bishop of Rome on October 25, 1187.

In both preferences, the cardinals were expressing their unhappiness with Urban III's virulently anti-imperial policy. Gregory VIII immediately moved to restore harmony to papal-imperial relations and then became principally concerned with preparations for another crusade, prompted by the news of a Muslim victory at Hattin in Galilee and then the shocking report of the capture of Jerusalem itself (October 2, 1187). He sent legates to much of Europe to preach the crusade. Gregory VIII fell ill and died in Pisa on December 17, 1187.

172 CLEMENT III

December 19, 1187–March 1191

The pontificate of Clement III was dominated by preparations for the Third Crusade (1189–92). Born Paolo Scolari, he was the cardinals' second choice when they voted in Pisa two days after the death of Gregory VIII in that city. (Their first choice, Cardinal Teobaldo of Ostia, declined.)

The new pope arranged to return the papacy to Rome after a six-year exile. The senators acknowledged his sovereignty and restored papal revenues and the right to mint coins. In return, Clement III had to make substantial annual and special-occasion payments to the commune and leave the administration of the city largely to it. Peace was also restored with the empire. The Papal States, occupied by the emperor's son Henry since 1186 as a reprisal against Urban III, were returned to the Holy See, although the empire reserved some proprietary rights.

Clement III made these concessions because of financial difficulties and also because he wanted to devote his time and energies to the preparation of the Third Crusade, which would have to be coordinated by the emperor Frederick. Like his predecessor,

Gregory VIII, he urged the Crusaders to adopt a penitential dress and diet, and he sent legates throughout
Europe not only to preach the crusade, but also to
promote harmony among Christian nations. As a result, the papacy enhanced its role as an instrument of
unity. The exact date of the pope's death in mid or late
March 1191 is unknown. He was buried in the Lateran,
but no trace of his tomb remains.

173 CELESTINE III

ca. 1106–98, pope April 14, 1191–January 8, 1198

Already eighty-five when unanimously elected,
Celestine III had a surprisingly long, if undistinguished, reign of nearly seven years. Born Giacinto
Bobo, he was cardinal-deacon of Santa Maria in Cosmedin at the time of his election in late March, having
been at that rank for forty-seven years. He was ordained a priest and a bishop on April 13 and 14 (Easter),
respectively, and took the name of his old friend and
patron, Celestine II (1143–44).

Celestine III's pontificate was dominated by his relations with the new young king of Germany, Henry
VI, who was waiting outside the city limits to receive
the imperial crown, promised by Gregory VIII. With
some reluctance the aged pope crowned Henry on
April 15. Upon the emperor's return to Germany, he
began arbitrarily making appointments of bishops
to various dioceses and imprisoned the English king,
Richard the Lion-hearted, although Richard was under

papal protection as a returning Crusader. But the pope took no direct action against the emperor, not even for these last two outrages.

By now the pope was already in his nineties, and at Christmas 1197 he indicated his wish to resign provided the cardinals elected his close collaborator, Cardinal Giovanni of Santa Prisca. They rejected his proposal, and he died a few weeks later, on January 8, 1198. He was buried in the Lateran.

174 INNOCENT III

> ca. 1160/1–1216, pope February 22, 1198–July 16, 1216
> (The Vatican's official list begins his pontificate on
> January 8, the day of his election, but he was not
> consecrated Bishop of Rome until February 22.)

Innocent III was one of the most important and powerful popes in the entire history of the Church, and his pontificate is considered the summit of the medieval papacy. Indeed, as pope he claimed authority not only over the whole Church, but over the whole world as well. Born Lotario di Segni, he was made a cardinal-deacon of SS. Sergio and Bacco in 1190 and was unanimously elected pope at age thirty-seven on the day of Celestine III's death. He was ordained a priest on February 21 and consecrated and crowned Bishop of Rome the next day.

When two rival candidates to succeed Henry VI as king of Germany applied to the pope for the imperial crown, he maintained his right to intervene because he alone could bestow the crown and because he had to choose the man best suited to the needs and interests of the Church. Innocent intervened elsewhere as well. He excommunicated King John of England for refusing to recognize Stephen Langton as archbishop of Canterbury, acquired as papal fiefs Aragon, Portugal, Sicily, and Poland, and made his authority felt in Scandinavia, Spain, the Balkans, Cyprus, Armenia, and Prussia.

Although Innocent III was a masterful political pope, he also had a clear ecclesiastical agenda: the Fourth Crusade (1202–4), church reform, and the combating of heresy. When the crusade failed (Constantinople fell in 1204), he appealed in 1213 for another one and fixed the date at the Fourth Lateran Council (1215) for 1217. The clergy were to contribute one-twentieth of their income toward it while the pope and cardinals were to contribute a tenth.

More than twelve hundred prelates and many representatives of lay princes attended the Fourth Lateran Council in 1215. Its seventy decrees included a definition of the Eucharist in terms of transubstantiation (the sacramental changing of the bread and wine at Mass into the Body and Blood of Christ), the condemnation of heresies, the requirements that all Catholics make an annual confession and that Jews and Muslims wear distinctive dress, and a universal four-year truce in preparation for the next crusade.

In the summer following the council, Innocent III died suddenly of a fever on July 16, 1216, in Perugia and was buried there at the cathedral of San Lorenzo. In 1891 Pope Leo XIII (1878–1903), himself a former bishop of Perugia, had Innocent III's remains transferred to the basilica of St. John Lateran in Rome.

175 HONORIUS III

July 24, 1216–March 18, 1227

Old and frail when elected pope, Honorius III continued the reform program of Innocent III. Born Cencio Savelli, he was cardinal-priest of SS. John and Paul when elected pope in Perugia two days after Innocent III died there, on July 18, 1216. He was consecrated as Bishop of Rome in Perugia on July 24.

Honorius III's pontificate was principally concerned with the new crusade proclaimed by Innocent III and the Fourth Lateran Council (1215). But the Fifth Crusade (1217–21) ended, like the previous one, in failure. Honorius III had crowned Frederick II, king of Germany, as emperor in 1220 in order to facilitate his participation in the next crusade, but Frederick instead left Rome to settle problems in Sicily. The emperor only agreed to embark on the crusade in 1225 because of the pope's threat to excommunicate him if he failed to set out by the summer of 1227.

On December 22, 1216, Honorius III formally approved the Dominican order; on December 29, 1223, he approved the rule of the Franciscan order, and on January 30, 1226, the rule of the Carmelites. He died on March 18, 1227, and was buried in the basilica of Santa Maria Maggiore (St. Mary Major).

176 GREGORY IX

ca. 1170–1241, pope March 19, 1227–August 22, 1241

Gregory IX was the pope who established the papal Inquisition. Born Ugolino da Segni, he was the nephew of Innocent III; he was cardinal-bishop of Ostia and Velletri when elected pope the day after the death of his predecessor, Honorius III. He was crowned two days later, on March 21.

Gregory IX proved to be a strong supporter of the Franciscans (he had been their protector before his election) and the Dominicans, canonizing his personal friend Francis of Assisi (d. 1226) in 1228. In 1231 he made heretics liable to the death penalty at the hands of the civil authorities and instituted the papal Inquisition under the direction of the Dominicans, who would act with his direct "apostolic authority."

Most of his pontificate was marked by the ongoing and deep-seated tensions between Gregory IX and the emperor Frederick II. The emperor had delayed embarking on the Sixth Crusade according to the timetable set during the previous pontificate and was duly excommunicated. After more conflict, the pope and the emperor achieved a peace at Ceprano in July 1230 whereby the emperor made concessions in Sicily and promised not to violate the papal territories, and the pope, in his turn, lifted the excommunication. The uneasy truce held, more or less, for several years, but tensions erupted in 1236 when the emperor asked the pope to excommunicate his enemies in the Lombard League. Gregory IX refused and in 1239 once again excommunicated the emperor. Frederick then invaded the Papal States and surrounded Rome.

Gregory IX summoned a general council to meet in Rome on Easter, 1241. But the emperor intercepted all the bishop-delegates traveling to Rome from outside of Italy. Imperial ships captured the ships carrying the French bishops and cardinals and imprisoned all those on board. In the suffocating August heat, with the emperor's forces still surrounding the city, the pope died on August 22, 1241, and was buried in St. Peter's. The emperor withdrew to Sicily to await future developments.

177 CELESTINE IV

October 25–November 10, 1241

An aged and sick man, Celestine IV died about two weeks (or sixteen days) after being elected. His was the third, and possibly even the second, shortest pontificate in history (Urban VII, twelve days; Boniface VI, possibly fifteen days; the exact length of Boniface VI's and Celestine IV's pontificates is impossible to determine).

Born Goffredo Castiglioni, he was cardinal-bishop of Sabina when elected pope. After Gregory IX's death, the ten available cardinals were divided between those who supported the late pope's hostile attitude toward the emperor and those who deplored it. A Roman senator, Matteo Rosso Orsini, who was effectively the absolute ruler of Rome, confined the cardinals in wretched conditions until they agreed on a candidate. As the days dragged on, some of the cardinals became ill and one died. On October 25, after two months of virtual house arrest, the cardinals elected Goffredo, who took the name Celestine IV. Two days later, the new pope fell ill, and he eventually died on November 10, probably before being crowned and performing any official papal acts. He was buried in St. Peter's.

178 INNOCENT IV

ca. 1200–54, pope June 28, 1243–December 7, 1254 (The Vatican's official list begins his pontificate on June 25, the day of his election, but he was not consecrated Bishop of Rome until June 28.)

Innocent IV was the first pope to approve the use of torture in the Inquisition to extract confessions of heresy. Born Sinibaldo Fieschi, he was a distinguished canon lawyer when elected pope at Anagni after a vacancy of eighteen months. The delay in the election was caused by the emperor Frederick II, who, still smarting under the excommunication imposed on him by Gregory IX in 1239, wanted to be sure that the new pope would be sympathetic to him.

Although he possessed many of the same leadership qualities that Gregory IX had, Innocent IV did not have Gregory's temperament—or virtue. He followed the principle "The end justifies the means." While the emperor was scheming to have his excommunication lifted in return for various concessions to the Holy See, the distrustful pope fled secretly in the summer of 1244 to Lyons, where he was under the

protection of King Louis I of France. Between June 26
and July 17, 1245, he held the First Council of Lyons,
which found the emperor guilty in absentia of perjury, sacrilege, and heresy and then deposed him. The
excommunication against him was renewed in April
1248, and the emperor died at the end of 1250.

Innocent IV returned triumphantly to Rome in the
following year and immediately tangled with the emperor's son, Conrad IV, in the hope of regaining Sicily as a papal fief. After Conrad died (1254), the pope
annexed Sicily to the Papal States and moved his residence to Naples, where he died less than two months
later, on December 7, 1254, just as a rebellion was
being raised against papal rule in Sicily. His original
tomb was in the basilica of Santa Restituta in Naples,
which was incorporated into the cathedral in the thirteenth century.

179 ALEXANDER IV

December 12, 1254–May 25, 1261

Alexander IV's pontificate was characterized by constant conflict with political powers, in which the papacy
generally came out second best. Born Rinaldo dei Conti
di Segni, a nephew of Gregory IX (1227–41), Alexander
was cardinal-bishop of Ostia when elected pope in Naples on December 12, 1254, five days after the death of
Innocent IV.

From the outset of his pontificate, Alexander IV
was faced with the new Sicilian revolt, and he excommunicated its leader, Manfred, the illegitimate son of

the late emperor Frederick II. A military effort to recapture Sicily for the papacy failed and most of the Papal States came under Manfred's control. Alexander IV could not even reside in Rome for most of his pontificate, given the power struggles there. He spent most of his time in Viterbo and died there on May 24, 1261, around the time that his archenemy Manfred was being elected a senator in Rome. The pope was buried in Viterbo's cathedral of San Lorenzo.

180 URBAN IV

French, ca. 1200–1264,
pope August 29, 1261–October 2, 1264

The pontificate of Urban IV left no lasting image in papal history, having failed to resolve or even improve a number of continuing political problems inherited from previous popes. Jacques Pantaléon, the son of a shoemaker, was patriarch of Jerusalem and was visiting the Curia on business when he was elected in Viterbo on August 29, 1261, to succeed Alexander IV, who had died in that city. The new pope took the name Urban IV, perhaps in honor of Urban II (1088–99), who was also French.

Urban's first move was to replace the hostile Manfred as head of the kingdom of Sicily and to eliminate the power of the Hohenstaufen dynasty from Italy. Within a few months he recovered most of the Papal States (lost by his predecessor) in the south and began rebuilding papal prestige in the north. In June 1263, Urban IV offered the kingdom of Sicily and southern Italy to the French king's brother Charles in return for a large sum of money, an annual tribute, and guarantees of freedom for the Church in those territories and of military assistance when needed. When Manfred heard of the arrangement, he resumed military operations in Tuscany, Campagna, and the Papal States. The pope had to take refuge in Orvieto, where he was compelled to modify the treaty with Charles and to accept Manfred's election as a Roman senator. When Orvieto itself was threatened militarily, the pope retreated to Perugia, where he died on October 2, 1264. He was buried in Perugia's cathedral of San Lorenzo.

181 CLEMENT IV

French, February 5, 1265–November 29, 1268

During his pontificate, Clement IV decreed that appointments to all benefices in the West were papal appointments, thereby preparing the way for the present, relatively recent system in which the pope makes all episcopal appointments. Born Guy Foulques, son of a successful French judge, he was a widower with two daughters and was cardinal-bishop of Sabina at the time of his election, on February 5, 1265, as pope in Perugia, the city where his predecessor, Urban IV, had died. He took the name Clement IV and was crowned, also in Perugia, on February 15. As pope he resided first in Perugia and then in Viterbo, but never in Rome because of hostile conditions there.

On the political front, he completed his predecessor's expulsion of the Hohenstaufen dynasty from

Italy and the installation of Charles of Anjou as king of Sicily and Naples in place of the papal enemy Manfred, the illegitimate son of the deceased emperor Frederick II. (Charles was crowned in St. Peter's in 1266 by five cardinals appointed by the pope.) The pope then borrowed large sums of money to finance a military campaign against Manfred. A strong French army defeated and killed Manfred at Benevento in 1266. Ironically, now that the pope had gotten rid of the Hohenstaufen dynasty, he found himself and the papacy under the threat of a new aggressive force in Italy, the Angevin house in the person of Charles of Anjou.

Clement IV died in Viterbo on November 29, 1268, and was buried in the Dominican convent of Santa Maria in Gradi outside the walls of the city. His remains were transferred in 1885 to the basilica of San Francesco in Viterbo.

182 GREGORY X, BL.

1210–76, pope March 27, 1272–January 10, 1276 (The Vatican's official list begins his pontificate on September 1, 1271, the day of his election, but he was not consecrated as Bishop of Rome until March 27, 1272.)

Gregory X is famous for the manner in which he was elected to the papacy—in the extraordinary conclave in Viterbo in which the civil authorities locked the cardinals in the papal palace and then, on the advice of Bonaventure (d. 1274), the minister general of the Franciscans, removed its roof and threatened them with starvation if they did not quickly proceed to the election of a successor to Clement IV. (It had taken them nearly three full years already!) Born Teobaldo Visconti, Gregory was not yet a priest or a cardinal when elected to the papacy on September 1, 1271. He was archdeacon of Liège and was away at the time in Acre (Akko, in modern-day Israel) on a crusade in the Holy Land with the future King Edward I of England. Teobaldo reached Viterbo on February 10, 1272, more than five months after his election, and then went to Rome. He was ordained a priest on March 19 and consecrated as Bishop of Rome in St. Peter's on March 27, 1272.

Because of his background as a Crusader, Gregory X made the liberation of the holy places the central theme of his brief pontificate. He convened a general council whose agenda was threefold: a new crusade, reunion with the Greek Church, and reform of the clergy. Gregory X also invited the Byzantine emperor Michael VIII Palaeologus to send delegates, which he did. The council opened at Lyons on May 7, 1274, and the Greek delegates assented to the primacy of the Holy See and to the Roman creed. At the council's fourth session (July 6) the pope formally ratified the (short-lived) union of the Latin and Greek Churches. In addition to establishing a system for financing the crusade (which was never launched), the council decreed that, once there is a vacancy in the Holy See, the cardinals must assemble within ten days after the pope's death in the place where he died and proceed to the election of a successor without any further contact with the outside world.

After crossing the Alps, the pope visited various northern Italian cities to settle local disputes, but he came down with a severe fever and died at Arezzo on January 10, 1276. Gregory X's name was later added to the Roman Martyrology during the pontificate of Benedict XIV (1740–58). Feast day: January 9.

183 INNOCENT V, BL.

French, ca. 1224–76, pope January 21–June 22, 1276

Innocent V was the first Dominican pope, and the still current papal custom of wearing a white cassock may have begun with him when he decided to continue wearing his white Dominican habit as pope. Innocent V was the second of four individuals to occupy the papacy in the year 1276. Born Pierre de Tarentaise, he was a renowned and well-published theologian and cardinal-bishop of Ostia when unanimously elected to the papacy on January 21, 1276, in Arezzo, where Gregory X had died. The new pope went as soon as possible to Rome, arriving on February 22. He was immediately enthroned in the Lateran and then crowned on February 25.

Innocent V's election signaled the desire for a change of course in papal policy. The Curia wanted to move away from Gregory X's cultivation of the Germans in order to counterbalance the domination of Italy by Charles of Anjou, king of Sicily. Accordingly, on March 2

Innocent V confirmed Charles as a Roman senator and as imperial vicar in Tuscany and asked Rudolf, the king of Germany, to postpone his trip to Rome.

His handling of relations with the East was generally inept. He almost apologized to the Byzantine emperor Michael VIII Palaeologus for Charles's plans for recapturing Constantinople on the grounds that it had been forcibly taken away from the Latins. Innocent VI died on June 22. He was buried in St. John Lateran Basilica and beatified by Pope Leo XIII in 1898. Feast day: June 22.

184 HADRIAN [ADRIAN] V

ca. 1205–76, pope July 11–August 18, 1276

Hadrian V's pontificate was noted for its brevity (five weeks) and for the fact that he died before he could be ordained a priest (he was a deacon at the time of election) and consecrated and crowned as pope. Canonically, he may have been a legitimate pope—the Vatican's official directory, the *Annuario Pontificio,* so regards him—because during this period acceptance of valid election was sufficient. But theologically he could not have been pope, because the pope is, first and foremost, the Bishop of Rome and, since Hadrian was not yet a bishop, he could not have become the Bishop of Rome until consecrated as such.

Born Ottobono Fieschi, he was a nephew of Innocent IV (1243–54) and cardinal-deacon of the church of San Adriano (the name he would take as pope) at the time of his election. He had also served as a very successful papal legate to England and returned to Rome to become one of the most respected and influential members of the College of Cardinals. On the day after his election, he assembled the cardinals in the Lateran and suspended the rules for a papal election laid down by Gregory X (1272–76), promising to develop new ones. A few days later he left Rome to escape the oppressive summer heat and went to Viterbo, north of Rome, where he became seriously ill and died on August 18. Hadrian V is memorialized in Dante's *Divine Comedy* as a temporary inhabitant of purgatory for the sin of avarice (*Purgatory* 19.88–145).

185 JOHN XXI

Portuguese, ca. 1210/15–77,
pope September 8, 1276–May 20, 1277

John XXI was the first and only Portuguese pope, the first and only medical doctor to be pope, and the fourth canonically recognized individual to occupy the Chair of Peter in the year 1276. He is numbered as John XXI, although no pope took the name John XX. There may have been confusion at the time created by the fact that as many as ten popes had taken the name John in the tenth and eleventh centuries.

Born Pedro Julião (better known as Peter of Spain, or Petrus Hispanus), he was cardinal-bishop of Tusculum when elected pope in Viterbo ten days after Hadrian V's death in that town. He was crowned on September 15. The new pope had taught medicine at the new University of Siena and served as the personal physician of Pope Gregory X (1272–76). He was also an accomplished scholar who left the details of policy making to Cardinal Giovanni Gaetano, the future Pope Nicholas III (1277–80). In a reversal of the anti-imperial approach of Innocent V (January 21–June 22, 1276), John XXI refrained from confirming Charles of Anjou, king of Sicily, as a Roman senator and imperial vicar in Tuscany and sought to reconcile Charles with King Rudolf I of Germany in order to prepare the way for Rudolf's coronation as emperor. John XXI was mortally injured when the ceiling of his study fell in on him, and he died on May 20, 1277. He was buried in the Duomo (cathedral) of Viterbo.

186 NICHOLAS III

> 1210/20–80, pope December 26, 1277–August 22, 1280
> (The Vatican's official list begins his pontificate on
> November 25, the day of his election, but he was not
> consecrated Bishop of Rome until December 26.)

Nicholas III was the first pope to make the Vatican Palace his residence. He also had the unfortunate distinction of having been placed in hell in the *Divine Comedy* by the Italian poet Dante for nepotism and avarice (*Inferno* 19.61ff.). Born Giovanni Gaetano of the noble Orsini family, he had been archpriest of St. Peter's and a cardinal-deacon in the title of San Nicolò in Carcere for more than thirty years when elected pope in the papal palace in Viterbo on November 25, 1277, after a deadlock of six months. He took the name Nicholas III, probably in honor of Nicholas I (858–67). He re-

turned immediately to Rome the day after his election
and on the day after Christmas, 1277, was consecrated
as Bishop of Rome and crowned.

A goal of Nicholas's pontificate was to restore the
political independence of the Holy See in Italy. Therefore, he persuaded Charles of Anjou to resign as imperial vicar of Tuscany and not to seek reappointment
as a Roman senator when his term expired, and he
decreed that in the future no prince may become a
member of the senate without the pope's permission.
Meanwhile, he negotiated with King Rudolf I a formal
renunciation of imperial claims on papal territories in
Romagna, which had the effect of enlarging the Papal
States and establishing boundaries that would remain
more or less in place until the dissolution of the Papal
States (except for Rome) in 1860. Nicholas III tried unsuccessfully to restore unity between the Latin and
Greek Churches, on Rome's terms. He died on August 22, 1280, of a stroke at his new summer residence
in Soriano, near Viterbo. His body was taken back to
Rome and buried in the Orsini chapel of St. Nicholas,
whose construction he had directed, in St. Peter's.

187 MARTIN IV

*French, ca. 1210/20–85, pope March 23, 1281–March 28,
1285 (The Vatican's official list begins his pontificate
on February 22, the day of his election, but he was not
consecrated Bishop of Rome until March 23.)*

Martin IV was actually the second Pope Martin (Popes
Marinus I and II were incorrectly given as Martin II

and III in the official lists of the thirteenth century). Born Simon de Brie, he was cardinal-priest of Santa Cecilia when elected pope in Viterbo after six months of animosity and intrigue between forces sympathetic to Charles of Anjou, king of Sicily, and those hostile to him. Simon was elected through powerful pressure exerted by Charles. The Romans, however, refused the new pope entrance into the city, so he had to be crowned in Orvieto, where he spent most of his pontificate. He was consecrated as Bishop of Rome and crowned and enthroned in Orvieto on March 23. He took the name Martin in honor of the patron saint of France, Martin of Tours (d. 397).

Martin IV's election represented a complete rejection of his predecessor's policies. Thus, when the Romans elected the new pope senator for life (a position Nicholas III had secured for himself while forcing Charles to relinquish his membership in the senate), Martin IV transferred the office to Charles and effectively handed over control of the Papal States to him as well. Unlike his predecessors, Martin IV supported Charles's efforts to recover Constantinople for the West by military means, and in 1281 he excommunicated the Byzantine emperor Michael VIII Palaeologus as a schismatic, even though the emperor had done all in his power to accommodate himself to the demands of the Holy See. Thus was the formula of union for the Latin and Greek Churches forged at the Second Council of Lyons in 1274 effectively annulled. Martin IV died in Perugia on March 28, 1285, and was buried in the cathedral of San Lorenzo in Perugia.

188 HONORIUS IV

*1210–87, pope May 20, 1285–April 3, 1287 (The Vatican's
official list begins his pontificate on April 2, the day
of his election, but he was not consecrated Bishop of
Rome until May 20.)*

The pontificate of Honorius IV, the grandnephew of
Honorius III (1216–27), was without particular shape
or distinction. Born Giacomo Savelli, he was the elderly and arthritic cardinal-deacon of Santa Maria in
Cosmedin when unanimously elected pope in Perugia
four days after the death of Martin IV. His election was
received with enthusiasm in Rome, and he was consecrated as Bishop of Rome and crowned in Rome itself
on May 20.

Since most of the cardinals were French, the new
pope was responsive to their wishes to retrieve Sicily for the Angevins (the house of Anjou). A crusade launched against the Spanish rule of Sicily by
the French king, Philip III, led to Philip's death. Ultimately, Sicily was lost. The pope resumed contacts
with the German king Rudolf I and set the date of his
coronation as emperor for February 2, 1287, but when
the papal legate to the Diet of Würzburg (March 16–
18) was rebuffed in his efforts to secure financial contributions on the occasion of the planned coronation,
the event was postponed. The coronation never took
place. Honorius IV died in Rome on April 3, 1287, and
was buried in St. Peter's, but his remains were later
transferred by Paul III (1534–49) to the Chiesa dell'
Aracoeli, to be placed next to those of his mother.

189 NICHOLAS IV

1227–92, pope February 22, 1288–April 4, 1292

Nicholas IV was the first Franciscan pope. Born Girolamo Masci, he was a Franciscan friar and the pastorally attentive cardinal-bishop of Palestrina when he was unanimously elected in the new papal palace on the Aventine Hill on February 15, 1288. He took the name Nicholas IV in honor of Nicholas III, who had made him a cardinal. He was crowned on the same day.

Unlike his predecessor, Nicholas IV was unable to reside without interruption in Rome during his pontificate because of intermittent civil disorders that were stirred in part by his own blatant favoritism toward the Colonna family, for which he was roundly mocked. But Nicholas IV had no more success in manipulating political developments in Sicily than his predecessor had. Nothing came either of his efforts to mount another crusade to liberate the holy places in Palestine from the Muslims. He is known in history, however, as a missionary pope for having sent his fellow Franciscan friar Giovanni di Monte Corvino to the court of the Great Kubla Khan, an initiative that led to the first establishment of the Catholic Church in China. Nicholas IV died on April 4, 1292, and was buried in Santa Maria Maggiore.

190 CELESTINE V, ST.

1209/10 (or 1215?)–96, pope August 29–December 13, 1294 (The Vatican's official list begins his pontificate on July 5, the day of his election, but he was not consecrated Bishop of Rome until August 29.)

Celestine V is best known for being constantly, and erroneously, identified as the only pope ever to have resigned from the papacy. There were two other popes before him (Pontian and Silverius), and possibly a third and fourth (John XVIII and Benedict IX), who resigned from the papacy for one reason or another. A fifth pope, Gregory XII, resigned in 1415 in order to help bring to an end the Great Western Schism (1378–1417).

Born Pietro del Murrone in the Abruzzi region of Italy, the eleventh child of peasant parents, he was a simple hermit under the Rule of St. Benedict at the time of his election as pope, at about the age of eighty-five, in Perugia after a vacancy of twenty-seven months. He was hailed as the "angel pope" based on a thirteenth-century dream of a pope who would usher in the age of the Holy Spirit. Pietro took the name Celestine V. Charles II, king of Sicily and Naples, saw to it that the new pope took up residence in Naples rather than in Rome, as the Curia demanded.

From Naples Celestine did whatever Charles ordered him to do, placing his men in key positions in the Curia and the Papal States and creating twelve cardinals whom Charles proposed. Uneducated (he could not speak Latin) and generally befuddled, he proved an inept administrator. As Advent approached,

Celestine sought to resign and consulted Cardinal Benedetto Caetani (who would succeed him as Boniface VIII), a noted canon lawyer, about the possibility. Caetani helped him prepare resignation documents, and on December 13, Celestine V abdicated, causing much controversy. When Caetani himself was elected, he feared that Pietro could be made a rallying point for a schism, so he kept the former pope confined to the tower of Castel Fumone, east of Ferentino, where he died on May 19, 1296. Feast day: May 19 (not observed universally).

191 BONIFACE VIII

> ca. 1235–1303, pope January 23, 1295–October 11, 1303
> (The Vatican's official list begins his pontificate on
> December 24, 1294, the day of his election, but he was
> not consecrated Bishop of Rome until January 23, 1295.)

Few popes in history have made greater claims for the spiritual and temporal powers of the papacy than Boniface VIII. As such, he was the last of the medieval popes and one of the three most powerful medieval popes, along with Gregory VII (1073–85) and Innocent III (1198–1216).

Born Benedetto Caetani, he was cardinal-priest of San Martino and possessor of many lucrative benefices at the time of his election as pope on Christmas Eve in Naples, eleven days after the resignation of Celestine V. A renowned canon lawyer, he arranged for the abdication of his predecessor, for which he was bitterly criticized by the Spiritual Franciscans (those who called for the literal and uncompromising observance of the rule of poverty). He took the name Boniface VIII (there had been an antipope Boniface VII in 974 and again in 984–85, but no officially recognized pope with that number). By all accounts, he was a man of exceedingly irascible temperament, given to outbursts of impatience and rage and bent on the acquisition of wealth and power for himself and his family.

Boniface VIII made a lasting contribution to the field of canon law, but most of his pontificate was taken up with political matters. He tried and failed to restore Charles II of Naples to the throne of Sicily (seized earlier by rebels) and to mediate disputes between Venice and Naples, and Scotland and England. His attempts to end hostilities between France and England opened a more serious conflict between himself and Philip IV (Philip the Fair) of France. Both countries were financing the war by taxing their clergy, a practice forbidden by canon law without the consent of the pope (Fourth Lateran Council, 1215). In an effort to stop the practice, Boniface VIII issued one of the most famous of papal bulls, *Clericis laicos,* on February 25, 1296, which began with the assertion, "The laity have always been hostile to the clergy." Philip retaliated by curtailing papal revenues from France, and the pope backed down.

Meanwhile, the pope was having problems on his home front. The Colonna family, which had supported Boniface's election, now resented his highhanded, autocratic style of governance, were opposed to his Sicilian policy, and questioned the validity of Celestine V's resignation and Boniface's election.

When a convoy bearing papal treasure was highjacked in 1297, Boniface ordered the two Colonna cardinals to hand over to him three strategic family castles. When they refused, Boniface VIII deposed and excommunicated the two. Boniface proclaimed 1300 a Jubilee year and granted plenary indulgences (the remission of all temporal punishment in purgatory) to the many pilgrims to Rome and the apostolic shrines. He began dressing in imperial regalia, declaring himself as much an emperor as a pope.

In the fall of 1301 the conflict with Philip was reignited. The king had imprisoned the bishop of Parmiers and demanded his reduction to the lay state. Boniface VIII viewed the king's action as an intrusion upon his spiritual authority. The pope condemned the king's action and summoned the Church's leadership to Rome for a synod in November 1302. Following the synod, Boniface VIII published his second famous bull, *Unam sanctam,* on November 18, 1302, which stated, among other claims, that "outside this [Catholic] Church there is neither salvation nor remission of sins" and that "it is altogether necessary to salvation for every human creature to be subject to the Roman Pontiff."

Philip responded with a vitriolic personal attack on the pope and called for a council to depose him. After preparing a bull of excommunication against the king, the pope moved from Rome to Anagni. The palace there was stormed by a band of mercenaries under the head of the Colonna family, and the pope was arrested. He was rescued by the citizens of Anagni (the city of his birth) and returned to Rome on September 25, 1303, but he died a broken man less than three weeks later, on October 12, and was buried in the crypt of St. Peter's Basilica.

192 BENEDICT XI, BL.

1240–1304, pope October 22, 1303–July 7, 1304

Benedict XI's pontificate was marked by his weak acquiescence to the demands of the king of France; he appeased the king's desire to have a council denounce the memory of Boniface VIII by revoking ecclesiastical censures and penalties on the royal family and the French court and almost completely withdrawing Boniface's bull *Clericis laicos* concerning temporal taxation of clergy. Born Niccolò Boccasini, of an ordinary working-class family, he was the cardinal-bishop of Ostia and a Dominican (he had been master of the order) when unanimously elected pope in Rome on October 22, 1303. He chose the name Benedict, after his predecessor's baptismal name, as a show of support and solidarity with the powerful but tragic Boniface VIII. The new pope had been one of two cardinals who had faithfully stood with Boniface during the assault upon him at Anagni. He was crowned on October 27, 1303, in Rome.

Benedict XI has been described by historians as a scholarly but weak man who felt at ease only with his fellow Dominicans. Indeed, he appointed only three cardinals during his pontificate, all Dominicans. A man of peace, he immediately lifted Boniface VIII's excommunication of the two Colonna cardinals, but without restoring their properties or cardinalatial rank. The pope's gesture only partially satisfied the Colonna partisans, and it exasperated the Bonifacians. The factional conflict that erupted afterward forced Benedict XI to leave Rome for Perugia in April 1304. On July 7, 1304, the pope died of acute dysentery in Perugia and was buried in the church of San Domenico. He was beatified by Pope Clement XII in 1736. Feast day: July 7.

193 CLEMENT V

French, ca. 1264–1314, pope June 5, 1305–April 20, 1314

With Clement V's pontificate began the seventy-year "Babylonian captivity" of the papacy in Avignon, France. Born Bertrand de Got, he was archbishop of Bordeaux when elected pope in Perugia on June 5, 1305, after an eleven-month deadlock between pro–Boniface VIII cardinals opposed to King Philip IV of France and the pro-French, anti-Boniface cardinals allied with the Colonna family. He took the name Clement V out of respect for the previous Pope Clement (IV, 1265–68), who was also French. He intended at first to be crowned at Vienne, where he hoped to mediate a peace between the English and French kings, thereby preparing the way for another crusade to liberate the holy places in Palestine from the Muslims. But instead King Philip IV had Clement V crowned in his presence at Lyons on November 15, some five months after his election. Clement V entered office afflicted with cancer and had to withdraw from public view for months at a time.

After wandering around Provence and Gascony for the first several years of his pontificate, Clement V finally settled with the Curia at the Dominican priory in Avignon, because the town belonged not to the French king but to his vassals, the Angevin kings of Naples, and offered easy access to the sea. Meanwhile, the king renewed the pressure for a general council to condemn his old nemesis Boniface VIII. After stalling, the pope finally relented and agreed to open the case on February 2, 1309. The king suspended the proceedings in April 1311, but he exacted a staggeringly high price from the pope. The Colonna cardinals who had been excommunicated by Boniface VIII were completely rehabilitated and fully compensated, Boniface's acts against French interests were annulled, and Celestine V was canonized. Also, because Philip coveted the wealth of the Knights Templar, a religious order devoted to the liberation of the holy places in Palestine from Muslim control, Clement V was forced (at the council of Vienne, 1311–12) to condemn the order and rule that all of its property should be transferred to the Knights of St. John of Jerusalem (the Hospitallers, known today as the Knights of Malta). In effect, however, King Philip IV held their considerable property until his own death in 1314.

Clement V died of stomach cancer on April 20, 1314, in Roquemaure, near Carpentras, while traveling to his birthplace, Villandraut. By the time of his death, the papal treasury had been depleted from excessive personal use. He was buried in a parish church at Uzeste, about three miles from his place of birth.

194 JOHN XXII

French, ca. 1244–1334,
pope August 7, 1316–December 4, 1334

John XXII, the second of the Avignon popes, was born
Jacques Duèse (of Cahors) and was cardinal-bishop of
Porto at the time of his election to the papacy on August 7, 1316, in Lyons, more than two years after the
death of his predecessor, Clement V. Evidently, the
cardinals had some difficulty deciding upon a candidate, given the conflicting political currents, and the
seventy-two-year-old Cardinal Duèse was obviously a
compromise choice. He was crowned in Lyons on September 5 by Cardinal Napoleone Orsini. His electors
obviously considered him a transitional pope, given his
age. His pontificate lasted more than eighteen years!

Although small of stature and in weak health, this
elderly pope plunged into his new duties with uncom-
mon energy and enthusiasm. He restored efficiency
to the Curia and financial stability to the Church. He
extended the powers of the papacy over appointments
to benefices and redrew diocesan boundaries. To improve the flow of revenue into the Holy See (which
was Rome, not Avignon, however), he created a new
system whereby each country would pay the first
year's revenue of a benefice to the pope.

In 1318 he intervened in the ongoing dispute between the Conventual and Spiritual Franciscans, coming down on the side of the former. He banned the
Spirituals' simplified habit and ordered them to obey
their superiors and accept as legitimate the storing up

of provisions. Twenty-five recalcitrants were handed over to the Inquisition, and four were actually burned at the stake in 1318.

Because of the German king Louis IV's aggressively antipapal actions in Italy, the pope excommunicated him in 1324. Whereupon Louis called for a council to denounce the pope for heresy because of his attitude toward the Spiritual Franciscans' understanding of evangelical poverty. Louis entered Rome in January 1328, had himself crowned emperor by the captain of the Roman people, deposed the pope for heresy, and had a Spiritual Franciscan elected pope. The antipope took the name Nicholas V and installed himself! (He later submitted to John XXII and was pardoned.)

In 1331–32, the pope delivered four sermons that were to haunt him for the remaining years of his pontificate. He had said that the saints would not see God face-to-face until after the final judgment—in opposition to the traditional doctrine that the saints enjoy the Beatific Vision immediately after death. Louis IV plotted with Cardinal Orsini toward the pope's condemnation and deposition at a general council, but the pope fell ill. On his deathbed, he modified his position. Before the final judgment, he said, the saints see God face-to-face as clearly as their condition allows, and he insisted that he never held the contrary view except as a personal opinion he was prepared to reject if it were contrary to the faith of the Church. John XXII died on December 4, 1334, at age eighty-nine and was buried in the cathedral of Notre-Dame-des-Doms in Avignon.

195 BENEDICT XII

> *French, 1285–1342, pope January 8, 1335–April 25, 1342*
> *(The Vatican's official list begins his pontificate on De-*
> *cember 20, 1334, the date of his election, but he was not*
> *consecrated Bishop of Rome until January 8, 1335.)*

Benedict XII was the third of the Avignon popes. Born
Jacques Fournier, of poor parents, he was a Cistercian,
cardinal-priest of the church of Santa Prisca, and the
former counselor of his predecessor, John XXII, when
elected pope on December 20, 1334, in Avignon. He was
consecrated as Bishop of Rome and crowned by Cardinal Orsini on January 8, 1335, in the Dominican church
in Avignon. Almost immediately after his coronation,
Benedict XII was pressured by envoys from Rome to return the papacy there. But the majority of cardinals and
the French king himself were against the move, and the
continued political unrest in Rome and the Papal States
gave much practical strength to their argument.

Benedict XII had come into office with a reputation
as a learned theologian and an indefatigable inquisitor,
skilled at extracting confessions from alleged heretics,
some of whom were burned at the stake. Soon after
his coronation, he dismissed large numbers of clerics
from the papal court at Avignon and sent them back
to their benefices (income-producing ecclesiastical offices). He was convinced that clergy should remain
in residence at their pastoral posts and that wandering monks should return to their monasteries. In 1336
Benedict settled a controversy that had stirred the last
years of the previous pontificate. He ruled that the in-

tuitive, face-to-face vision of the divine essence (the Beatific Vision) occurs immediately after death for those who die in a state of grace.

Benedict XII encountered a number of problems on the political front. He could not prevent the outbreak of the Hundred Years' War (1337–1453) between England and France or terminate hostilities after it began, so his hopes were dashed for the launching of another crusade to liberate the holy places in Palestine from Muslim control. His open favoritism toward French policy, of course, created much resentment in England. He also failed to defend the integrity of papal territories in Italy, losing control over Romagna, the March of Ancona, and even Bologna. Relations with the emperor Louis IV of Germany were full of mutual hostility. Benedict XII died on April 25, 1342, and was buried in the cathedral of Notre-Dame-des-Doms in Avignon.

196 CLEMENT VI

French, 1290/91–1352,
pope May 7, 1342–December 6, 1352

The fourth—and most partisanly French—of the Avignon popes, Clement VI was born Pierre Roger. A Benedictine, he was archbishop of Rouen, chancellor of France, and cardinal-priest of the church of Santi Nereo e Achilleo when he was elected pope by some seventeen cardinals meeting in Avignon on May 7, 1342. Elected unanimously, the more easygoing and worldly Cardinal Roger represented a change from the austere and rigid Benedict XII. He chose the name Clement to make the point that power should be exercised with clemency and was crowned on Pentecost Sunday, May 19, in the Dominican church in Avignon.

About six months after his election, Clement received a delegation from Rome, begging him to return to the city. The delegation also petitioned for a reduction in the interval between Jubilee years. In the bull granting the request, *Unigenitus*, the pope defined the treasury of merits, a vast reserve of merit built up by Christ and the saints that can be applied to individuals, upon the recitation of certain prayers and the performance of certain spiritual works, to offset the burden of sin. The means by which these merits are applied came eventually to be called indulgences. Disputes over the sale of indulgences were a major factor in provoking the Protestant Reformation some two centuries later.

The pope rejected the appeal to return to Rome and actually purchased the city of Avignon and enlarged the papal palace. Unfortunately, Clement VI's pontificate was modeled less on the example of the Apostle Peter, whose successor he claimed to be, than on that of a worldly prince. His court was bathed in luxuries, and charges were raised about his own sexual life. He shamelessly conferred church offices and gifts on relatives, friends, and fellow countrymen. Clement VI's lavish expenditures eventually depleted the papal treasury. In 1348–49 when the Black Death hit Avignon itself, the pope defended the Jews against the charge that they were responsible for it. Clement VI died on December 6, 1352, after a short illness. He was buried at first in the cathedral, but his body was moved in April to the Benedictine abbey of La Chaise-Dieu.

197 INNOCENT VI

French, 1282–1362,
pope December 18, 1352–September 12, 1362

The pontificate of Innocent VI, the fifth of the Avignon popes, was marked by much activity, both ecclesiastical and political, but with little lasting effect. Born Étienne Aubert, he was cardinal-bishop of Ostia when elected pope in Avignon on December 18, 1352. As usual, the cardinals wanted not a carbon copy of the old pope, but rather a wholly new style and approach. The new pope, already seventy-two, was crowned in the Avignon cathedral by the senior cardinal-deacon on December 30.

In spite of his age and unstable health, he immediately revived the reformist spirit of Benedict XII (1335–42). Once again, clergy were required to reside in their benefices (income-producing ecclesiastical offices), candidates for office had to establish their credentials for the position, and no one could hold more than one benefice at a time. The pope also gave his support to the reformist agenda of the Master of the Dominican order and was particularly severe with the Spiritual Franciscans (those who insisted that a Franciscan should own absolutely nothing), turning some of them over to the Inquisition to be imprisoned or even burned at the stake. Innocent VI died on September 12, 1362, and was buried in Holy Trinity chapel, in the charterhouse of Villeneuve-lès-Avignon, which he had built.

198 URBAN V, BL.

> *French, ca. 1310–70, pope November 6, 1362–December 19, 1370 (The Vatican's official list begins his pontificate on September 28, the day of his election, but he was not consecrated Bishop of Rome until November 6.)*

The sixth—and probably the best—Avignon pope was Urban V. Born Guillaume de Grimoard, he was a Benedictine monk, a canon lawyer, abbot of Saint-Victor in Marseilles, and papal legate in Italy—but not a cardinal—when elected pope in Avignon on September 28, 1362. The cardinals at first elected the brother of Pope Clement VI (1342–52), but he declined. When they could not agree on one of their own number, they turned to the deeply spiritual Abbot Grimoard and elected him unanimously.

Retaining his black Benedictine habit and rule of life, Urban V continued his predecessor's reformist agenda. He reduced even further the luxury of the papal court and combated the holding of more than one benefice (income-producing ecclesiastical office) at a time. He also exhausted the papal treasury once again by his generous support of impoverished students, of colleges, and of artists and architects. He founded new universities in Orange (southern France), Kraków, and Vienna.

Urban V sincerely hoped to return the papacy once and for all to Rome. He had good reasons to do so, apart from its historic connection with the Apostle Peter; there he could better organize a crusade and renewed efforts toward reunion with the East. Although the pope's skilled legate had managed to restore the allegiance of the Papal States, Rome itself was in chaos and the Vatican was uninhabitable. Nevertheless, on April 30, 1367, against the strong objections of the French cardinals and the Curia, Urban V left Avignon. After a brief stay in Viterbo, he entered Rome with an impressive military escort on October 16. He remained there for three years. In September 1368, he created seven new cardinals: six French and only one Roman. The next month the emperor Charles IV arrived in the city for discussions with the pope, who crowned his queen as empress.

At the end of his pontificate, Urban V, at the urging of the French cardinals and because of the unsettled situation in Italy, again fled Rome for Avignon (1370). After arriving there, he fell gravely ill and died on December 19. His tomb in the cathedral became the center of a cult. Urban V was beatified by Pope Pius IX in 1870. Feast day: December 19.

199 GREGORY XI

French, 1329/30–78, pope January 4, 1371–March 27, 1378 (The Vatican's official list begins his pontificate on December 30, 1370, the day of his election, but he was not consecrated Bishop of Rome until January 4, 1371.)

The last of the Avignon popes and the last French pope, Gregory XI returned the papacy to Rome under pressure from St. Catherine of Siena (d. 1380). Born Pierre Roger de Beaufort, he was appointed to the College of Cardinals (as cardinal-deacon of the church of Santa Maria Nuova) by his uncle, Pope Clement VI (1342–52), at the age of eighteen or nineteen. Although he repeatedly tried to refuse, Cardinal Pierre Roger was unanimously elected to the papacy in Avignon on December 30, 1370, at the age of forty-two.

Gregory XI's pontifical agenda was straightforward enough: to return the papacy to Rome, to mount another crusade to liberate the holy places in Palestine from Muslim control, to bring about reunion with the Eastern Church, and to replenish the depleted papal treasury. Gregory formed a league of cities against the papal nemesis, the Visconti of Milan, in 1371 and placed an interdict on the family in early 1373. (An interdict is an ecclesiastical penalty that prohibits persons from participating in public worship and from the reception of the sacraments.) Because Florence had been angered by the Holy See's reasserting papal power in central Italy and withholding food supplies during a shortage in 1374–75, it lead a revolt against the Papal States. The pope imposed an interdict on Florence and sent an army of mercenaries under the command of Cardinal Robert of Geneva (later the antipope Clement VII), which reconquered the Papal States.

Catherine of Sienna spent the summer of 1376 in Avignon and finally persuaded Gregory XI to return the papacy to Rome. In spite of the pleas of his relatives, the French cardinals, and the Curia, the pope left the city for good on September 13. He set sail from Marseilles on October 2 but did not reach Corneto (now Tarquinia) until December 6 because of stormy seas. It was only on January 17, 1377, that Gregory XI entered Rome and took up residence in the Vatican.

After his return to Rome, however, the situation in Italy went from bad to worse. Peace negotiations with Florence broke down because the pope's demands were too severe, and hostility toward the pope in Rome intensified because of Cardinal Robert of Geneva's particularly brutal attack on Cesena the previous February. Gregory XI retreated to Anagni, where he died on March 27, 1378, on the eve of the Great Western Schism (1378–1417). He was buried in the church of Santa Maria Nuova.

200 URBAN VI

ca. 1318–89, pope April 8, 1378–October 15, 1389

Urban VI was one of the most unstable popes in history and the last noncardinal to be elected pope; his intransigence and unreasonableness provoked the French cardinals into electing an antipope, thus beginning the Great Western Schism of 1378–1417.

Born Bartolomeo Prignano, he was archbishop of Bari when elected pope on April 8, 1378, in the first papal conclave to be held in Rome since 1303. And a tumultuous conclave it was. The Roman people gathered outside the Vatican Palace demanding a Roman, or at least an Italian, pope. At one point, some of the crowd actually gained entrance into the palace to lobby the cardinal-electors directly, and rioting broke out. All but one of the cardinals voted for Archbishop Prignano. He had been regarded as a conscientious and efficient administrator, having served for twenty years as a leading figure in the Curia in Avignon and then as regent of the papal chancery after Gregory IX returned to Rome. He was enthroned as Urban VI on Easter Sunday, April 18.

That summer the new pope alienated the very cardinals who had elected him by making abusive remarks and by threatening to appoint enough Italian cardinals to tip the balance of the college in favor of the Italians. As he began to manifest a darker side of his personality, including uncontrollable tirades, the French cardinals withdrew to Anagni. After a failed attempt to reach an accommodation with the new pope, they published on August 2 a declaration that the April election was invalid because it was conducted not freely but under threat of mob violence. The French cardinals invited Urban VI to abdicate. Five days later (August 9) they sent out a notice to the Christian world that the pope had been deposed as incompetent and as an intruder. They moved then from Anagni to Fondi, where they elected the French king's cousin, Cardinal Robert of Geneva, as pope on September 20. His coronation as Clement VII on October 31 began the Great Western Schism (1378–1417). A later council ended the schism, but never settled the controversy over Urban's and Clement's claims to the papacy.

Europe's loyalties were divided between the two competing claimants, who fought each other on two fronts: the spiritual and the temporal. First, they excommunicated one another, and then they sent armed mercenary forces against each other. Urban's forces won the decisive battle near Marino in April 1379, captured Castel Sant'Angelo, and secured control of the city of Rome. Clement retreated south to Naples and then to Avignon in June, where he established a papal court full of pomp and luxury. The two men had no direct contact after that. Clement died of apoplexy on September 16, 1394.

Since Urban VI had no doubt about the legitimacy of his own claim to the papacy, he responded with indifference to appeals to find a solution to the crisis. He was mainly preoccupied with securing the kingdom of Naples for one of his nephews. With the Papal States in a state of anarchy, Urban VI died the next year, on October 15, 1389, probably of poisoning. He was buried in St. Peter's. The antipope Clement VII was still alive in Avignon, but there was no interest in recognizing him in order to end the schism.

201 BONIFACE IX

*ca. 1350–1404, pope November 9, 1389–October 1, 1404
(The Vatican's official list begins his pontificate on November 2, the day of his election, but he was not consecrated Bishop of Rome until November 9.)*

The second of the popes in the Roman line during the Great Western Schism (1378–1417), Boniface IX ruled like a benevolent despot in a pontificate marred by nepotism and simony (the buying and selling of ecclesiastical offices and spiritual benefits, such as indulgences). Born Pietro Tomacelli, he was cardinal-priest of the church of Santa Anastasia when he was elected pope by fourteen Roman cardinals on November 2, 1389. He was consecrated as Bishop of Rome and crowned on November 9. As in many other instances, Boniface IX was completely different from his predecessor, Urban VI, in style and temperament. He had a pleasant personality and was a skilled and practical leader.

The new pope was immediately excommunicated by the Avignon pope (the antipope Clement VII), and he, in turn, excommunicated his rival in France. Boniface IX won his first major struggle with Clement VII on the battlefield, regaining the allegiance of the kingdom of Naples. The pope also regained control over northern Italian territories lost during the previous pontificate. At first the pope's relations with the Romans were very amicable, so relieved were they to have been liberated from the erratic and dyspeptic rule of Urban VI. But the atmosphere soon changed, and Boniface IX had to move to Perugia and then to Assisi. But when the Romans began to worry that the pope might once again remove the seat of the papacy from Rome, they relented and welcomed him back to the city.

Boniface IX did nothing to deal with the schism in the Church. He cultivated his ties with Germany and England while ignoring all appeals for a resolution of the division. Clement VII died in 1394. The new

Avignon pope, Benedict XIII, deeply convinced of the legitimacy of his own claim to the papacy, nevertheless tried to open the channels of communication with Rome, but Boniface again refused. Although an able, even outstanding, administrator, Boniface IX was infamous for his blatant nepotism and financial skullduggery. He died on October 1, 1404, and was buried in the crypt of St. Peter's Basilica.

202 INNOCENT VII

ca. 1336–1406, pope October 17, 1404–November 6, 1406

The third of the popes in the Roman line during the Great Western Schism (1378–1417), Innocent VII rebuffed all efforts to resolve the crisis. Born Cosimo Gentile de' Migliorati, he was for ten years the papal tax collector in England, then cardinal-priest of Santa Croce in Gerusalemme and archbishop of Bologna when elected pope by eight cardinals in Rome on October 17, 1404.

Although the new pope and the other cardinals had taken an oath at the conclave to do everything in their power to end the schism, Innocent VII refused Benedict XIII's request for a face-to-face meeting. Toward the end of the year, however, Innocent yielded to pressure from Rupert, the newly elected king of Germany, to summon a council, but civil unrest in Rome ultimately caused it to be called off entirely. Innocent VII appealed to Ladislas, king of Naples, to put down a revolt, but the pope had to swear that he would not enter into any agreement with the Avignon pope that did not recognize Ladislas's title to Naples. But after several months of Ladislas's rule in Rome, the people were ready to welcome Innocent back in early March 1406. The pope had to impose the penalty of excommunication on Ladislas to get him to vacate Castel Sant'Angelo, but after Ladislas and his troops left, the pope named him defender and standard-bearer of the Church! Innocent VII died two months later and was buried in St. Peter's.

203 GREGORY XII

ca. 1325–1417, pope December 19, 1406–July 4, 1415 (The Vatican's official list begins his pontificate on November 30, the day of his election, but he was not consecrated Bishop of Rome until December 19.)

The fourth and last of the popes in the Roman line during the Great Western Schism (1378–1417), Gregory XII was the last pope to resign from the papacy. Born Angelo Correr, he was cardinal-priest of San Marco and papal secretary when elected pope, at age eighty-one, by fourteen cardinals on November 30, 1406. He was crowned on December 19. Along with the other cardinals, the new pope had sworn during the conclave that, if elected, he would abdicate—on condition that the Avignon pope, Benedict XIII, would also abdicate—and that he would create no new cardinals. A meeting with Benedict XIII was set to be held by the following November 1 at the latest. But then pressure began to be applied to the elderly pope by the kings of Naples, Hungary, and Bohemia as well as by his nephews, who enjoyed the benefits of kinship with a reigning pope. The negotiations dragged on for months, and it became increasingly evident to Gregory XII that Benedict XIII had no intention of abdicating the Avignon throne.

In 1408 Gregory XII broke his pledge and created four new cardinals, causing most of his cardinals to abandon him and join with Benedict's cardinals; together the cardinals convened the Council of Pisa, which met in the Duomo (or cathedral) on March 25, 1409, and formally deposed both Gregory XII and Benedict XIII as schismatics, intractable heretics, and perjurers. They declared the Holy See vacant, and on June 26 elected a new pope, Alexander V.

Meanwhile, Gregory XII opened his own council and excommunicated both Benedict XIII and Alexander V. Alexander V died suddenly on May 3, 1410, and the Council of Pisa elected Cardinal Baldassare Cossa to succeed him. He took the now famous name John XXIII. After the Council of Constance (1414–18) deposed John XXIII on May 29, 1415, it sought to open negotiations with Gregory XII with a view to his abdication, which he agreed to. On July 4, 1415, Gregory resigned from the papal office. (The Avignon pope, Benedict XIII, still refused to abdicate, but the council declared him a heretic and deprived him of all rights to the papacy.) Three weeks before the election of Martin V, which ended the Great Western Schism, Gregory XII, already beyond the age of ninety, died at Recanati (October 18, 1417) and was buried in its cathedral.

204 MARTIN V

> *1368–1431, pope November 21, 1417–February 20, 1431*
> *(The Vatican's official list begins his pontificate on*
> *November 11, the day of his election, but he was not*
> *consecrated Bishop of Rome until November 21.)*

With Martin V's election to the papacy, the Great
Western Schism (1378–1417) finally came to an end.
Born Oddo Colonna, he was cardinal-deacon of San
Giorgio in Velabro when unanimously elected pope in
Constance on November 11, 1417 (the feast of St. Martin), after an unusual three-day conclave in which
twenty-two cardinals and thirty representatives of the
five nations present at the Council of Constance (1414–
18) participated and voted (the first—and last—papal
conclave since 1058 to include lay electors). Martin V's
election effectively ended the schism, even though first
Benedict XIII (the Avignon antipope) and then his successor, Clement VIII, held out until their followings
dwindled to insignificance. But Gregory XII's abdication
and then John XXIII's acceptance, under duress, of his
own deposition by the council were the decisive events
that cleared the way for the almost universal acknowledgment of Martin V as the only legitimate pope.

Although Martin V was publicly committed to carrying out the reforms of the Council of Constance,
he was also interested in strengthening the canonical
and financial status of the papacy. He brought loyal-
ists from Rome and Avignon alike into the Curia, but
he failed to remove abuses and he maintained papal
rights over benefices.

Concerned about the chaos that had developed in the Papal States during the course of the schism (1378–1417), Martin V resisted pressures to make his papal residence in Germany or in Avignon and on May 16, 1418, left Constance for Rome. Once there, he quickly negotiated an agreement with Queen Joanna II of Naples, and her troops were withdrawn from the city. In 1424 papal troops defeated the dominant ruler of central Italy in the battle of L'Aquila, and in 1429 they crushed by force of arms a revolt by Bologna. Now free to reorganize the Papal States with the support of his troops, Martin V recovered the lost papal treasury, thereby enriching not only the Holy See but also his Colonna relatives. Martin V died of apoplexy on February 20, 1431, before the council at Basel, which he had called, began. He was buried in the basilica of St. John Lateran.

205 EUGENIUS [EUGENE] IV

*ca. 1383–1447, pope March 11, 1431–February 23, 1447
(The Vatican's official list begins his pontificate on
March 3, the day of his election, but he was not
consecrated Bishop of Rome until March 11.)*

Born Gabriele Condulmaro, Eugenius IV was the nephew of Pope Gregory XII (1406–15), who had appointed him cardinal-priest of San Clemente in 1408. At the time of his unanimous election to the papacy on March 3, 1431, Cardinal Condulmaro was governor of the March of Ancona and of Bologna. He was consecrated as Bishop of Rome and crowned in St. Peter's Basilica on the following Sunday, March 11.

The new pope's preoccupation at the start of his pontificate was the reformist Council of Basel, which Martin had called. The council opened on July 23, 1431, and Eugenius IV dissolved it on December 18, using sparse attendance as an excuse. But the council refused to disperse. Meanwhile, the Papal States were occupied by hostile lay powers, and a revolt erupted in Rome in May 1434. Eugenius IV had to flee the city in disguise. He went to Florence, where he would reside until 1443.

On June 9, 1435, the Council of Basel decreed the end of annual papal taxes, causing the pope to denounce their actions. But the final rupture between Eugenius IV and the council came on an issue to which both were committed, namely, the reunion of the Latin and Greek Churches. The great majority of the council delegates favored Basel itself, or Avignon, or Savoy for the negotiations, while the Greeks favored Constantinople. The pope preferred an Italian city. He won over the Greeks to his point of view, and the council was transferred to Ferrara on September 18, 1437, opening on January 8, 1438. The council moved to Florence the following January, ostensibly because of the outbreak of plague, but the more plausible reason was financial—the pope had accepted full responsibility for the entire Byzantine delegation. An act of union between the Latin and Greek Churches (entitled *Laetentur coeli*, July 6, 1439) was forced on the Byzantine emperor John VIII Palaeologus because of the imminence of a Turkish invasion. The terms of the union included the legitimacy of the use of the *Filioque* (Lat., "and of the Son") in the creed, a phrase vehemently opposed by the East because it undercut the unique status of God the Father.

Those conciliar delegates who remained in Basel after the transfer of the council to Ferrara and then to Florence first suspended and then deposed Eugenius IV on January 24, 1438, and June 25, 1439, respectively. The pope replied on September 4, 1439, challenging the ecumenicity of the earlier phases of the Council of Constance and condemning the Council of Basel. On November 5, 1439, those remaining in Basel elected a layman, Amadeus VIII, the duke of Savoy, as an antipope, Felix V. Felix V abdicated on April 7, 1449. He was the last of the antipopes.

In the spring of 1443, when Eugenius IV recognized the claims of Alfonso V of Aragón to the throne of Naples, Alfonso ordered his bishops to withdraw their support from the antipope Felix V and made possible the pope's return to Rome from Florence in September, after an absence of some nine years. It is said that, as he lay dying, Eugenius IV expressed regret that he had ever left the monastery he had lived in during his youth. He was at first buried in the crypt of St. Peter's next to the tomb of Eugenius III, but his body was eventually moved to the church of San Salvatore in Lauro in Rome.

206 NICHOLAS V

1397–1455, pope March 6, 1447–March 24, 1455

Nicholas V was the first of the Renaissance popes, a patron of literature, the arts, and architecture. He amassed a great personal library (which upon his death became the basis of the Vatican Library), had many classical and patristic Greek authors translated into Latin, and sponsored the rebuilding and decoration of numerous churches and other structures in Rome. Born Tommaso Parentucelli, he was archbishop of Bologna, a cardinal-priest of Santa Susanna, and a papal legate in Germany when elected pope on March 6, 1447, as a compromise choice. He was crowned on March 19 with the tiara of St. Sylvester.

Nicholas V had almost immediate success in areas where his less patient and less politically skilled predecessor, Eugenius IV, had failed. He restored order in the city of Rome, rid the Papal States of mercenary troops, and won (or bought) back the allegiance of various cities. He ratified the agreement Eugenius had reached with the German Church and court, and in the Concordat of Vienna (1448) King Frederick III recognized papal rights to annual taxes (annates) and over church appointments in Germany. On March 19, 1452, Nicholas V crowned the German king Frederick III as emperor in St. Peter's, the last imperial coronation to take place in Rome. In June 1453 the news of the sack of Constantinople by the Turks (on May 29) sent shock waves through the whole of Europe. Nicholas tried to mount a crusade in September, but to no avail. Weakened by gout, Nicholas V died on March 24, 1455. He was buried in St. Peter's, near the tomb of his predecessor, Eugenius IV.

207 CALLISTUS [CALIXTUS] III

Spanish, 1378–1458, pope April 8, 1455–August 6, 1458

The first Spanish pope, Callistus III created two of his nephews cardinals, one of whom would become the second—and last—Spanish pope, the infamous Alexander VI (1492–1503). Born Alfonso de Borja (Borgia, in Italian), he was cardinal-priest of the church of Santi Quattro Coronati as well as bishop of Valencia when elected pope on April 8, 1455, as a compromise candidate between the competing Colonna and Orsini factions—and a presumably safe one, given his health (he was weakened by gout) and age (seventy-seven). He was crowned in St. Peter's Basilica on April 20.

Callistus III immediately threw himself into his new responsibilities, organizing a crusade to liberate Constantinople from the Turks (captured in May 1453). Although there were some initial successes in the pope's campaign against the Turks, Christian rulers in the West, preoccupied with domestic concerns, were generally indifferent to the cause. Like many seemingly pious individuals, Callistus III was a stubborn man who tolerated no opposition from anyone, including his cardinals. His heavy-handed methods of raising money for the crusade and his blatant nepotism angered and embittered many. He enlisted Spanish commanders to lead troops in the Papal States and filled the Curia with Spanish appointees from Valencia and Catalonia. Although he annulled the sentence of heresy against Joan of Arc, he also revived harsh anti-Jewish legislation banning communication between Christians and Jews.

Callistus III died on August 6, 1458. Upon his death, the Italians vented their wrath upon the Catalans, who fled in terror. Callistus III was buried originally in the chapel of San Andrea in St. Peter's, but his body was transferred in 1610 to the church of Santa Maria di Monserrato, the Spanish church in Rome.

208 PIUS II

1405–64, pope August 19, 1458–August 15, 1464

The third of the Renaissance popes and a renowned humanist in his own right, Pius II encouraged the arts and literature and promoted the lavish pageantry associated with the papacy of this period. He also canonized St. Catherine of Siena (his home region) in 1461. Born Enea (Aeneas) Silvio Piccolomini, he had been a firm opponent of Pope Eugenius IV (1431–47) and secretary and principal adviser to the antipope Felix V (1439–49). In 1445, with encouragement from King Frederick III of Germany, whose imperial poet (poet laureate) and secretary he had become, Piccolomini severed his connection with the antipope Felix V and reconciled himself with Eugenius IV. Callistus III made him a cardinal in 1456 in gratitude for his efforts in reconciling the king of Aragón and Naples with the pope. Cardinal Piccolomini was elected pope on August 19, 1458, at the chronological age of fifty-three, but he was already prematurely old. He chose the name Pius in honor of the Roman poet Virgil's "pius Aeneas." He was crowned on September 3.

Pius II immediately called for a crusade against the Turkish advance, but his proposals for raising troops and money met with strong opposition, and the attempt failed. Feeling a diminution of papal influence, he published legislation forbidding the submission of papal acts to general councils on appeal. He continued to have difficulties in France, Germany, and Bohemia. When in October 1463, the pope called for a crusade, this time one that he himself would lead, again the Christian rulers withheld their support. Although by now seriously ill, the pope took the cross in St. Peter's in June 1463 and headed for Ancona, which he had previously designated as the rendezvous point. When he arrived, he found only a handful of Crusaders. As the Venetian galleys came into view, Pius died, on August 15, 1464, at age fifty-nine. He was buried in the chapel of San Andrea in St. Peter's, but his body was transferred in 1614 to the church of Sant'Andrea della Valle, also in Rome.

209 PAUL II

1417–71, pope August 30, 1464–July 26, 1471

One of history's least popular popes, Paul II reneged on his promise to the cardinals who elected him to promote the reform of the Church, angered humanists for his treatment of scholars, and was absorbed in luxury, sport, and entertainment. Born Pietro Barbo, he was the nephew of Pope Eugenius IV (1431–47), who saw to his rapid rise in the Church—from archdeacon of Bologna to bishop of Cervia and then of Vicenza, protonotary of the Roman church, and then, at age twenty-three, cardinal-deacon. Upon Pius II's death in August 1464, the cardinal-electors were looking for a different kind of pope, someone less self-indulgent and more committed to reform. The cardinals swore themselves to a pact defining the next pope's agenda and calling for a general, or ecumenical, council within three years' time. Cardinal Barbo was unexpectedly elected on August 30 on the first ballot and immediately declared that the pact provided only guidelines for his pontificate, not mandates. When he forced the cardinals to modify them, he also lost their trust. He was crowned on September 16.

Paul II was among the worst of the Renaissance popes: a vain, intellectually shallow, ostentatious playboy. He was a promoter of carnivals, to whose expense he forced Jews to contribute. When he decreed on April 19, 1470, that, beginning with 1475, there would be a Holy Year every twenty-five years, his motive was hardly religious or spiritual. He loved festivities. Like his predecessors, Paul II tried to mount a crusade against the Turks, but his efforts bore little fruit. Paul II died suddenly of a stroke at age fifty-four on July 26, 1471. He was buried in St. Peter's.

210 SIXTUS IV

1414–84, pope August 25, 1471–August 12, 1484 (The Vatican's official list begins his pontificate on August 9, the day of his election, but he was not consecrated Bishop of Rome until August 25.)

Sixtus IV transformed the city of Rome from a medieval to a Renaissance city, built the Sistine Chapel, and established the Vatican archives, but he also blatantly practiced nepotism (making six nephews cardinals), established the Spanish Inquisition, annulled the decrees of the reformist Council of Constance (1414–18), was personally involved in a conspiracy that included murder, and helped prepare the way for the Protestant Reformation.

Born Francesco della Rovere in poverty, he was educated by Franciscans and joined the order early in his life. A celebrated preacher and respected theologian, he became minister general of the Franciscans in 1464 and was appointed cardinal of San Pietro in Vincoli in 1467. In the confusion following Paul II's sudden death at age fifty-four, Cardinal della Rovere quickly emerged as the favorite. He was consecrated as Bishop of Rome and crowned on August 25 in St. Peter's Square, the first time such a ceremony was held there.

Soon after his election, Sixtus IV named two of his young nephews cardinals (one of whom would become Pope Julius II) and advanced and enriched a number of other relatives. Like many of his predecessors, he was eager for a crusade against the Turks, but he too was faced with the general indifference of Christian rulers in Europe.

Sixtus IV was preoccupied during much of his pontificate with the well-being of the Papal States. In 1478 he was drawn by one of his nephews into the Pazzi conspiracy, in which Giuliano de' Medici was killed and his brother Lorenzo wounded. (That same year he established the Spanish Inquisition, later sought to check its abuses, and then confirmed the infamous Tomás de Torquemada as grand inquisitor.) This murderous act drew the pope into a useless and scandalous war with Florence (1478–80), and then he incited Venice to attack Ferrara—only to change sides and impose spiritual penalties on Venice. The princes and cities of Italy forced the pope to accept the Peace of Bagnolo in 1484, leaving him with no additional territories and much trouble in Rome and Latium.

Although his vain military expeditions and his unseemly generosity toward his family depleted the papal treasury and forced him to resort to dubious forms of revenue raising like the sale of indulgences, Sixtus IV reigned as a Renaissance prince. He built churches, attracted painters, sculptors, and musicians to Rome, and opened the Vatican Library to scholars. He died on August 12, 1484, and was buried in St. Peter's, where his bronze tomb is considered a masterpiece.

211 INNOCENT VIII

1432–92, pope August 29, 1484–July 25, 1492

With the pontificate of Innocent VIII, the papacy sunk to the depths of worldliness—a fitting prelude to the most notorious pontificate in history, that of Alexander VI. Born Giovanni Battista Cibò, he was the bishop of Molfetta and a cardinal-priest of Santa Cecilia (and the father of three illegitimate children prior to ordination) when elected pope in a conclave filled with intrigue and bribery. He was crowned on September 12.

Innocent VIII's papal court was indistinguishable from that of any contemporary prince, and his cardinals (appointed mostly by Sixtus IV) lived in the grand style. Because of the enormous financial debts left by his predecessor, the new pope created new and unnecessary offices in the Curia and elsewhere in order to sell them to the highest bidders.

As in the case of almost every pope before him, Innocent VIII's efforts to mount a crusade against the Turks went nowhere. As Innocent VIII's pontificate neared its end, there was jubilation in Rome over the news that the Moors had been expelled from Granada (January 2, 1492). In gratitude, the pope awarded the Spanish king Ferdinand V (and his wife, Isabella of Castile) and his successors the title "Catholic Kings." Upon the pope's death on July 25 (with Christopher Columbus less than three months from landfall in America), the Papal States were in a condition of anarchy. It is said that, as he lay dying, he begged the cardinals to elect a successor better than himself. They surely did not! Innocent VIII was buried in St. Peter's.

212 ALEXANDER VI

Spanish, 1431–1503, pope August 26, 1492–August 18, 1503 (The Vatican's official list begins his pontificate on August 11, the day of his election, but he was not consecrated Bishop of Rome until August 26.)

Alexander VI was the most notorious pope in all of history. His pontificate was marked by nepotism, greed, and unbridled sensuality. Born Rodrigo de Borja y Borja (Borgia in Italian) near Valencia, he was the nephew of Pope Callistus III (1455–58), who named him a cardinal-deacon at age twenty-five and the next year vice-chancellor of the Holy See, a position that made it possible for him to amass such wealth that he was accounted the second richest cardinal. He also lived an openly promiscuous life, fathering several children before and after his election to the papacy. Rodrigo had hoped to succeed Sixtus IV to the papacy in 1484 but had to wait for the next conclave in 1492 to realize his ambition, although not without the help of generous bribes and promises of lucrative appointments and benefices. Therefore, his election in the Sistine Chapel on August 11, 1492, was simoniacal (i.e., purchased). Alexander VI was crowned in St. Peter's on August 26.

Although the new pope seemed to make a strong beginning, restoring order in Rome and promising reform of the Curia and a crusade against the Turks, it soon became evident that the consuming passions of his pontificate would be gold, women, and the interests of his family. He named his son Cesare, at age eighteen, a cardinal, along with the brother of the current papal mistress. He also arranged several marriages for his daughter Lucrezia and often left her in charge of the papacy, as virtual regent, when he was away from Rome. The pope's main political preoccupation during his pontificate was the transformation of the Papal States and central Italy into a family enterprise. The means employed included assassinations, seizures of properties, and the creation of cardinals for a high price.

The political act for which Alexander VI is best remembered occurred in 1493 when he drew a line of demarcation between Spanish and Portuguese zones of exploration in the New World. The ecclesiastical act for which he is also remembered was his excommunication, torture, and execution in 1498 of the famous Florentine preacher and reformer Girolamo Savonarola, who had been denouncing papal corruption and calling for a council to reform the Church and depose Alexander VI.

In June 1497, when his favorite son, Juan, was murdered and suspicion centered on Cesare, Alexander VI was so shattered that he resolved to dedicate himself thereafter to church reform. But his resolution could not withstand the continued temptations of the flesh and the demands of his family. In August 1503 he and his son Cesare were at dinner hosted by a cardinal. Both ingested a poison evidently meant for their host. The pope died, but his son survived. Alexander VI was buried first in the chapel of San Andrea in St. Peter's, and then in 1610 his remains were transferred to the Spanish church of Santa Maria di Monserrato in Rome.

213 PIUS III

> ca. 1439–1503, pope October 1–18, 1503 (The Vatican's
> official list begins his pontificate on September 22, the
> day of his election, but apparently, although he had
> been appointed archbishop of Siena, he had not yet
> been ordained a priest or a bishop; his consecration as
> Bishop of Rome did not occur until October 1.)

A compromise candidate in poor health, Pius III died only seventeen days after his consecration and coronation as pope. Taking the day of his episcopal consecration as the beginning of his pontificate, his was possibly the fourth shortest pontificate in history, and even the second or third shortest because of the difficulty in determining the exact dates for Boniface VI (896) and Celestine IV (1241).

Born Francesco Todeschini-Piccolomini, he was a nephew of Pope Pius II (1458–64), who appointed him archbishop of his home city of Siena at age twenty-one and a few weeks later made him cardinal-deacon of San Eustachio. He was placed in charge of Rome and the Papal States when his uncle Pius II embarked on a crusade in 1464 and was for many years cardinal-protector of England and Germany and then papal legate to Germany. At the time of his election, Pius III was in poor health (afflicted with gout) and prematurely old, both of which made him an attractive candidate to provide the Church with a bit of breathing space following Alexander VI's pontificate. But the new pope's reign proved to be even shorter than the cardinals themselves had expected. He died on October 18 and was buried in the chapel of San Andrea in St. Peter's. Pius III's remains were transferred in 1614 to the church of Sant'Andrea della Valle in Rome.

214 JULIUS II

*1443–1513, pope November 1, 1503–February 21, 1513
(The Vatican's official list begins his pontificate on
October 31, but he was actually elected the next day,
November 1.)*

A patron of artists, a politician, and a warrior, Julius II was born Giuliano della Rovere of impoverished but noble parents. He was, like so many other popes, a nephew of a previous pope, in this case Sixtus IV (1471–84), and, like these others, he benefited greatly from favors granted by his uncle the pope. As a cardinal he fathered three daughters. He was elected unanimously in a single day, November 1, 1503, with the help of substantial bribes and promises of ecclesiastical preferments, especially to Cesare Borgia.

Apart from his interest in art and architecture, Julius II was a thoroughly political, even military, pope, far removed from the example of the Apostle Peter and the mandate of Jesus Christ. He restored and enlarged the Papal States, forced the still dangerous Cesare

Borgia out of Italy, won back most of Romagna, and in 1506, in full armor and in the lead, captured Perugia and Bologna from their tyrannical rulers. In 1508, having joined the League of Cambria (France, Germany, and Spain), he defeated Venice so completely that it had to surrender Rimini and Faenza as well as all taxation rights. Fearing French domination in northern Italy and concerned about the need for Venetian assistance against the Turks, Julius II then made peace with Venice and, to win the support of Spain, recognized Ferdinand II of Aragón as king of Naples, disregarding France's claims on it. Later, having formed the Holy League with Venice and Spain, he drove the French from the Papal States.

Julius II paid little attention to ecclesiastical, much less spiritual, concerns. He did, however, issue a fateful dispensation to Henry VIII of England enabling him to marry his brother's widow, Catherine of Aragón, establish the first dioceses in South America, and convene the ecumenical council Lateran V (May 1512).

Julius II is perhaps best remembered for his patronage of great artists like Michelangelo, Raphael, and Bramante. The pope commissioned Bramante to prepare plans for the new St. Peter's Basilica, and he assisted at the laying of the cornerstone on April 18, 1506. In a historically momentous decision, Julius II arranged to finance the construction by the sale of indulgences, thereby lighting the match that ignited the Protestant Reformation. Julius II died of fever on February 21, 1513, and was buried in the church of San Pietro in Vincoli.

215 LEO X

1475–1521, pope March 17, 1513–December 1, 1521
(The Vatican's official list begins his pontificate on
March 9, the day of his election, but he was not
consecrated Bishop of Rome until March 17.)

The Protestant Reformation began during the pontificate of Leo X, in large part because of his decision to sell church offices and indulgences in order to pay off debts incurred through personal extravagance, military campaigns, and the construction of St. Peter's Basilica. Born Giovanni de' Medici, son of Lorenzo the Magnificent, he was tonsured (i.e., admitted to the clerical state) at age seven, was named a cardinal-deacon of Santa Maria in Dominica at age thirteen, and was the effective ruler of Florence at the time of his election to the papacy on March 9, 1513, at age thirty-seven.

A Renaissance prince who loved books, music, art, hunting, and the theater, Leo X made Rome once again the cultural center of the Western world. Politically, he was concerned with preserving Italy, and especially his beloved Florence, from foreign domination. To do so, he entered into an unpopular treaty with France in 1515 (after a series of French military victories in Italy, including Milan). Leo X surrendered Parma and Piacenza in return for Florence's independence, under Medici control. To finance his military expeditions, the projected crusade against the Turks, and the construction of the new St. Peter's, Leo X had to borrow money on a mammoth scale and to sell church offices, including cardinals' hats. For the construction of the new basilica he renewed the sale of indulgences authorized by Julius II, and then he arranged a highly lucrative (but simoniacal) deal with Albrecht, the archbishop of Brandenburg and Mainz, for the indulgence to be preached in his dioceses. When the Dominican John Tetzel (d. 1519) began preaching the indulgence in January 1517, the Augustinian monk Martin Luther (d. 1546) posted his famous Ninety-five Theses of protest on the church door in Wittenberg. In 1520, Leo published a bull condemning Luther, which Luther publicly burned. Leo then excommunicated Luther on January 3, 1521.

Unfortunately, Leo X and the Curia did not comprehend the significance of these reform movements or of the Church's urgent need to root out corruption and abuses. When Leo X died suddenly of malaria on December 1, 1521, Italy was in political turmoil, northern Europe was about to erupt in an explosion of religious conflict, and the papacy was in great debt. Leo X was buried first in St. Peter's, but his remains were transferred in 1536 to the basilica of Santa Maria sopra Minerva, where a great monument to him was erected.

216 HADRIAN [ADRIAN] VI

Dutch, 1459–1523,
pope January 9, 1522–September 14, 1523

The first pope of the Catholic Counter-Reformation, Hadrian VI was the only Dutchman to serve as pope and the last non-Italian until John Paul II (1978–2005).

He is also one of only two popes in the second Christian millennium to retain his baptismal name as pope (Marcellus II did the same in 1555). Born Adrian Florensz Dedal in Utrecht, he was, like Jesus, the son of a carpenter. He was cardinal-archbishop of Utrecht when unanimously elected to the papacy on January 9, 1522, with the support of the emperor Charles V. He came to Rome by sea to underscore his independence from both France and the empire. Accordingly, he was not crowned until August 31.

From the outset of his pontificate, Hadrian VI saw his task as one of containing the Reformation by attending to the reform of the Church's central administration and of uniting the Christian West against the Turks. Both were to end in failure. First, he was badly received by the Roman people, who resented his belt-tightening economies. Because the cardinals were also unhappy, having expected some generous "payoffs" for their election of him, they refused to cooperate with his attempts at reforming the Curia. Hadrian VI's legate at the Diet of Nuremberg (December 1522) was instructed to acknowledge that blame for the disorder in the Church lay primarily with the Curia itself—an admission that historians have described as the first step in the Catholic Counter-Reformation.

Hadrian VI's hopes for a crusade against the Turks foundered diplomatically, in spite of the fall of Rhodes to the Turks in December 1522 and the impending threat to Hungary. The pope had alienated Charles V by remaining neutral in Charles's fight against Francis I of France. Then he alienated Francis by arresting

Cardinal Soderini, an ally of the French king. Francis stopped the flow of money from France to Rome and prepared to invade Lombardy. This forced the pope into a defensive alliance with the empire, England, Austria, Milan, and other Italian cities. A little over a month later, Hadrian fell seriously ill and died in September 14, 1523. He was buried first in the chapel of San Andrea in St. Peter's between the tombs of Pius II and Pius III. His remains were transferred ten years later to the German national church of Santa Maria dell'Anima in Rome.

217 CLEMENT VII

1478–1534, pope November 19, 1523–September 25, 1534

During Clement VII's pontificate, the Protestant Reformation continued to spread across northern Europe and into England. Born Giulio de' Medici, the illegitimate son of Giuliano de' Medici, he was cardinal-archbishop of Florence and vice-chancellor of the Holy See when unanimously elected (actually, proclaimed) pope on November 19, 1523, after a conclave of six weeks' duration.

Politically, the new pope was mainly concerned with preserving his family's hold on Florence and the papacy's on the Papal States. He flip-flopped in his loyalties; he first supported Francis I of France, then sought alliance with emperor Charles V, and then joined a military league against the emperor. As a result, the emperor invaded Italy and sacked Rome on May 6, 1527. The pope escaped to Castel Sant'Angelo but was forced to surrender and was imprisoned for over six months. Clement VII came to recognize that his interests lay with the emperor. The reconciliation of pope and emperor was sealed by Charles V's coronation at Bologna on February 24, 1530, the last imperial coronation by a pope, and by the restoration of Medici rule in Florence.

In June 1526, the Diet of Speyer rejected the Edict of Worms (1521), which had banned Martin Luther's writings. In doing so, Speyer gave the Reformers valuable breathing space. Clement fumbled an opportunity to confront the Lutheran challenge when he refused to call a general council to deal with the crisis. He also mishandled Henry VIII's divorce from Catherine of Aragón, first appearing to be sympathetic to the English king's request for a dispensation, then pronouncing a deferred sentence of excommunication on Henry on July 11, 1533, and voiding his divorce and remarriage. The English Church went into schism. Clement VII died on September 25, 1534, and was buried in the basilica of Santa Maria sopra Minerva.

218 PAUL III

1468–1549, pope October 13, 1534–November 10, 1549

A leading pope of the Counter-Reformation, Alessandro Farnese was sixty-seven, dean of the College of Cardinals, and cardinal-bishop of Ostia when unanimously elected pope on October 13, 1534, after a two-day conclave. He wanted to take the name Honorius IV, but the cardinals objected, and he chose instead the name

Paul III after the man who was pope when he was born. He was crowned on November 3.

Paul III was a Renaissance pope in the fullest sense of the word. He loved to hunt, patronized artists and writers (he commissioned Michelangelo to complete the *Last Judgment* in the Sistine Chapel), and staged splendid balls and carnivals. His nepotism was also in the Renaissance tradition. He named two of his grandsons cardinals at ages fourteen and sixteen and then gave them important church offices. On the other hand, he also made some excellent appointments to the College of Cardinals, including Gian Pietro Carafa (later Paul IV). On December 17, 1538, the pope excommunicated Henry VIII and placed England under interdict (an ecclesiastical penalty that prohibited the administration of the sacraments). England drifted farther away from Rome. At the same time, however, the pope promoted the reform of religious orders and the development of new ones, including the Society of Jesus (Jesuits), which he formally approved on September 27, 1540.

Paul is listed among the popes of Catholic reform because of his efforts toward the renewal of the Church, culminating in his convening the Council of Trent in 1545. The pope was represented by various legates. The first seven sessions of the council were concerned with the relationship between Scripture and tradition, original sin, justification, and the seven sacraments. Eventually, when tension flared again between the pope and the emperor, the pope had no option but to suspend the eighth session on February 1, 1548. Paul III died of violent fever on November 10,

1549, at age eighty-one and was buried in St. Peter's. His tomb by Michelangelo's student Giacomo della Porta is considered one of the basilica's finest.

219 JULIUS III

1487–1555, pope February 8, 1550–March 23, 1555

During Julius III's pontificate, the Council of Trent was reconvened for a year (1551–52). Born Giovanni Maria de' Ciocchi del Monte, he was elected pope as a compromise candidate on February 8, 1550, in a conclave that lasted ten weeks. Before election, Cardinal Ciocchi del Monte had been an assistant (chamberlain) to Julius II, which is why he chose his name.

In spite of his strong canonical background, Julius III proved to be a typical Renaissance pope, given to hunting, banqueting, the theater, advancing the interests of his family, and an assortment of other sensual pleasures. Because of a preelection oath he had sworn with other cardinals at the conclave, he reconvened the Council of Trent on May 1, 1551, with the gratitude and support of the emperor Charles V. King Henry II of France, however, forbade French participation. There were several sessions (eleven through sixteen), some of which were attended by German Protestants. But the council had to be suspended once again because of the German-French war precipitated by the pope's effort to expel the pro-French Ottavio Farnese (Paul III's grandson) from Parma.

The pope retired to his luxurious new villa (Villa Giulia, at the Porto del Popolo), where he spent most of his time on idle pursuits, interrupted by occasional ventures into church business. For example, when the Catholic Queen Mary succeeded Edward VI to the English throne on July 6, 1553, Julius III appointed Cardinal Reginald Pole, a relative of the queen, as legate in England. On November 30 Pole solemnly absolved England from the papal interdict placed upon it by Julius III's predecessor, Paul III. The pope died of gout on March 23, 1555, and was buried in the crypt of St. Peter's.

220 MARCELLUS II

1501–55, pope April 10–May 1, 1555 (The Vatican's official list begins his pontificate on April 9, the day of his election, but he was not consecrated Bishop of Rome until the following day.)

Marcellus II was one of only two popes in modern times to retain his baptismal name as pope (the other was Hadrian VI in 1522). Born Marcello Cervini, he served as cardinal-priest, papal legate, copresident of the Council of Trent, and head of the Vatican Library. As head of a reform commission, he was so critical of the nepotism and lifestyle of his predecessor, Julius III, that he had to retire to his diocese. Few papal elections held out such high promise for reform. Unanimously elected on April 9, 1555, and consecrated a bishop and crowned the next day (even though opposed by the emperor), he drastically reduced the expenses for his coronation and decreased the size of the Curia. He gathered all the reform documents prepared under

Julius III with the intention of promulgating them in a single papal bull. After only twenty-one days as Bishop of Rome, Marcellus died of a stroke on May 1 and was buried simply in the crypt of St. Peter's Basilica. He is memorialized in Palestrina's *Missa Papae Marcelli*.

221 PAUL IV

1476–1559, pope May 23, 1555–August 18, 1559

At first hailed as a reformer, Paul IV soon showed himself to be a pope in the old medieval style: authoritarian, triumphalistic, censorious, and intolerant. He created the Index of Forbidden Books. Born Gian Pietro Carafa, he had been a model bishop of Chiete (or Theate), where he founded a religious order known as the Theatines, dedicated to a life of strict poverty and to church reform. Although known as a reformer, he was hostile to all efforts at reconciliation with the Lutherans, and as head of the reactivated Inquisition he exercised his authority with unusually brutal severity. He was appointed a cardinal in 1536 and dean of the College of Cardinals in 1553. The conclave of some forty cardinals was divided between pro-French and pro-imperial factions, so the conclave turned finally to their seventy-nine-year-old dean, Cardinal Carafa, and unanimously elected him pope on May 23, 1555.

Paul IV did not fare well in political-ecclesiastical matters. Upon the death of Queen Mary I of England in 1558, for example, he insisted on the restitution of all church properties and demanded that Queen Elizabeth I submit all of her claims to him. The

fortunes of Protestantism in England were immeasur-
ably aided by the pope's behavior. On the positive side,
Paul IV was generally careful in his choice of cardinals, and he insisted that bishops reside in their dioceses and monks in their monasteries. Upon his death
on August 18, 1559, rioting crowds destroyed the headquarters of the hated Inquisition and released its prisoners. The pope's statue on the Capitol was toppled
and disfigured. Paul IV was buried in the basilica of
Santa Maria sopra Minerva.

222 PIUS IV

1499–1565, pope December 25, 1559–December 9, 1565

In contrast to the severe and autocratic Paul IV, Pius
IV was warm and friendly and revived the Renaissance
tradition of papal generosity toward artists, architects,
and scholars. Born Gian Angelo de' Medici (no relation
to the famous Florentine family), he had held a number of diplomatic and political positions under Paul III
(1534–49), including governor of Parma, archbishop of
Ragusa, and cardinal-priest. Cardinal de' Medici was
elected pope by acclamation on Christmas Eve. The
vote was canonically confirmed on Christmas morning, December 25, 1559. Pius IV was crowned on January 6, 1560.

Pius IV immediately rehabilitated Cardinal Giovanni
Morone, who had been imprisoned by Paul IV under
suspicion of heresy, revoked the arrest warrants for va-
grant monks, reined in the Inquisition, and began re-

vision of the complicated Index of Forbidden Books. Although Pius IV indulged in a favorite Renaissance practice of nepotism, one of his choices proved remarkably fortunate. Within a week of his coronation, he appointed his young lay nephew Carlo Borromeo (d. 1584) as cardinal-archbishop of Milan, where he proved himself an able and committed reformer. Borromeo was canonized in 1610.

The most important initiative of Pius IV's pontificate, however, was his reconvening, after a ten-year suspension, of the Council of Trent in 1562 and his guiding the council to a successful conclusion the following year. The council adjourned on December 4, 1563, at its twenty-fifth session, and Pius IV formally confirmed its decrees in his bull *Benedictus Deus* on June 30, 1564.

Then began the difficult task of implementing the council's decrees. The pope established a congregation of cardinals to supervise their enforcement and ordered bishops present in Rome to return to their dioceses. In March 1564, he published the council's Index of Forbidden Books. Since the council had left the question of Communion in both kinds (consecrated bread and consecrated wine) to the pope, Pius IV allowed the practice of offering the chalice to the laity at the discretion of the bishops in regions where Protestantism was strong. After suffering over a long period of time with gout, Pius IV died on December 9, 1565. He was buried first in St. Peter's, but in January 1583 his remains were transferred to the church of Santa Maria degli Angeli, which he had built.

223 PIUS V, ST.

1504–72, pope January 7, 1566–May 1, 1572

Pius V enforced the decrees of the Council of Trent, published the *Roman Catechism*, reformed the Roman Missal and the Roman Breviary (Divine Office), and excommunicated Queen Elizabeth I of England. Although later canonized as a saint, he was a harsh enforcer of orthodoxy and probably an anti-Semite.

Born Antonio Ghislieri of poor parents, he was a shepherd until he became a Dominican at age fourteen, taking as his religious name Michele. After ordination to the priesthood as a Dominican (1528), he served as an inquisitor for Como and Bergamo. Because of his zealousness, he rapidly rose to become the protégé of Cardinal Gian Pietro Carafa (later Paul IV), who made him a bishop, then cardinal, and then grand inquisitor of the Roman Inquisition. Cardinal Alessandrino (so called after his native city, Alessandria) was elected pope on January 7, 1566, after a nineteen-day conclave. Pius V was crowned on January 19. He did away with the traditional pomp and feasting, insisting that they were anachronistic and offensive to the poor.

The new pope's agenda was simple and straightforward: to implement the decrees of the Council of Trent, which had adjourned two years earlier. First, he imposed strict standards of lifestyle on himself, those in the Curia, and the city of Rome itself. Faithful to Trent's decrees, he published the *Roman Catechism* in 1566, a revised Roman Breviary in 1568, and a revised

Roman Missal in 1570. He restricted the use of indulgences and dispensations.

Pius V's intense commitment to stamp out heresy led him to an inordinate reliance upon the Inquisition and its often inhuman methods. Many distinguished individuals were tried and sentenced under Pius V, but he still blamed himself for being too lenient! He was also unusually severe on the Jews. Pius V's political activities were largely counterproductive. His one significant achievement on the political-military front was the victory of his Holy League (with Spain and Venice) over the Turkish fleet at Lepanto in the Gulf on Corinth on October 7, 1571. The victory ended Turkish superiority in the Mediterranean.

Pius V died on May 1, 1572, at age sixty-eight and was buried first in St. Peter's; in 1588 his remains were transferred to a splendid tomb in the basilica of Santa Maria Maggiore (St. Mary Major). He was beatified on May 1, 1672, by Clement X and canonized on May 22, 1712, by Clement XI. Feast day: April 30.

224 GREGORY XIII

1502–85, pope May 13, 1572–April 10, 1585

Gregory XIII is best known for the Gregorian calendar (1582), still in use today, which reformed the Julian calendar by dropping ten days and introducing a leap year every fourth year. Born Ugo Buoncompagni, he was ordained a priest at about the age of forty. Given his strong legal and administrative experience, he undertook diplomatic missions for Paul IV in 1556. He took an active part in the Council of Trent from 1561 to 1563 and, in recognition of his services there, was created a cardinal-priest of San Sisto in 1565 and papal legate to Spain. His successful mission in Spain won the admiration of King Philip II, who exerted great influence on Cardinal Buoncompagni's election as pope on May 13, 1572, after a conclave of less than twenty-four hours. He took the name Gregory XIII out of respect for St. Gregory the Great (590–604), whom he had regarded as his protector since infancy.

The new pope had a more accommodating personality than his predecessor. On the other hand, Gregory XIII, influenced by St. Charles Borromeo (d. 1584), was also determined to promote the decrees of the Council of Trent and Catholic reform generally. He placed a high priority on bishops' living in their dioceses, and he transformed nunciatures from purely diplomatic posts to instruments of church reform. To ensure a better-educated clergy, he established at great expense colleges in Rome and in other cities and entrusted them largely to the Jesuits. In Rome, he reconstructed and generously endowed the Roman College (1572), which was later named the Gregorian University in his honor.

But like his predecessor, Pius V, there was a hard side to Gregory XIII as well. Thus, when news of the St. Bartholomew's Day massacre of Huguenots (Calvinists) in France reached Rome in late August 1572, he celebrated with thanksgiving services. He encouraged Philip II of Spain to launch an attack on Elizabeth I of England and, failing that, actively supported plots to assassinate her. In the last years of his pontificate, he faced serious disorder and banditry in Rome and the Papal States. Gregory XIII died on April 10, 1585, and was buried in St. Peter's.

225 SIXTUS V

1520–90, pope April 24, 1585–August 27, 1590

Sixtus V set the maximum number of cardinals at seventy, a total not exceeded until the pontificate of John XXIII (1958–63), reorganized the Roman Curia in a fashion that remained unchanged until the Second Vatican Council (1962–65), and instituted the practice of bishops visiting the Holy See at least once every five years to submit reports on the state of their dioceses.

Born Felice Peretti, a farmworker's son, he joined the Franciscans at age twelve, was ordained a priest, earned a doctorate in theology, and soon earned a reputation as a great preacher. He served as inquisitor for Venice, vicar general of the Franciscan order, and bishop of Sant'Agata dei Goti before his appointment by Pius V as cardinal in 1570. By now living in semiretirement, he was an unknown quantity at the conclave following Gregory's death—except to a small but powerful circle of friends, who exploited a division in the College of Cardinals and saw to his unanimous election as pope on April 24, 1585. He took the name Sixtus V out of respect for his fellow Franciscan Sixtus IV (1471–84). He was crowned on May 1.

The new pope immediately addressed the problem of lawlessness in the Papal States. Employing the

harshest repressive measures, including public execu-
tions and the exposure of bandits' heads on the bridge
of Sant'Angelo, he finally brought the situation under
control over a period of two years. He also replen-
ished the papal treasury by shrewd economic and ag-
ricultural policies, raising taxes, selling church offices,
and floating loans. He was one of the richest and most
financially independent princes in Europe. However,
he made no headway against the Turks, saw the Spanish Armada defeated by the English, and failed to stem
the tide of Protestantism in France.

Sixtus V's building projects in Rome transformed
it from a Renaissance to a Baroque city. He died on
August 27, 1590, at age sixty-nine, after several successive attacks of malaria. On hearing the news of his
death, Roman mobs toppled his statue on the Capitol.
He was buried in the basilica of Santa Maria Maggiore
(St. Mary Major).

226 URBAN VII

1521–90, pope September 15–27, 1590

The pontificate of Urban VII was one of the shortest
in history. Born Giovan Battista Castagna, he served as
papal legate to France, a curial official, archbishop of
Rozzano, governor in the Papal States, an active par-
ticipant in the Council of Trent (1562–63), nuncio to
Spain, governor of Bologna, consultor (later inquisitor general) to the Holy Office, and a cardinal-priest
of San Marcello al Corso (1583). When he was elected
pope on September 15, 1590, many had great hopes that

his would be a reformist but temperate pontificate. Although he had been in good health, the new pope contracted malaria the night after his election and died before his coronation could take place. Urban VII was buried in the basilica of Santa Maria sopra Minerva in Rome. He left a large amount of money for the care of impoverished girls.

227 GREGORY XIV

1535–91, pope December 5, 1590–October 16, 1591

The pontificate of Gregory XIV was one of the least popular and least successful in history, marred as it was by bad administration and by plague, food shortages, and lawlessness in Rome. Born Niccolò Sfondrati, he was named bishop of Cremona at age twenty-five and was appointed a cardinal in the title of Santa Cecilia in 1583. Although he had little curial experience, he was elected pope with the support of the pro-Spanish cardinals from a list of seven candidates after a faction-ridden conclave of more than two months. He took the name of the pope who made him a cardinal, Gregory, and was crowned on December 8.

Although only fifty-five, he was physically weak and often in pain. The state of his health and his own insecurity about his lack of experience in the Curia led him to name his own twenty-nine-year-old nephew, Paolo Emilio Sfondrati, cardinal-secretary of state. Paolo, however, was more interested in his own and his family's well-being than in that of the Church. Resentment developed quickly among the other cardinals.

Problems in the city of Rome—especially food shortages—were exacerbated by his nephew's incompetent administration. As he grew progressively weaker, Gregory XIV continued to fulfill his papal responsibilities from a sickbed. He called for the enforcement of residency requirements for bishops and arranged for the revision of Sixtus V's defective edition of the Vulgate Bible. Gregory XIV died on October 16, 1591, and was buried in St. Peter's, in the Gregorian chapel next to the tomb of Gregory XIII.

228 INNOCENT IX

1519–91, pope October 29–December 30, 1591

The third pope elected in a space of thirteen months, the elderly Innocent IX served only two months. Born Giovanni Antonio Facchinetti, he was bishop of Nicastro, took an active part in the last phase of the Council of Trent (1562–63), and was papal nuncio in Venice. Although he was on Spain's list of acceptable candidates, even the anti-Spanish cardinals acceded to his election because of his age and fragile health. He was elected on October 29, 1591, and was crowned on November 3.

The new pope, as expected, pursued a pro-Spanish policy like his predecessor, Gregory XIV. Accordingly, he provided financial and military support to keep the pressure on the still Protestant Henry IV, king of France. He also took steps to deal with the persistent problem of lawlessness in Rome. Innocent IX fell ill on December 18 but insisted on making a pilgrimage to the seven pilgrimage churches of Rome. He died a few days later, on December 30, and was buried in a simple tomb in the crypt of St. Peter's Basilica.

229 CLEMENT VIII

1536–1605, pope February 3, 1592–March 3, 1605 (The Vatican's official list begins his pontificate on January 30, the day of his election, but he was not consecrated Bishop of Rome until February 3.)

The fourth pope elected within the space of only sixteen months, Clement VIII (born Ippolito Aldobrandini) served in a number of curial posts under Pius V (1566–72) and Sixtus V (1585–90), who made him a cardinal-priest in the title of San Pancrazio in 1585. Although not a favorite of the pro-Spanish party, he had enough of its support to be elected on January 30, 1592. The pope-elect was consecrated as Bishop of Rome on February 3 and crowned on February 9. He took the name Clement because his friend Philip Neri (the later canonized founder of the Oratorians) had once predicted that he would become pope someday and would take that name.

An ascetical person afflicted with gout, Clement VIII lived a traditionally pious and austere life, traveling on foot each month to the seven pilgrimage churches of Rome. Although he had been a strong critic of nepotism when he himself was a cardinal, he named his nephews Cinzio and Pietro Aldobrandini to the College of Cardinals and turned the affairs of the Church over to them almost entirely. He also appointed a fourteen-year-old grandnephew to the college.

Clement VIII at least attempted to carry forward the reform movement launched by the Council of Trent (1545–63). He promoted the reform of religious houses, published a corrected version of the Vulgate Bible, and issued revised editions of a number of liturgical books. However, he also expanded the Index of Forbidden Books, including a ban on all Jewish books. He increased the severity of the Inquisition, which, during his pontificate, sent more than thirty people to the stake, including the former Dominican philosopher Giordano Bruno (1600).

In 1595 Clement VIII recognized the now Catholic Henry IV as king of France, which had the effect of freeing the papacy from Spanish domination. He also endorsed proposals that were subsequently accepted by the Synod of Brest-Litovsk (1596), whereby millions of Orthodox Christians in Poland would join the Roman Catholic Church while retaining their liturgy. Clement VIII died on March 3, 1605, and was buried in St. Peter's. In 1646 his remains were transferred to a magnificent tomb in the Borghese Chapel in the basilica of St. Mary Major.

230 LEO XI

1535–1605, pope April 1–27, 1605

A nephew of Leo X (1513–21), Leo XI was old and in poor health when elected, and he served less than a month. Born Alessandro Ottaviano de' Medici, he was a favored disciple of St. Philip Neri (d. 1595), was named bishop of Pistoia, then archbishop of Florence, cardinal, papal legate to France, cardinal-bishop of Albano, and cardinal-bishop of Palestrina. He was elected pope on April 1, 1605, with strong support from France and equally strong opposition from Spain. Cardinal de' Medici took the name Leo XI out of respect for his uncle, Leo X, and was crowned on April 10. He became sick while taking possession of the Lateran Basilica (the pope's cathedral as Bishop of Rome) and died before the end of the month, on April 27. He was buried in St. Peter's.

231 PAUL V

1552–1621, pope May 16, 1605–January 28, 1621

Born Camillo Borghese, Paul V served in the Roman Curia, was sent on a diplomatic mission to Spain, and was named a cardinal at age forty-four in the title of Sant'Eusebio in 1596, bishop of Iesi in the March of Ancona (1597–99), and vicar (i.e., the effective bishop) of Rome and inquisitor in 1603. His election to the papacy on May 16, 1605, at age fifty-three the youngest cardinal, was a great surprise to most people, but he was seen as an acceptable compromise between rival factions in the conclave of fifty-nine cardinals and so elected. He was crowned on May 29 and took possession of the Lateran Basilica (the pope's cathedral in Rome) on November 6.

The new pope immediately had problems with the contemporary political powers, Catholic as well as Protestant, because of his inflated view of papal authority, particularly in the temporal order. Some

Italian states yielded to him at first (Savoy, Genoa, Naples), but Venice resisted. Only the intervention of King Henry IV of France prevented the defection of Venice to Protestantism. When the English Parliament required Catholics to swear an oath denying the pope's right to depose princes, Paul V denounced the oath and forbade English Catholics to take it. In France, the pope's condemnation of Gallicanism (the view that the French Church is largely autonomous from Rome) provoked the Estates-General to declare that the French king derives his authority from God alone.

Unfortunately for his memory and place in history, Paul V is best remembered for having censured the famous astronomer Galileo Galilei (d. 1642) for advocating the scientific theory espoused by the great Polish astronomer Nicolaus Copernicus (d. 1543) that the earth revolves around the sun, not vice-versa. The Inquisition declared the theory incompatible with Sacred Scripture and ordered Galileo not to teach or seek to prove the theory. Copernicus's works were placed on the Index of Forbidden Books. (Galileo was brought before the Inquisition again in 1633, forced to renounce his position, and placed under house arrest for the remainder of his life. In 1979 John Paul II conceded that the Church had erred in its judgment against Galileo and in 1984 made all the relevant documents public.)

In Rome, Paul V completed the nave, façade, and portico of St. Peter's, erected many fountains, and improved the water supply. He died of a stroke on January 28, 1621, and was buried first in St. Peter's and then in the magnificent Borghese Chapel in the basilica of St. Mary Major.

232 GREGORY XV

1554–1623, pope February 9, 1621–July 8, 1623

The first Jesuit-trained pope, Gregory XV (born Alessandro Ludovisi) held a variety of posts in the Roman Curia, served in diplomatic missions, became archbishop of Bologna in 1612, and was named a cardinal-priest in the title of Santa Maria in Trastevere in 1616 in recognition of his successful efforts in negotiating a peace between Savoy and Spain. In the conclave that followed Paul V's death, the cardinals turned to Cardinal Ludovisi, who was sixty-seven and in frail health. He accepted and was elected by acclamation on February 9, 1621. He took the name Gregory XV in honor of Gregory XIII. He was crowned on February 14.

The new pope moved to reform the system of papal elections out of concern for the external influences brought to bear upon them. In two separate decrees in 1621 and 1622, he ordered that elections should normally occur after the conclave has been closed off from the public and that voting should be conducted by secret written ballot (a practice that remains in force today). In order to coordinate the Church's widespread missionary efforts, Gregory XV established the Sacred Congregation for the Propagation of the Faith in 1622 and assigned thirteen cardinals to it. The new congregation became a virtual headquarters of the Counter-Reformation since the missionary efforts were directed not only to non-Christian lands but to those now under the control of Protestantism.

Gregory XV canonized Teresa of Ávila, Philip Neri, and the two great Jesuits Ignatius of Loyola and Francis Xavier. He died in the Quirinale Palace on July 8, 1623, and was buried first in St. Peter's Basilica; his remains were later moved (in 1634) to the newly completed church of Sant'Ignazio in Rome.

233 URBAN VIII

1568–1644, pope August 6, 1623–July 29, 1644

Although known for consecrating the new St. Peter's Basilica in 1626 and for selecting Castel Gandolfo as a papal summer residence (still in use today for that purpose), Urban VIII was a reckless nepotist who too often placed his family's interests ahead of the Church's. Born Maffeo Barberini of wealthy parents, he served in the Roman Curia, then as nuncio to France (twice) and titular archbishop of Nazareth. In 1606 he was named a cardinal and eventually became prefect of the Signatura of Justice, the highest court in the Church's judicial system. He was elected pope on August 6, 1623, with fifty out of fifty-five votes after a literally and figuratively heated conclave, in which twelve of the cardinals became gravely ill with malaria. He was crowned on September 29. The new pope appointed a brother and two nephews to the College of Cardinals, promoted other brothers to lucrative positions, and generally enriched all of his relatives so extravagantly that he suffered pangs of conscience in old age.

Urban VIII's pontificate overlapped with the Thirty Years' War (1618–48), fought mainly in Germany. On one side were the German Protestant princes and foreign powers (France, Sweden, Denmark, England), and on the other was the Hapsburg empire (Austria, Spain, Bohemia, and most of Italy). Although Urban VIII strove to maintain neutrality in the conflict between France and Spain, his sympathies were clearly with France because he feared Hapsburg domination in Italy. But the pope and the Catholic Church paid a high price for such one-sided "neutrality" in that war. The Counter-Reformation in the empire was over.

To promote the Church's missionary work, he founded the Urban College of Propaganda in Rome (1627). In a bull dated April 22, 1639, he prohibited slavery of any kind among the Indians of Brazil, Paraguay, and the entire West Indies. It was also under Urban VIII that Galileo Galilei (d. 1642), although a personal friend, was condemned for a second time and forced to renounce the Copernican system under threat of torture (1633). In 1642 the pope censured the views of Cornelius Jansen (d. 1638) as expressed in his work *Augustinus.* The work was controversial because its understanding of the relationship between grace and free will, with its apparent depreciation of free will, seemed closer to Protestantism than the Catholic tradition.

When Urban VIII died on July 29, 1644, the Roman people, disgusted with his extravagances and shameless nepotism, were utterly jubilant. He was buried in St. Peter's, and his monument was done by the great Bernini himself.

234 INNOCENT X

1574–1655, pope September 15, 1644–January 7, 1655

Born Giovanni Battista Pamfili, Innocent X served for a long time as a judge of the Roman Rota and papal nuncio to Naples and then to Spain. He was elected pope on September 15, 1644, after a conclave lasting thirty-seven days because of the torrid Roman heat and the outbreak of malaria among the cardinals. He took the name Innocent X in honor of his uncle, Cardinal Innocenzo del Bufalo. The new pope was crowned on October 4. Innocent X appointed none of his relatives to fill the now traditional role of the cardinal-nephew (the pope's most trusted adviser), but a much more sinister influence in his papal court was his ambitious and greedy widowed sister-in-law, Donna Olimpia Maidalchini. Innocent X did nothing without consulting her.

The Thirty Years' War (1618–48) came to an end during Innocent X's pontificate, but he was unhappy with the terms of peace (the Peace of Westphalia) because they seemed to make too many concessions to the Protestants. The war between France and Spain continued in spite of the peace, and the pope tended to favor Spain because it was a declining power that posed less of a threat to the Church in Italy.

Innocent X continued his predecessors' support of the missions. He increased the authority of the Congregation for the Propagation of the Faith and elevated the Dominican College in Manila to university status. With regard to Jansenism, a movement based largely in France that seemed more Protestant than Catholic because of its seeming depreciation of human free will, he established a commission in 1651 to examine Cornelius Jansen's *Augustinus*. The pope himself participated in some of the commission's sessions. On May 31, 1563, he published a bull, *Cum occasione,* that unconditionally condemned five propositions extracted from the work.

Innocent X died in the Quirinale Palace on January 7, 1655, and was buried in St. Peter's with simple ceremonies, but his remains were transferred in 1730 to the Pamfili family crypt in the church of Sant'Agnese.

235 ALEXANDER VII

1599–1667, pope April 7, 1655–May 22, 1667

Born Fabio Chigi, Alexander VII served a vice-legate in Ferrara, bishop of Nardò, inquisitor and apostolic delegate in Malta, and, for thirteen years, papal nuncio in Cologne. He was named secretary of state by Innocent X and later made a cardinal and bishop of Imola. Cardinal Chigi was elected pope on April 7, 1655, after a conclave that lasted some eighty days and against the strong initial opposition of France. He took the name Alexander VII in honor of the great twelfth-century pope Alexander III (1159–81) and was crowned on April 18.

Although the new pope began his pontificate by forbidding his own relatives from visiting Rome, by the next year he relented, with the encouragement of the Curia, and showered favors of all kinds upon his family: church offices, palaces, estates, and money. Alexander's relations with France were sour from the start and, because he was without allies, he had to accept the terms of the Treaty of Pisa (1664) and submit to the king's wishes on episcopal appointments. His relations with other foreign powers were mixed.

The most important achievement of Alexander VII's pontificate was in the realm of the missions, not politics. He decreed on March 23, 1656, that the Jesuit missionaries in China be allowed to use Chinese rites and, over three years later, dispensed the native Chinese clergy from having to pray the Divine Office in Latin. The same year he also confirmed Innocent X's condemnation in 1653 of the five propositions in Cornelius Jansen's *Augustinus,* insisting against Jansen's defenders that the five propositions were, in fact, to be found in the *Augustinus.* (The Jansenists held that the role of free will in salvation is, for all practical purposes, negated by the overriding power of God's grace.)

Alexander VII commissioned the great sculptor and architect Bernini to enclose St. Peter's Square within two grand semicircular colonnades. He died on May 22, 1667, and was buried in St. Peter's in a tomb designed by Bernini himself.

236 CLEMENT IX

1600–1669, pope June 20, 1667–December 9, 1669

Clement IX's brief and undistinguished pontificate was preoccupied with politics, but he does have the distinction of having created the comic opera as a dramatic form. He wrote poetry and religious drama, some of which was publicly performed.

Born Giulio Rospigliosi, he spent his early years in the Roman Curia and then was appointed titular archbishop of Tarsus and papal nuncio to Spain. In 1653 he was named governor of Rome and then secretary of state and cardinal-priest of San Sisto under Alexander VII (1657). In spite of the French government's hostility to Alexander VII, Cardinal Rospigliosi maintained a mutually respectful relationship with the French court. Thus, upon Alexander VII's death, he had expected not only the support of Spain, but also that of France. Since the cardinals wanted someone capable of mediating between the two nations, they gladly turned to Rospigliosi, who was elected on June 20, 1667. He took the name Clement IX and was crowned on June 26.

Unlike many of his predecessors, the new pope gave very little to his relatives. That was probably the only real achievement of his pontificate: to have liberated the papacy, if only for a short time, from the corrupting grip of nepotism. Otherwise, his pontificate was mired in political maneuvering that had little or no positive outcome. Thus, Clement IX was forced to allow the French crown a free hand in ecclesiastical appointments. The pope's involvement in peace negotiations between France and Spain showed that he was no match for the crafty Hugues de Lionne, France's foreign minister. The "peace" was interpreted as a sign of papal weakness in the face of French pressure. The pope died on December 9, 1669, following a stroke in the Quirinale Palace. He was buried first in St. Peter's, but his remains were transferred in 1680 to the basilica of St. Mary Major.

237 CLEMENT X

1590–1676, pope April 29, 1670–July 22, 1676

Born Emilio Altieri, Clement X served in the nunciature in Poland, then as bishop of Camerino and nuncio to Naples, secretary of the Congregation of Bishops and Regulars (members of religious orders), and a consultor of the Holy Office (formerly the Inquisition). After a faction-ridden conclave of almost five months, with France and Spain exercising vetoes of certain candidates (the royal veto was abolished by Pius X in 1904), Cardinal Altieri, at age seventy-nine, was elected as a compromise candidate on April 29, 1670.

Deeply concerned about the Turkish threat to Poland, Clement X and Cardinal Odescalchi (later Innocent XI) gave financial assistance to John Sobieski (d. 1696), who defeated the Turks at the Dniester (November 11, 1673) and was elected king the following May. Relations with King Louis XIV of France were no better in Clement X's pontificate than in his predecessor's. The king confiscated church property and diverted income from religious houses. When Louis XIV later claimed an unrestricted right to make appointments to church offices and to receive the income of vacant dioceses and abbeys, the pope said nothing— leaving the problem for his successor to deal with.

Clement X canonized an unusually large number of saints, including Cajetan, the founder of the Theatines, the Jesuit Francis Borgia, and Rose of Lima, South America's first canonized saint. He also beatified Pope Pius V and the Spanish mystic John of the Cross. He died on July 22, 1676, at the age of eighty-six and was buried in St. Peter's, where his statue by Ercole Ferrata is situated.

238 INNOCENT XI, BL.

1611–89, pope September 21, 1676–August 12, 1689

Although regarded as the outstanding pope of the seventeenth century, Innocent XI manifested Jansenist and anti-Jesuit leanings. Born Benedetto Odescalchi, he held a series of appointments in papal service before being named a cardinal-deacon, then legate of Ferrara, and bishop of Novara. Generous to the poor, he resigned his diocese in 1654 because of ill health and lived quietly in Rome while working in the Curia. He was surprised, therefore, when the cardinals elected him after another faction-ridden conclave of two months' duration. He accepted election only after the cardinals subscribed to his program of reform. Cardinal Odescalchi took the name Innocent XI out of respect for the pope who created him a cardinal (Innocent X) and was crowned on October 4.

The new pope imposed severe reductions in the papal budget and called for evangelical preaching and catechesis, the strict observance of monastic vows, careful selection of priests and bishops, and the frequent reception of Holy Communion. So ascetical was he in his personal life, that many suspected him of Jansenist leanings (that is, a rigid approach to the moral life). It was not surprising, therefore, that he condemned sixty-five laxist propositions in 1679 (laxism held that a Catholic could follow any moral course as long as there was at least some good reason for doing so).

On the political front, Innocent XI was in constant conflict with King Louis XIV of France. Innocent rejected the king's right to make appointments to church offices and to receive the income of vacant dioceses and abbeys. He also rejected the Gallican Articles, which the king ordered the French clergy to adopt on March 19, 1682, and refused to ratify the appointment of bishops who did adopt them. The Articles denied papal authority in temporal affairs or over kings, asserted the superiority of ecumenical councils over the pope, and reaffirmed ancient liberties of the French Church. The king thought the pope might be more cooperative because of his (Louis's) brutal campaign against the Huguenots. But the pope was appalled by the inhumanity of the king's persecution. In January 1688, Innocent XI secretly informed Louis XIV that he and his ministers were excommunicated. The following September the king occupied the papal territories of Avignon and Venaissin and imprisoned the papal nuncio. Open schism was avoided only by the intervention of François Fénelon (d. 1715) and the accession of William of Orange to the English throne.

Although the Romans resented the pope's austerity measures during his lifetime, many revered him

after his death on August 12, 1689. He was buried in
St. Peter's under the altar of San Sebastiano. Innocent
XI was eventually beatified by Pius XII in 1956. Feast
day: August 12.

239 ALEXANDER VIII

1610–91, pope October 6, 1689–February 1, 1691

Elected at age seventy-nine, the worldly Alexander
VIII was greeted by the Romans as a welcome contrast
to the austere Innocent XI. Born Pietro Ottoboni, he
served in the Roman Curia, as a governor in the Papal
States, and as a judge in the Roman Rota before being
made a cardinal, then bishop, and then grand inquisitor of Rome and secretary of the Holy Office. The
cardinals decided that the elderly Cardinal Ottoboni's
experience and character made him the logical choice.
He was elected pope on October 6 and chose the
name Alexander VIII out of deference to the nephew
of Alexander VII (1655–67), Cardinal Flavio Chigi, who
had led the support for Ottoboni's election. The lavish personal style of the new pope was in stark contrast to that of his ascetical predecessor, Innocent XI.
Alexander VIII also revived the papal practice of nepotism that had gone into eclipse during the previous
two pontificates.

Alexander VIII made some effort toward reconciliation with King Louis XIV of France (for which he
incurred the hostility of the emperor Leopold I). In
return for Louis's withdrawal of his occupation forces
in the papal territories of Avignon and Venaissin and

other concessions, the pope named the bishop of
Beauvais to the College of Cardinals, even though he
had participated in the antipapal Gallican assembly
of 1682. The pope also accepted the French ambassador to Rome, who had been rejected by Innocent
XI. However, the pope and the king continued to dis-
agree over the issue of the power of appointment of
bishops. Alexander VIII died on February 1, 1691, and
was buried in St. Peter's under a sumptuous monument by Arrigo di San Martino.

240 INNOCENT XII

1615–1700, pope July 12, 1691–September 27, 1700

Innocent XII was a reformist pope in the style of his
hero, Innocent XI, striking especially at nepotism.
Born Antonio Pignatelli, he served in the Roman
Curia, as governor of Viterbo, and as nuncio to Tuscany, Poland, and Vienna. The conclave following
Alexander VIII's death lasted five months because of
the divisions between and within the pro-French and
pro-imperial factions. Under pressure of the unbear-
able summer heat and the impatience of the Roman
people, Cardinal Pignatelli was elected as a compromise candidate on July 12, 1691, taking the name
Innocent XII out of respect for the pope who named
him a cardinal and whose style he hoped to emulate as
pope. He was crowned on July 15.

The new pope introduced economies in the administration of Rome and the Papal States, reformed
the judicial system, insisting on impartial justice for

everyone, reduced (but did not eliminate) the sale of church offices, and declared that all of the poor and the needy were his "nephews." But his most significant initiative was his decree *Romanum decet pontificem* (June 22, 1692), which mandated that popes may never grant estates, offices, or revenues to relatives and that if such relatives are poor, they should be treated like others in need.

On the political front, Innocent XII broke the fifty-year deadlock between France and the Holy See. The pope ratified the appointment of bishops nominated by the king and accepted royal administration of vacant dioceses. In return the king promised to revoke the requirement that French clergy subscribe to the antipapal Gallican Articles. Innocent XII died on September 27, 1700, and was buried in a simple tomb in St. Peter's Basilica. A monument designed by Ferdinando Fuga with a sculpture by Filippo della Valle was later erected in 1746.

241 CLEMENT XI

1649–1721, pope November 30, 1700–March 19, 1721
(The Vatican's official list begins his pontificate on
November 23, the day of his election, but he was not
consecrated Bishop of Rome until November 30.)

Born Giovanni Francesco Albani, Clement XI served in the Roman Curia and as governor in various parts of the Papal States, was secretary of papal briefs, and was named a cardinal-deacon in the title of Santa Maria in Portico in 1690 (he was not ordained a priest for another ten years, just before his elevation to the papacy). The conclave that followed Innocent XII's death lasted forty-six days, divided once again between pro-French and pro-imperial factions. Albani was elected unanimously on November 23, 1700, at age fifty-one, as a compromise candidate with the support of independent cardinals who were committed to a nonpolitical pope. He was consecrated as Bishop of Rome on November 30 and crowned on December 8. He took the name Clement XI because the day he accepted election was the feast of St. Clement, pope and martyr.

At the instigation of King Louis XIV, the new pope would play a key role in the repression in France of Jansenism (a morally rigid movement that emphasized the workings of divine grace to the practical exclusion of human free will). In 1708 the pope condemned 101 propositions in a book by Jansenist leader Pasquier Quesnel. After Louis XIV's death, the Jansenist leaders called for a council to determine their orthodoxy. The pope refused the appeal and excommunicated the Jansenist leaders.

Clement XI was also committed to the missionary enterprise of the Church. A particular problem festered in the Chinese mission, however. In their pastoral ministry, the Jesuit missionaries were using Chinese rites, such as the cult of Confucius and of ancestors (justifying them on the grounds that they were civic in nature). Alexander VII had approved the use of Chinese rites in 1656. On November 20, 1704, Clement XI accepted the judgment of the Holy Office (formerly the Inquisition) that missionaries in China were prohibited from using Chinese rites and repeated the judgment in 1715. Clement's action proved disastrous to the Church's missionary outreach in China. Clement's action was not reversed until 1939, by Pius XII. Clement XI died on March 19, 1721, and was buried, according to his expressed wish, under the pavement of the Coro Chapel in St. Peter's.

242 INNOCENT XIII

1655–1724, pope May 8, 1721–March 7, 1724

Innocent XIII's short and unproductive pontificate was marked by constant illness and personal aversion to the Jesuits. Born Michelangelo de' Conti, he served in the Roman Curia, held three governorships in the Papal States, was nuncio to Switzerland, and was named a cardinal-priest of Santi Quirico e Giulitta in 1706. After that he was named bishop of Osimo and then Viterbo, resigning the latter because of poor health. He was unanimously elected pope on May 8, 1721, after a lengthy conclave in which the emperor, through his delegate, vetoed the favored candidate, who had been Clement XI's secretary of state. Cardinal Conti took the name Innocent XIII out of respect for Innocent III (1198–1216), from whose family he was descended. He was crowned on May 18 and took possession of his cathedral church, the Lateran Basilica, on November 16.

Although educated by the Jesuits in Rome, the new pope developed a keen dislike of the Society of Jesus while serving as nuncio in Portugal. He even thought of suppressing the order because of its lack of compliance with Clement XI's ban (in 1704 and 1715) against the use of Chinese rites. But he also reaffirmed Clement XI's condemnation of the Jansenists, fierce adversaries of the Jesuits. On the political front, Innocent XIII mollified the emperor Charles VI by investing him with the kingdoms of Naples and Sicily (which Clement XI had refused to do) and placated the French regent by appointing his minister to the College of Cardinals. Innocent XIII died on March 7, 1724, and was buried in a simple tomb in St. Peter's Basilica. No monument marks his resting place.

243 BENEDICT XIII

1649–1730, pope May 29, 1724–February 21, 1730

Born Pietro Francesco Orsini, Benedict XIII renounced his inheritance as a youth and joined the Dominicans. Through the machinations of his influential family, he was named a cardinal in 1672 at age twenty-three and archbishop of Benevento in 1686. He was unanimously elected pope on May 29, 1724, as a compromise candidate after the pro-French, pro-Spanish, and pro-Hapsburg factions failed over nine weeks to elect their own favored candidates. Cardinal Orsini at first took the name Benedict XIV, in honor of another Dominican pope, Blessed Benedict XI (1303–4), but changed the number to XIII because the previous bearer of the name Benedict had been an antipope (1394–1417) during the Great Western Schism. Benedict XIII was crowned on June 4.

In the most fateful—and unfortunate—decision of his pontificate, the new pope retained his archdiocese of Benevento after accepting election as Bishop of Rome. (Pluralism, holding more than one church office at a time, was considered an abuse around the time of the Protestant Reformation.) Benedict XIII devoted himself to the pastoral care of Rome—he consecrated churches, visited the sick, administered the sacraments, and even gave religious instruction—but undermined his own reform efforts by opening his pontificate to unsavory influences from Benevento. Benedict XIII brought in Niccolò Coscia, his chancellor and secretary in Benevento, and made him a cardinal in 1725, against the protests of many cardinals. Coscia, in turn, appointed cronies from Benevento to influential positions and had one of his own underlings made secretary of state. As a result of Coscia's unscrupulous behavior, papal interests in Sicily and Sardinia were undermined, and the finances of the Papal States were in a state of collapse.

In spite of his personal and pastoral sincerity, Benedict XIII was profoundly unpopular with the Roman people, particularly because of their hatred of Coscia and his cronies. When the pope died, at age eighty-one, on February 21, 1730, the Romans erupted in a rage against the Beneventans, who barely escaped with their lives. Benedict XIII was buried first in St. Peter's, but his remains were transferred in 1738 to the basilica of Santa Maria sopra Minerva, long associated with the Dominican order.

244 CLEMENT XII

1652–1740, pope July 12, 1730–February 6, 1740

Born Lorenzo Corsini, Clement XII renounced his inheritance after his father's death in 1685 and, with the aid of influential relatives, entered the service of the Roman Curia. Lorenzo remained in Rome as treasurer of the apostolic chamber and in 1706 was named a cardinal-deacon in the title of Santa Susanna. He was elected on July 12, 1730, at age seventy-eight, after a four-month-long conclave. He took the name Clement XII out of respect for Clement XI, who had made him a cardinal.

The new pope was often bedridden with gout and became blind in the second year of his pontificate, forcing him to rely excessively on his cardinal-nephew Neri Corsini. Clement XII revived the papal lotteries to raise much needed revenue for the Papal States, placed new taxes on imports, restricted the export of valuables, and issued paper money.

On the political front, the Catholic powers continued to ignore the papacy, as they had under Clement XI. The emperor Charles VI declared his own sovereignty over Parma and Piacenza (traditional papal fiefs). The Papal States were overrun by Spanish armies, which then recruited troops from Rome, inspiring a revolt among the people. In 1736 Spain and Naples broke off diplomatic relations with the Holy See. To restore those relations, the pope had to recognize Don Carlos of Spain as king of the Two Sicilies.

With the help of his family's wealth, Clement XII beautified Rome, including the Piazza di Trevi, and the Trevi Fountain itself, one of the city's most popular tourist attractions today. Clement XII died on February 6, 1740, just shy of his eighty-eighth birthday. He was buried in the magnificent Corsini chapel (which he had commissioned) in the basilica of St. John Lateran.

245 BENEDICT XIV

1675–1758, pope August 17, 1740–May 3, 1758

Born Prospero Lorenzo Lambertini of noble but poor parents, Benedict IX was secretary of the Congregation of the Council (1708–27), Promoter of the Faith (in charge of canonizations), and archbishop of Ancona (1727) and was named a cardinal in 1728. In 1731 he became archbishop of Bologna, his birthplace, where he proved a successful and much admired pastor. He was elected pope after the longest conclave in modern times (six months) on August 17, 1740, having emerged as a candidate only at the very end and to everyone's surprise. He took the name Benedict XIV in memory of the pope, Benedict XIII, who named him a cardinal. He was crowned on August 22 in St. Peter's.

The new pope was conciliatory by nature and politically realistic. He signed concordats with Sardinia, Naples, Spain, and Austria, all containing substantial concessions to the rulers. The pope established two curial congregations, one to select worthy men as bishops and the other to answer bishops' questions directed to the Holy See. He promoted improved clerical training, episcopal residentiality, and pastoral visitation. He addressed such topics as these in a circular letter written to all the bishops of the Catholic world. Entitled *Ubi primum,* it concerned the duties of bishops and is generally regarded as the first papal encyclical (December 3, 1740). A month before his death, he instructed the patriarch of Lisbon to investigate the Jesuits in that country, because of the many (false) complaints he had been receiving about them.

Although Benedict XIV was a man of his time theologically and spiritually, many Protestants and agnostic scholars respected him for the breadth of his scholarly interests and for his support of the arts and sciences. The great Voltaire (d. 1778) even dedicated his tragedy *Mahomet* to the pope, which caused some consternation in conservative Catholic circles. Benedict XIV died on May 3, 1758, and was buried in St. Peter's, where he is memorialized by a striking monument by Pietro Bracci, erected through the financial contributions of the sixty-four cardinals he had created during his pontificate.

246 CLEMENT XIII

1693–1769, pope July 6, 1758–February 2, 1769

Born Carlo Rezzonico of an extremely rich commercial family in Venice, Clement XIII served first in the Roman Curia, as a governor in the Papal States, and then as auditor of the Rota (a judicial body that handles mostly marriage cases) for Venice. He was named a cardinal-deacon in the title of San Niccolò in Carcere in 1737 and was appointed bishop of Padua in 1743, where he modeled himself on St. Charles Borromeo (d. 1584) and was regarded by some as a saint. On July 6, after animated debate and a conclave of some fifty-three days, Cardinal Rezzonico was elected pope by cardinal-electors who wanted a pope very different from Benedict XIV and not anti-Jesuit. He took the name Clement XIII in honor of his patron, Clement XII, and was crowned on July 16.

The new pope faced some old business from the previous pontificate, specifically an investigation of charges against the Jesuits in Portugal. The Bourbons in France, Spain, Naples, and Parma were now waging a full-scale offensive against the Society of Jesus. (At the time, the Jesuits had 23,000 members, 800 residences, 700 colleges, and 270 missions.) Portugal's powerful minister, the Marquis de Pombal, hated the Jesuits, mainly because he viewed them as a threat to the monarchy and because of their interference with Portugal's economic designs on South America. Pombal thereupon confiscated Jesuit assets in Portugal and its colonies and then imprisoned some Jesuits and deported others to the Papal States in 1759. When Clement XII protested, his nuncio was expelled, and diplomatic relations were broken for a decade. France followed Portugal's lead, abolishing the Society of Jesus in 1764, and again the pope resisted.

On January 7, 1765, Clement XII published a bull, *Apostolicum pascendi munus*, reaffirming his support for the Society, applauding its accomplishments, and insisting that an assault upon the Jesuits was tantamount to an assault upon the Church itself. The pope invoked Pius V's bull of 1568, *In coena Domini*, which condemned state control of the Church. France occupied the papal enclaves of Avignon and Venaissin. In January 1769, Spain, France, and Naples were demanding that the pope suppress the order. Although he had no intention of doing so, he summoned a special consistory of cardinals for February 3, but he suffered a stroke and died the day before it was to meet. Clement XIII was buried in St. Peter's Basilica.

247 CLEMENT XIV

*1705–74, pope May 28, 1769–September 22, 1774
(The Vatican's official list begins his pontificate
on May 19, the day of election, but he was not
consecrated Bishop of Rome until May 28.)*

Born Giovanni Vincenzo Antonio Ganganelli, he adopted his father's name, Lorenzo, as his religious name upon entering the Franciscans. He was a professor of theology, college rector, and a consultant to the Holy Office (formerly the Inquisition) before being named a cardinal in the title of San Lorenzo in Panisperna in 1759 by Clement XIII, who referred to him as a Jesuit in the clothes of a Franciscan. He was elected pope on May 19, 1769, after a contentious conclave in which the Catholic powers (particularly the Bourbon monarchs in France, Spain, Naples, and Parma) threatened to veto a pro-Jesuit candidate. Upon election,

Ganganelli took the name of the pope (Clement XIII) who had appointed him to the College of Cardinals. He was crowned on June 4.

The new pope began to distance himself now from the Jesuits, with whom he had once been friendly. He knew that his first order of business would be to satisfy the Catholic powers' thirst for Jesuit blood. Clement XIV temporized for four years, hoping that the Jesuit problem would somehow resolve itself. But in the spring of 1773 the Bourbon states warned the pope that they would break diplomatic relations with Rome if he did not act against the Jesuits. On July 21, 1773, the pope issued the bull *Dominus ac Redemptor noster,* which completely dissolved the Society of Jesus. The superior general, Lorenzo Ricci, and his assistants in Spain, Italy, Portugal, Germany, and Poland were imprisoned in the Castel Sant'Angelo for questioning the decision. The Jesuit order was crushed everywhere except in Prussia and Russia, whose sovereigns forbade the promulgation of the papal bull. The Catholic school system in Europe and the missionary effort abroad suffered incalculable harm—all to satisfy the political and economic interests of grasping, nominally Catholic rulers.

Elsewhere on the political front, Clement XIV failed to stop the partitioning of Poland among Prussia, Russia, and Austria in 1772, but he made politically astute moves regarding England by welcoming members of the royal family in Rome and by playing down papal support for the exiled Catholic Stuarts. Clement XIV died in his summer residence, the Quirinale Palace, on

September 22, 1774, and was buried at first in St. Peter's. In 1802 his remains were transferred to the Church of the Holy Apostles, where they were entombed in a magnificent monument by Antonio Canova.

248 PIUS VI

> *1717–99, pope February 22, 1775–August 29, 1799*
> *(The Vatican's official list begins his pontificate on*
> *February 15, the day of his election, but he was not*
> *consecrated Bishop of Rome until February 22.)*

Pius VI's pontificate was the third longest in history, after Pius IX (1846–78) and Leo XIII (1878–1903). Born Giovanni Angelo Braschi of aristocratic parents of modest means, he served as secretary to Cardinal Antonio Ruffo in several different posts and then as private secretary to Benedict XIV (1740–58). He was appointed a cardinal-priest in 1773 by Clement XIV. He was elected pope at the 134-day conclave following the death of Clement XIV, because he was perceived to be pro-Jesuit by the pro-Jesuit cardinals and anti-Jesuit by the anti-Jesuit cardinals. He was fifty-seven and took the name Pius because he had a particular devotion to St. Pius V (1566–72).

The event that cast the darkest shadow over his pontificate was the French Revolution. At first the pope was cautious, although he regarded the revolution as an act of rebellion against a divinely sanctioned social order and a conspiracy against the Church. But in 1791, he denounced the oath of loyalty the new regime imposed on the clergy and condemned the Civil Constitution as well as the Declaration of the Rights of Man (1789). He declared the ordinations of the new state bishops sacrilegious and suspended priests, bishops, and abbots who had taken the civil oath. Diplomatic relations between France and the Holy See were immediately broken off, and France annexed the papal enclaves of Avignon and Venaissin.

Matters, however, went from bad to worse. A French general was killed during a riot in Rome and the Directory (the revolutionary leaders in Paris) ordered the occupation of the Papal States. General Louis Berthier entered Rome on February 15, 1798, proclaimed the Roman Republic, deposed Pius VI as head of state, and forced him to withdraw to Tuscany. When war broke out again, the Directory was concerned that troops would attempt to rescue the pope, so they had him moved from Florence on March 28, 1799, to Turin, then across the Alps to Briançon, and then to Valence. Pius VI died a prisoner in Valence at age eighty-one on August 29, 1799, and was buried in a local cemetery. Many thought that the papacy had at last come to an end with his death, that Pius VI was indeed "the last pope," but he had left careful instructions for the holding of the next conclave under emergency conditions.

249 PIUS VII

1742–1823, pope March 14, 1800–August 20, 1823

Pius VII's pontificate was the sixth longest in history, after Pius IX (1846–78), John Paul II (1978–2005), Leo XIII (1878–1903), Pius VI (1775–99), and Hadrian I (772–

95). Born Luigi Barnabà Chiaramonti of noble parents,
he joined the Benedictines at age fourteen, taking the
name Gregorio, was a professor of theology in Parma
and at San Anselmo's in Rome, was named bishop of
Tivoli in 1782 and then bishop of Imola in 1785, when
he was also named a cardinal by Pius VI. After Pius
VI's death, and with Rome now occupied by troops
from the kingdom of Naples, the cardinals chose
Venice, which was under Austrian protection, for the
conclave. It opened on December 1 with thirty-four
cardinals in attendance. A fourteen-week deadlock was
broken when the choice fell on the Benedictine bishop
of Imola, and he was elected on March 14, 1800. He
took the name Pius VII in honor of his predecessor.

The new pope resisted pressure to move the seat
of the papacy to Vienna. He left for Rome on July 3
and named an outstanding cardinal, Ercole Consalvi,
to be his secretary of state. By the time the new pope
reached Rome, after a difficult journey by sea and land
arranged by the Austrian emperor, the Austrian troops
had been defeated by Napoleon Bonaparte at the
battle of Marengo in northwest Italy on June 14. Pius
VII soon persuaded Austria and Naples to withdraw
from occupied papal territories. The pope and Cardinal Consalvi then negotiated a concordat with Napoleon, now First Consul of the new French Republic,
on July 16, 1801. The concordat restored Catholicism
in France, although with limitations later appended by
Napoleon.

Pius VII reached a similar agreement with the new
Italian Republic in 1803 but failed in his attempt to do

so with Germany. Against the advice of the Roman Curia, the pope went to Paris to take part in Napoleon's coronation as emperor on December 2, 1804. The gesture was not reciprocated. Napoleon did not modify the limitations he had placed on the Church and the pope. And when the pope insisted on remaining neutral in the renewed European wars and refused to support the blockade of England, Napoleon occupied Rome on February 2, 1808.

The pope was arrested on July 5 and placed in virtual solitary confinement in Savona. He at first refused to approve the investiture of bishops nominated by Napoleon, but later succumbed to great pressure and agreed verbally to their investiture by metropolitan archbishops. After being taken secretly from Savona to Fountainebleau, the exhausted pope was forced to sign a draft convention that included an implied renunciation of the Papal States. Napoleon published the document as if it were the final version. Two months later the pope retracted his signature, and the following year, with Napoleon having suffered major defeats in Russia and then Leipzig, Pius VII was sent back to Savona and released on March 10, 1814.

On August 7, 1814, the feast of St. Ignatius of Loyola (now celebrated on July 31), in spite of protests from the Catholic powers, Pius VII restored the Society of Jesus, after having regularized its status in Russia and Naples in 1801 and 1804, respectively. After falling and breaking his thigh some six weeks earlier, Pius VII died on August 20, 1823, two years after his nemesis, Napoleon Bonaparte, and was buried in St.

Peter's. His longtime, faithful secretary of state, Cardinal Consalvi, had a grand monument by Antonio Canova erected in Pius VII's memory.

250 LEO XII

1760–1829, pope September 28, 1823–February 10, 1829

Leo XII's pontificate was an extremely conservative one: he condemned religious toleration, reinforced the Index of Forbidden Books and the Holy Office (formerly the Inquisition), reestablished the feudal aristocracy in the Papal States, and confined Jews once again to ghettos. Born Annibale Sermattei Della Genga of noble parents, he served after ordination to the priesthood in 1783 as private secretary to Pius VI. He was then ambassador to Lucerne, titular archbishop of Tyre, nuncio to Cologne and Bavaria, and special papal envoy in various other situations. While Pius VII was imprisoned by Napoleon in France, Cardinal Della Genga lived at the abbey of Monticelli, near Piacenza, as a virtual state prisoner. He was elected pope on September 28, 1823, after a conclave of some twenty-five days due to the votes of reactionary cardinals who were unhappy with the secretary of state's liberal policies and wanted a return to more traditional papal rule. After at first refusing election, Cardinal Della Genga relented and took the name Leo XII, in honor of Pope Leo the Great (440–61), to whom he had a special devotion. Leo XII was crowned on October 5.

The new pope shared the hard-line conservative views of those who elected him. Leo XII at once replaced the cardinal-secretary of state, Ercole Consalvi, with the conservative Cardinal Della Somaglia and established a Congregation of State to advise him on political and religious matters. The modern state that Cardinal Consalvi had been trying to establish in the Papal States, without prejudice to the rights and interests of the Church, was now dismantled in favor of a harsh police state, complete with press censorship, capital punishment, and secret societies that sniffed out the slightest hints of revolution.

At first the European powers were concerned that Leo XII's election signaled a reversal of Pius VII's more liberal attitude toward the world's growing political pluralism. Some of the new pope's early moves confirmed those fears, but he soon came to realize that the Church needed to have good relations with other countries. He came to adopt a more conciliatory policy toward the European powers than with his own subjects in the Papal States. His internal policy was designed to rejuvenate the spiritual vitality of the Church, but his agenda was shaped by a rigidly clericalist theology and spirituality and an overriding fear of, and hostility toward, the modern world. He died on February 10, 1829, and was buried in St. Peter's.

251 PIUS VIII

1761–1830, pope March 31, 1829–November 30, 1830

After Leo XII's generally reactionary pontificate, Pius VIII returned to the more liberal policies of Pius VII (1800–1823). He approved the decrees of the First

Council of Baltimore in the United States (1830). Born
Franceso Saverio Castiglioni of noble parents, he was
named bishop of Montalto in 1800 but was imprisoned
from 1808 to 1814 for refusing to swear allegiance to
the Napoleonic regime in Italy. Pius VII named him a
cardinal and bishop of Cesena in 1816. Following Leo's
death, the five-week conclave of 1829, dominated this
time by moderate cardinals, elected Castiglione on
March 31 with the backing of Austria and France and
in spite of his poor health. He took the name Pius VIII
in honor of his patron, Pius VII, and was crowned on
April 5.

   Although the new pope was committed to reviv-
ing the more liberal policies of Pius VII, his first and
only encyclical, *Traditi humiliati nostrae* (May 24, 1829),
blamed the breakdown of religion and the social order
on indifferentism, the activities of Protestant Bible societies, attacks on Catholic dogma and the sacredness
of marriage, and the existence of secret societies. On
the other hand, he revoked most of Leo XII's harsh
measures in the Papal States.

   He appointed Cardinal Giuseppe Albani, the man
most responsible for the pope's election in the conclave, as secretary of state. Albani was openly pro-
Austrian, which meant that Pius VIII's policies toward
the young churches in Latin America, formerly subject
to the Spanish crown, were actually less progressive
than Leo XII's. Pius VIII died on November 30, 1830,
and was buried in St. Peter's. Cardinal Albani erected a
monument to him, the work of Pietro Tenerani.

252 GREGORY XVI

1765–1846, pope February 2, 1831–June 1, 1846

A Camaldolese monk (and the last monk to be elected pope), Gregory XVI was one of the Church's most reactionary popes, banning railways in the Papal States and streetlights as well, lest people gather under them to plot against the authorities. He was the last nonbishop to be elected pope. Born Bartolomeo Alberto Cappellari, the son of an aristocratic lawyer, he entered a Camaldolese monastery at age eighteen, taking the name Mauro, was ordained in 1787, and became a professor of science and philosophy in 1789. In 1805 he became abbot of San Gregorio in Celio, was named vicar general of his order in 1823, and became a cardinal in 1826. At the difficult and laborious fifty-day conclave following the death of Pius VIII, Cardinal Cappellari was elected on February 2, 1831, with the support of the ultraconservative, or reactionary, cardinals. He took the name Gregory XVI, in honor of Gregory the Great (590–604). Since he was not yet a bishop, Gregory XVI was consecrated at once and then crowned on February 6.

The new pope was immediately confronted with a popular uprising in the Papal States and in Rome. The people were calling for greater freedom and an Italian republic. Gregory XVI sought aid from the conservative Austrian government, whose troops promptly crushed the revolts. But the other great European powers (Russia, England, France, and Prussia) intervened at that point and demanded substantial reforms in the Papal States. Gregory was prepared to concede on minor points but stood firmly against elected assemblies and lay-dominated councils of state. New disorders erupted, and Austrian troops were called in for a second time. France thereupon seized Ancona, and for seven years the Papal States were under military occupation.

Gregory XVI was as rigid in dealing with theological issues as he was in dealing with political ones. In his encyclical *Mirari vos* (August 15, 1832), a forerunner to Pius IX's famous Syllabus of Errors (1864), he denounced the concepts of freedom of conscience, freedom of the press, and separation of Church and state.

Gregory XVI, having headed the Congregation for the Propagation of the Faith (Propaganda) before his election as pope, was a strong promoter of the missions. During his pontificate some seventy dioceses and vicariates apostolic (local churches not yet ready to be made dioceses) were established, and almost two hundred missionary bishops were appointed. He encouraged the creation of a native clergy and a native hierarchy in mission lands. It is also important to note that Gregory XVI, however reactionary a pope he may have been, clearly denounced slavery and the slave trade in a papal brief, *In supremo* (1839).

Gregory XVI died on June 1, 1846, and was buried in St. Peter's, first in the crypt and then, in 1853, in the basilica proper, with a monument done by Luigi Amici and funded by the cardinals Gregory XVI had created during his pontificate.

253 PIUS IX, BL.

1792–1878, pope June 16, 1846–February 7, 1878

The pontificate of Pius IX, also known as Pio Nono ("Pius the Ninth"), was the longest thus far in the history of the papacy (thirty-one years and seven months). Elected as a moderate after Gregory XVI's reactionary pontificate, he soon established himself among the more reactionary popes of history.

Born Giovanni Maria Mastai-Ferretti, the son of a count and countess, after ordination to the priesthood he served on a diplomatic mission to Chile, administered the Hospice of San Michele in Rome, was named archbishop of Spoleto in 1827 and then bishop of Imola in 1832, and was proclaimed a cardinal in 1840. He was considered a liberal during his years as a bishop in Spoleto and Imola because he supported administrative changes in the Papal States and sympathized with the nationalist movement in Italy. After the death of Gregory XVI, the conclave was sharply divided between reactionary and liberal cardinals, who each supported their own candidate. Recognizing that the deadlock between the two candidates would not be broken, the conclave swung to the fifty-four-year-old Cardinal Mastai-Ferretti, who was elected pope on June 16, 1846, after a two-day conclave. The newly elected pope took the name Pius IX in honor of Pius VII (1800–1823), the pope who had encouraged his vocation to the priesthood. Pius IX was crowned on June 21.

Pius IX believed, like other popes before him, that the temporal sovereignty of the Holy See (the so-called

Patrimony of St. Peter) was indispensable to its spiritual independence—a belief that has since been amply disproved. The reason the Papal States were regarded as such an obstacle to Italian unification was that they stretched across the whole of central Italy, cutting off the south from the north. In any case, the last straw was his refusal to support the war to expel Austria from Italy in 1848. With the Papal States in a state of economic crisis, the pope was besieged by revolutionaries at the Quirinale Palace and was forced to flee in disguise to Gaeta on November 24. On February 9, 1849, Giuseppe Mazzini and his followers proclaimed the Roman Republic.

The pope appealed to the Catholic powers of Europe for help. French troops restored papal rule to Rome on July 15, and Pius IX returned to the city on April 12, 1850. He then established an antinationalist, paternalistic regime in the Papal States that alienated the educated citizenry and that his own counselor described as "reactionary and maladroit." But one after another, the pope lost several of the Papal States (Romagna, Umbria, the Marches). By September 1860, all of the Papal States, with the exception of Rome and its immediate environs, had been taken over by the new kingdom of Italy. On September 20, 1870, Italian forces under Victor Emmanuel occupied Rome. In an October plebiscite, Rome was incorporated into the Italian state. On May 13, 1871, the Law of Guarantees assured the pope of personal inviolability and left him with the Vatican and other buildings. But Pius IX refused to

accept the arrangement and never again set foot outside the Vatican, considering himself a prisoner there.

On December 8, 1854, Pius IX defined the dogma
of the Immaculate Conception of the Blessed Virgin
Mary (namely, that Mary was conceived without original sin), giving rise to a new wave of Marian devotions
throughout the Western world. In 1864 he published
the encyclical *Quanta cura* with the famous "Syllabus
of Errors" attached, which dealt with pantheism and
naturalism, the relationship between faith and reason (a censure of rationalism), and liberalism and the
rights of the Church. Then, in 1869 Pius IX convened
the First Vatican Council (1869–70) which, in its dogmatic constitution *Pastor Aeternus* and under intense
personal pressure from the pope himself, reaffirmed
the primacy of the pope over the universal Church
and defined his infallibility.

Ironically, by the time his record-long pontificate
ended and in spite of his own wishes, Pius IX had
witnessed the creation of what is now known as the
modern papacy, freed of the deadweight of temporal
sovereignty and exercising a more far-reaching spiritual authority perhaps than ever before in its history.
When Pius IX died on February 7, 1878, however, he
was exceedingly unpopular with the people of Rome
and the educated, even though he had been popular
with the Catholic masses, especially outside of Italy.
On July 13, 1881, there was a disruption of the procession accompanying his body from its original burial
place in St. Peter's to St. Lawrence's Outside the Walls.

A mob tried unsuccessfully to seize the body and throw it into the Tiber River. He was beatified in 2000 by Pope John Paul II.

254 LEO XIII

1810–1903, pope February 20, 1878–July 20, 1903

Leo XIII was the first of the truly modern popes, seeking to bring the Church into dialogue with the modern world, but also challenging the modern world to live up to the standards of the gospel with regard to social justice. His was the third longest pontificate in history, after that of Pius IX, his predecessor, and John Paul II (1978–2005).

Born Gioacchino Vincenzo Pecci, he served after ordination to the priesthood as governor of Benevento (1838–41) and then of Perugia (1841–43), where he had to engage in such activities as the control of banditry, the building of roads, and the establishment of a savings bank for farmers. Gregory XVI then sent him as papal nuncio to Belgium (1843–46), as titular archbishop of Damietta. After leaving Belgium, he was named bishop of Perugia in 1846 and a cardinal in the title of San Crisogono in 1853. In 1877, Pius IX invited Archbishop Pecci back to Rome as the chamberlain of the Holy Roman Church, the one who administers the Holy See when there is a vacancy in the Chair of Peter.

Pius IX died on February 7, 1878, and the conclave elected Cardinal Pecci on the third ballot. He took the name Leo XIII in honor of Leo XII (1823–29), although he had been a very conservative and unpopular pope. Leo XIII was already sixty-eight years old and in weak health when elected. Many probably saw him as a transitional pope following Pius IX's record-long pontificate. But Leo himself would be in office for over twenty-five years, dying at age ninety-three.

Although the new pope was much more of a moderate than his predecessor, Leo XIII continued many of Pius IX's policies regarding, for example, socialism, Communism, and Freemasonry. Where Leo XIII was least like Pius IX was in his understanding of the relationship between Church and society and his general openness to scholarship and the intellectual life. He devoted several encyclicals to the social order: in 1881 his encyclical *Diuturnum illud* gave tentative recognition to democracy. But one of the most important papal pronouncements in history was his social encyclical *Rerum novarum,* published on May 15, 1891. Although it strongly defended the right to private property (against socialism), it also insisted on the social responsibilities that accompany the private possession of property, namely, the obligation to pay workers a just wage and to honor workers' rights, especially the right to form trade unions.

At the same time Leo XIII was deeply concerned about recovering the Papal States and the temporal power of the Holy See. Some of his actions, however, were clearly counterproductive. Thus, by forbidding Catholics from participating in elections in the new Italian state, he undermined the capacity of the Church to influence political events.

Ecumenically, Leo XIII's record was mixed, but more negative than positive. On the one hand, he was the first pope to speak of non-Catholic Christians as "separated brethren" and invite Protestants and Orthodox to return to union with Rome without mentioning heresy or schism. On the other hand, he followed the dominant ecclesiology of the Counter-Reformation period, which emphasized the hierarchical and structural elements of the Church as well as the supreme authority of the pope.

A man of traditional Catholic piety and devotion, Leo XIII issued ten encyclicals on the Rosary and consecrated the entire human race to the Sacred Heart of Jesus during the Jubilee year of 1900. Leo XIII brought increased international prestige to the papacy after long years of reactionary and separatist papal attitudes toward the newly emerging modern world. He died on July 20, 1903. He was buried temporarily in St. Peter's, but his body was later transferred, according to his wishes, to the basilica of St. John Lateran.

255 PIUS X, ST.

1835–1914, pope August 4, 1903–August 20, 1914

Although Pius X was canonized a saint in 1954, his pontificate stands as one of the most controversial in the modern papacy. He assumed a negatively critical posture toward modern democratic governments and led a sometimes cruel and internecine campaign against Catholic theologians, biblical scholars, and historians (lumping them all under the umbrella of Modernism), from which the Church did not begin to recover until the Second Vatican Council (1962–65). On the other hand, Pius X was a deeply spiritual man in his personal life and is remembered as the "pope of frequent Communion," having lowered the age for First Communion to the "age of discretion" (approximately seven).

Born Giuseppe Melchiorre Sarto, the son of a village postman and a seamstress, he was ordained in 1858, working first as a country curate and pastor. By 1893, he had become a cardinal and patriarch of Venice. In Venice he devoted himself to pastoral tasks, generally steering clear of politics. Likewise, when Cardinal Sarto was elected pope on August 4, 1903, by adopting as his motto, "To restore all things in Christ" (Eph. 1:10), he made clear that he intended to be a pastoral rather than a political pope. Nevertheless, his "pastoral" outlook carried him inevitably into troubled political waters. He appointed a conservative secretary of state in order to reverse Leo XIII's more accommodating approach to secular governments. This led the following year to a diplomatic break with France. The pope adopted the same stance toward Portugal in 1911, while his support for Catholic minorities in Ireland and Poland angered England and Russia.

Pius X's "pastoral" concept also included defending the flock against heresy. In the encyclical *Pascendi Dominici gregis* he characterized Modernism as the "synthesis of all heresies" and also imposed an oath against Modernism on all clerics. He also gave encouragement to a network of informants known as the Sodalitium Pianum (League of St. Pius V) to report on instances of deviations from doctrinal orthodoxy wherever and by whomever they occurred, leading in many instances to dismissal from faculty positions, suspension from the priesthood, or excommunication from the Church.

On a more positive, less controversial, note, Pius X reorganized the Roman Curia, revised the Code of Canon Law, improved seminary curricula and catechetical instruction, established the Pontifical Biblical Institute, and restored Gregorian chant as the model of church music. After suffering a heart attack in 1913, Pius X died as World War I was beginning, on August 20, 1914, and was buried in a simple and unadorned tomb in the crypt of St. Peter's, in accordance with his wishes. He was the first pope to be canonized since Pius V (1566–72). Feast day: August 21.

256 BENEDICT XV

1854–1922, pope September 3, 1914–January 22, 1922

Although his pontificate was overshadowed by World War I, Benedict XV's greatest accomplishment may have been his calling to a halt the internecine war within the Church provoked by the vehement anti-Modernist campaign of his predecessor, Pius X. Benedict XV may well have been one of the finest popes in history, but surely one of the least appreciated, inside as well as outside the Church.

Born Giacomo della Chiesa, of patrician parents, he was not impressive in appearance because of an injury incurred at birth. One eye, one ear, and one shoulder were noticeably higher than the other. He was also short, extremely thin, stooped-shouldered, and slightly bluish in complexion and walked with a limp. Ordained in 1878, he served as secretary to Archbishop Mariano Rampolla, who was then nuncio to Spain. When Rampolla became cardinal-secretary of state in 1887, della Chiesa remained with him, becoming undersecretary of state in 1901, archbishop of Bologna in 1907, and finally being named a cardinal in 1914, shortly before Pius X's death.

After ten ballots on September 3, the votes for della Chiesa reached thirty-eight, sufficient for election. The newly elected pope took the name Benedict XV in memory of Prospero Lambertini, who like himself had been archbishop of Bologna when elected pope with the name Benedict XIV. The new pope immediately took stock of the financial status of the Holy See, determined to dispense as much money as possible to those in need. As the war clouds continued to gather across Europe and beyond, the pope maintained a strictly neutral posture, refusing to condemn any side—with the result that both sides accused him of partiality. He sought in various ways to alleviate the sufferings caused by war and proposed a seven-point peace plan in 1917, which was ignored by both the Allies and the Central Powers.

After the war Benedict XV pleaded for reconciliation among the nations and gave at least general support to the League of Nations. With regard to the status of the Holy See within Italy, he adopted a more moderate political course, allowing full participation by Catholics in the political process. He also authorized a secret meeting between the Italian dictator Benito Mussolini and Cardinal Gasparri in order to begin the process of regularizing the place of the Holy See in Italy (the result would be the Lateran Treaty of 1929).

Benedict promulgated the new Code of Canon Law, made the Congregation for the Oriental Churches autonomous (he dreamed of a reconciliation between the Eastern and Western Churches), and established the Pontifical Oriental Institute in Rome. But perhaps the most important and abidingly relevant achievement of his pontificate was his first encyclical, *Ad beatissimi Apostolorum* (November 1, 1914), in which he called a halt to the internecine warfare between so-called Integralist Catholics and progressive Catholics that had developed and intensified during the previous pontificate. In the end, he was a pope dedicated to healing and reconciliation, even if on the political front his ministrations were unappreciated. Benedict XV died unexpectedly at age sixty-seven of influenza that developed into pneumonia on January 22, 1922. He was buried in the crypt of St. Peter's.

257 PIUS XI

1857–1939, pope February 6, 1922–February 10, 1939

Pius XI was the first pope to use the radio as a means of communication and the first pope with a serious avocation of mountain climbing. Born Ambrogio Damiano Achille Ratti, he was ordained in 1879 and became pro-prefect of the Vatican Library in 1911 and prefect in 1914. Benedict XV appointed him in 1921 archbishop of Milan and a cardinal in the title of San Martino ai Monti (appropriate for a mountaineer). The next year, on February 6, 1922, he was elected pope as a compromise candidate. Ratti took the name Pius XI in honor of Pius IX, who had supported him in his early years of ecclesiastical formation, and of Pius X, who had called him to Rome for service in the Vatican Library.

Pius XI believed the Church should be active in the world, not isolated from it. His first encyclical promoted Catholic Action, or the participation of the laity in the apostolate of the hierarchy. He also had a strong commitment to missions. His requirement that every religious order engage in missionary work caused the number of missionaries to double during his pontificate. Pius XI's most lasting encyclical, still studied today as an important part of the corpus of Catholic social teachings, was *Quadragesimo anno* (1931), written on the occasion of the fortieth anniversary of Leo XIII's pioneering social encyclical *Rerum novarum* and in the midst of a terrible worldwide economic depression. Pius XI insisted that the right to private property is a qualified right—qualified by the demands of social justice and the common good.

Pius XI's political acts included concordats and other agreements with some twenty governments, improved relations with France, and the Lateran Treaty (February 11, 1929), reached with the Italian prime minister Benito Mussolini after lengthy, difficult negotiations. Through the treaty the Vatican recognized for the first time since 1870 the kingdom of Italy, with Rome as its capital. Italy, in turn, financially compensated the Vatican for the loss of the Papal States and recognized Catholicism as the official religion of the country. Vatican City State was established as a separate and independent political entity.

Outside of Italy, so intense was Pius XI's revulsion for and fear of Communism that he even entered into a concordat with the ostensibly anti-Communist National Socialist (Nazi) Germany in 1933, trusting Hitler's assurances that the rights of the Church would be respected. Between 1933 and 1936, however, Pius XI addressed thirty-four notes to the Nazi government to protest its growing oppression of the Church. Most of the notes went unanswered. The break came in 1937 when he ordered his encyclical *Mit brennender Sorge,* condemning Nazism as fundamentally racist and anti-Christian, to be read from every German pulpit. When Mussolini dissolved Catholic youth organizations in Italy in 1931, Pius XI issued an encyclical critical of Italian Fascism and broke with him completely in 1938 after his adoption of Hitler's racist doctrines. Pius XI died on February 10, 1939, at age eighty-one and after seventeen years as pope. He was buried in the crypt of St. Peter's Basilica.

258 PIUS XII

1876–1958, pope March 2, 1939–October 9, 1958

Pius XII's pontificate spanned the entire Second World War and the postwar period, when he devoted his en-

ergies to combating Communism through various
means, including the promotion of Marian piety and
devotion. Although largely traditional in his theological and pastoral views, Pius XII in fact laid much of the
groundwork for the renewal that came to full flower
in the Second Vatican Council (1962–65).

Born Eugenio Maria Giuseppe Giovanni Pacelli,
the son of a lawyer, he studied, like several previous
popes, at the Pontifical Gregorian University and the
Capranica College. Ordained in 1899, he served from
1904 to 1916 as assistant to Cardinal Pietro Gasparri. By
February 7, 1930, he had succeeded his mentor as secretary of state. In this new capacity, Cardinal Pacelli was
responsible for concluding concordats with Austria
and National Socialist (Nazi) Germany in 1933 (Hitler
would flagrantly violate the latter). An accomplished
linguist and world traveler, Cardinal Pacelli paid official visits to Argentina, France, and Hungary and
an extensive private visit to the United States in 1936,
which included a meeting with the newly reelected
president, Franklin D. Roosevelt.

With World War II about to erupt, Cardinal Pacelli
was elected pope on March 2, 1939, on the third ballot
of a one-day conclave. Pacelli was the best known of
all the cardinals, especially among the non-Italians, and
seemed to possess the diplomatic experience needed
at that troubled time. He was also the first secretary of
state elected to the papacy since Clement IX in 1667.

The new pope's central concern as he began his pontificate was world peace. "Nothing is lost by peace,"
he said, "everything is lost by war." When his efforts

failed and war broke out in earnest, Pius XII secured for Rome the status of an open city and he himself adopted an impartial stance. After Hitler occupied Rome on September 10, 1943, Vatican City became a sanctuary for many refugees, including Jews. However, Pius XII has been criticized severely for his failure to speak out and act more forcefully on behalf of the plight of the Jews.

Those who have written in defense of his wartime posture underscore his denunciation of the extermination of peoples based on race, albeit in general terms, his concern that stronger and more explicit denunciations would lead to even greater reprisals, and his personal support for efforts to render assistance and refuge to Jews. At the same time, however, in two separate statements (1944 and 1946) he implicitly exonerated Germany from any notion of collective guilt. The controversy will undoubtedly continue, but the judgment of history on this matter seems to have tilted against Pius XII. In a word, he could and should have done much more to protest the Holocaust.

Pius XII was remarkably productive and successful in his pastoral and ecclesiastical activities. There were few religious and moral topics he did not touch upon in his allocutions, encyclicals, and other pronouncements. His encyclical on the Church as the Mystical Body of Christ, *Mystici corporis* (1943), led the way for Vatican II's teaching that the church is the whole People of God, and *Mediator Dei* (1947), in calling for greater participation by the laity in worship, prepared the way for its many changes in the liturgical life of the

Church. There was also, however, a conservative, even reactionary, side to Pius XII's theological and pastoral agenda. In his encyclical *Humani generis* (1950), Pius XII condemned the so-called new theology and warned that once the pope had spoken on a controverted matter, theologians were no longer free to discuss it.

Because of the prevalence of radio, newsreels, and television, Pius XII became the best known pope in history to that date. By the time of his death at Castel Gandolfo on October 9, 1958, he had gained considerable credibility and influence for the papacy and the Catholic Church among non-Catholics throughout the world. Pius XII was buried in the crypt of St. Peter's Basilica.

259 JOHN XXIII, BL.

1881–1963, pope October 28, 1958–June 3, 1963

Perhaps the most beloved pope in all of history, John XXIII convened the Second Vatican Council (1962–65) and set the Catholic Church on a whole new pastoral course, emphasizing the role of the laity, the collegiality of bishops, the authentic faith and goodness of non-Catholic Christians and non-Christians, and the dignity of all human beings.

Born Angelo Giuseppe Roncalli, the third of thirteen children in a family of peasant farmers, he was ordained in 1904 and became secretary to his bishop in Bergamo. In 1921 Benedict XV appointed him national director of the Congregation for the Propagation of the Faith. Father Roncalli eventually became a protégé of Achille Ratti, the future Pius XI (1922–39), who launched him on a church diplomatic career, with postings in Greece and France during World War II. In 1953 he was named a cardinal in the title of Santa Prisca and the patriarch of Venice.

The voting in the conclave of 1958 to elect Pius XII's successor was quite close and went back and forth over three days, but Roncalli was elected on the eleventh ballot. He took the name John XXIII (there had also been an antipope by the name of John XXIII during the Great Western Schism of the fifteenth century) for a number of different reasons: it was his father's name, the name of the parish church where he was baptized, the name of numerous cathedrals around the world, including St. John Lateran, and the name of those closest to Jesus, John the Baptist and John the Evangelist.

He gave his first papal blessing from the central external balcony of St. Peter's Basilica, where he was received with great joy by the assembled throng. For the first time in history, the blessing was televised. John XXIII was crowned on November 4, the feast of St. Charles Borromeo, who was his model as a bishop. Later he reminded the congregation that he was not a prince surrounded by the signs of outward power, but "a priest, a father, a shepherd." More than any other pope since the earliest centuries, he recognized that he was, first and foremost, the Bishop of Rome. His example undoubtedly influenced John Paul II (1978–2005), who carried it to even broader levels of practice.

John XXIII abolished the limit of seventy and named twenty-three new cardinals to the College of Cardinals, increasing the international composition. The titles cardinal-priest and cardinal-deacon were done away with; henceforth cardinals would have to be or become bishops. On January 25, 1959, John XXIII proposed an ecumenical council (Vatican II, begun in October 1962 and completed under his successor, Paul VI), attributing the idea to a sudden inspiration of the Holy Spirit and referring to the council as a "new Pentecost."

John XXIII made it clear in his opening address to the council that it had not been called, as previous councils had been, to refute errors and to clarify points of doctrine. He acknowledged that the Church had punished those in error in the past with much severity, but he said that the most effective means of eradicating discord and of promoting harmony, peace, and unity is through the spreading everywhere of "the fullness of Christian charity." Official observers from eighteen non-Catholic Christian churches were present by invitation at the opening of the council. Although the pope himself did not attend the sessions, he intervened decisively on November 21, 1962, to rule that a theologically rigid document on revelation should be redrafted by a new, mixed commission of bishops. He adjourned the first session of the council on December 8, but would never live to see the opening of the second session the following September. He was already suffering from terminal stomach cancer, originally diagnosed on September 23, 1962.

His encyclicals reflected the pastoral and ecumenical tone of his pontificate. *Ad Petri Cathedram* (1959), on the themes of truth, unity, and peace, greeted non-Catholics as "separated brethren." *Mater et magistra* (1961) updated Catholic social teaching on property, the rights of workers, and the obligations of government. *Pacem in terris* (1963), published less than two months before his death, insisted that the recognition of human rights and responsibilities is the foundation of world peace. Many saw this encyclical as a sign that the pope harbored the hope of an eventual reconciliation between the West and the Communist East.

John XXIII made his last public appearance from the window of his apartment on Ascension Thursday, May 23, 1963. The next several days were filled with pain, but the pope remained conscious and communicative, making statements that were relayed around the world. When John XXIII died on the evening of June 3, 1963, the whole world reacted with profound sorrow. John XXIII was buried in the crypt of St. Peter's Basilica. He was beatified in 2000 by Pope John Paul II, and his body was transferred to the nave of St. Peter's.

260 PAUL VI

1897–1978, pope June 21, 1963–August 6, 1978

Paul VI continued the Second Vatican Council begun by John XXIII and became the first pope to travel around the globe by airplane. Although progressive in theology and social thought, his pontificate was marked by the ill-fated encyclical *Humanae vitae,* which condemned contraception.

Born Giovanni Battista Montini, son of a successful lawyer and politician, he was ordained in 1920 and served from 1922 in the Secretariat of State. In 1937 he was named assistant to the secretary of state, Cardinal Eugenio Pacelli (the future Pius XII), for internal church affairs. Monsignor Montini was appointed archbishop of Milan in November 1954. He was named a cardinal by John XXIII on December 15, 1958. Although he spoke only twice at the first session of the Second Vatican Council (fall 1962), Cardinal Montini was one of its behind-the-scenes leaders.

After John XXIII died on June 3, 1963, the conclave to elect his successor was the largest in history— eighty-one cardinals. After six ballots and much heated maneuvering between conservative and liberal factions, Cardinal Montini, at age sixty-five, finally got the two-thirds majority necessary for election. The newly elected pope chose the name Paul VI as a sign that he wanted to reach out to the modern Gentiles (that is, to the whole world) as Paul the Apostle had done. But his model as pope would not be John XXIII; it would be Pius XII, with whom he had worked so closely in the Secretariat of State.

Paul VI immediately announced that he would continue the council (he opened the second session on September 29), carry forward the revision of the Code of Canon Law, and work for the promotion of peace and justice in the temporal order and for the unity of the Christian family of churches. He admitted laymen as council auditors (women would be invited the following year) and invited the various non-Catholic Christian churches to send more observers. On January 4, 1964, he made an unprecedented trip by airplane to the Holy Land, where he met with the ecumenical patriarch Athenagoras I in Jerusalem. On September 6 he announced that lay and religious women would be invited to the council as auditors.

The difficult task of implementing the decrees of Vatican II now faced the pope. Although many were unhappy with the changes, Paul VI did not water them down. He established several postconciliar commissions and authorized the use of the vernacular in the Mass and the sacraments. He also approved a new Liturgy of the Hours (Divine Office, or Breviary) and new translations and revisions of other liturgical texts and rituals and reduced the eucharistic fast to one hour before the reception of Holy Communion.

In July 1968 Paul VI issued the fateful encyclical on birth control, *Humanae vitae,* which declared that every act of sexual intercourse within marriage must be open to the transmission of life. In other words, there can be no artificial means of contraception. The encyclical created a storm of protest all over the world, but especially in North America and Europe. Many were aware of the findings and recommendation of the Papal Birth Control Commission in 1966; namely, that the pope should change the teaching, acknowledging that our understanding of the natural law has matured. When he did not do so, there was profound shock and disappointment.

Although the birth control encyclical had cast a shadow over his pontificate, Paul VI pursued many other pastoral initiatives before and after the release of the encyclical. His *Evangelii nuntiandi* (1975), possibly the best document of his pontificate, links the process of evangelization with the Church's abiding concern for questions of social justice, human rights, and peace. The pope traveled widely, escaping an assassination attempt in Manila in 1970. In the last year of his life, Paul VI was profoundly shaken by the kidnapping and murder of his close friend Aldo Moro, former prime minister of Italy and prominent Christian Democratic leader. His last public appearance was to preside at Moro's funeral in the basilica of St. John Lateran. He died of a heart attack at Castel Gandolfo on August 6, 1978, and was buried in the crypt of St. Peter's Basilica.

261 JOHN PAUL I

1912–78, pope August 26–September 28, 1978

Although John Paul I was pope for only thirty-three days, his was not the shortest pontificate in history. There were ten (and possibly eleven) other popes who served for thirty-two days or fewer, the shortest being Urban VII, September 15–27, 1590, a pontificate of twelve days.

Born Albino Luciani, of poor working-class parents, he was ordained in 1935, did doctoral studies at the Gregorian University in Rome, and served as a curate in his home parish. In 1937 he was appointed vice-rector and a member of the teaching faculty of his diocesan seminary and served also as vicar general of his diocese. In 1958 he was appointed bishop of Vittorio Veneto; in 1973 he was named a cardinal in the title of San Marco. He was generally conservative in theology but sensitive to the poor and to social issues. This latter trait would later commend him to the Third World cardinals at the next papal conclave.

After the death of Paul VI on August 6, 1978, 111 cardinals entered the conclave to elect a successor—the greatest number of electors in history. The conclave would begin—and end—on Saturday, August 26. On the fourth and final ballot, Cardinal Luciani was elected. It was evident that the cardinals wanted a pastoral pope, someone not connected with the Roman Curia and someone different in style from the previous pope.

The new pope chose a double name, John Paul, the first pope in history to do so. He did so, he said, to honor the pope (John XXIII) who ordained him a bishop and who preceded him as patriarch of Venice and the pope (Paul VI) who named him a cardinal. The new pope broke a tradition of more than a thousand years' standing when he refused to be crowned with the triple tiara. He took possession of his cathedral, the basilica of St. John Lateran, on September 23. That was to be his last public appearance outside the Vatican.

Late in the evening of September 28, John Paul I died of a heart attack while reading in bed. His light was still on when his body was discovered early the next morning. Rumors about the cause of his death proliferated. Some charged that the pope had been poisoned to prevent him from exposing financial irregularities in the Vatican Bank. The failure to conduct an autopsy (linked to the mistaken idea that deceased popes cannot be embalmed) and the lack of truthfulness regarding the circumstances in which the body was discovered only served to feed such rumors. The most likely truth is that the pope died prematurely, just short of his sixty-sixth birthday, because he needed treatment for some serious health problems and did not seek or receive it. John Paul I was buried in the crypt of St. Peter's Basilica, just across the aisle from another short-reigned pope, Marcellus II, whose pontificate lasted only twenty-one days.

262 JOHN PAUL II

Polish, 1920–2005, pope October 16, 1978–April 2, 2005

The first Slavic pope in history and the first non-Italian since Hadrian VI (1522–23), John Paul II was the most traveled pope in history. Although he was committed to the Second Vatican Council (1962–65), in which he participated as a bishop, his pontificate was dedicated to the containment and even repression of progressive interpretations and implementations of the council. Although some have characterized him as the first postmodern pope, others have described his pontificate as restorationist, that is, one that sought to restore the more monarchical style of the papacy, with all effective authority centered in the Vatican.

Born Karol Wojtyła in Wadowice, Poland, in a family of modest means, he was a university student and then a manual laborer during the Nazi occupation of his homeland. He studied secretly for the priesthood during World War II and was ordained in 1946. In 1956, he was appointed professor of ethics at Lublin University. Two years later he was appointed auxiliary bishop of Kraków by Pius XII. On December 30, 1963, Paul VI appointed him archbishop of Kraków, and on June 26, 1967 he named him a cardinal. In spite of the Communist control of Poland, Cardinal Wojtyła was able to travel freely and frequently around the world: to the eucharistic congress in Philadelphia in 1976, to the Middle East, Africa, South and East Asia, and Australia.

When John Paul I died suddenly on September 28, 1978, after only thirty-three days as pope, the cardinals who quickly returned to Rome, in virtual shock, were now looking to elect someone with the physical vigor to withstand the requirements of the office. The public discussion before the conclave centered on the seventy-two-year-old ultraconservative Cardinal Giuseppe Siri of Genoa. A coalition of centrist cardinals agreed to support Cardinal Giovanni Benelli of Florence. But other members of the coalition, particularly the Brazilians, felt that it might be time for a non-Italian. Cardinal Franz Koenig of Vienna began to openly campaign on behalf of Cardinal Wojtyła. The next day, October 16, Cardinal Wojtyła's votes doubled on the fifth ballot. On the eighth ballot he was elected. The newly elected pope, at age fifty-eight, chose the name John Paul II because of his "reverence, love, and devotion" to John Paul and also to Paul VI, who had been his "inspiration and strength." Significantly, he made no reference to John XXIII, who was the first pope whom John Paul I intended to honor with his double name.

John Paul II viewed his election to the papacy as providential, a compensation for Polish sufferings during the nineteenth century and then under the Nazis and the Communists in the twentieth. In his view, his special mission was twofold: to bring the insights and values of the suffering Church of the East (especially Poland) to the comfortable churches of the West and to bring an end to what he and other conservative cardinals and bishops regarded as the postconciliar drift of the Church, a pointed criticism of Paul VI (1963–78).

In January 1979, at the Latin American Conference of Bishops meeting at Puebla, Mexico, he cautioned the bishops and their clergy against direct involvement in politics (taken as an indirect criticism of Latin American liberation theology). The message was clear: social justice, yes, but always within the confines of Catholic orthodoxy as interpreted by the pope and the Vatican. The triumphant tour of Mexico became a kind of paradigm for all subsequent papal trips and established John Paul II as a global superstar. At the time of his death the pope had made 104 pastoral visits abroad and 146 visits inside Italy.

John Paul II published several substantial encyclical letters. *Redemptor hominis* (1979) emphasized the dignity and worth of every human person and deplored

destruction of the environment and consumerism. In
Laborem exercens (1981), marking the ninetieth anniversary of Leo XIII's *Rerum novarum,* the pope viewed
human work as a form of collaboration in the creative
work of God and, therefore, of infinite dignity. *Sol-
licitudo rei socialis* (1987) emphasized the obligations
of rich and developed nations toward poor and unde-
veloped countries and the "preferential option for the
poor" as a guideline of moral action. John Paul II had
been profoundly convinced from the start of his pontificate that he was destined by God to lead the Catholic Church into the new millennium and that it would
be a millennium that would see the walls between the
various religious faiths of the world come down so
that there would be a united religious front against
atheism, materialism, and individualism.

Two major controversial encyclicals on moral theology appeared in 1993 and 1995, respectively: *Veritatis
splendor,* which was critical of theological dissent in
the public media, and of moral relativism, and *Evan-
gelium vitae,* which strongly condemned contraception, euthanasia, and abortion in language similar to
that employed in infallible teaching. Significantly, the
pope also condemned capital punishment, insisting
that there are, for all practical purposes, no sufficient
reasons ever to justify it. Also in 1995 he published an
encyclical remarkable for its openness on the sensitive topic of the papacy itself. In *Ut unum sint* he acknowledged that, although the Petrine office belongs
to the essential structure of the Church, the manner in
which the papal office is exercised is always subject to

criticism and improvement. He invited his readers, especially those in the other Christian churches, to enter into dialogue with him about the manner in which his office is exercised and to recommend ways in which its exercise might conform more faithfully to the gospel. His *Ordinatio sacerdotalis* (1994) insisted that the Church is not authorized to ordain women as priests.

Among the other major developments in this pontificate were the promulgation in 1983 of the revised Code of Canon Law, a project initiated by Pope John XXIII (1958–63); the publication, under the direction of Cardinal Joseph Ratzinger, of the Catechism of the Catholic Church in 1992 (the English translation was delayed until 1994 because of complaints from ultraconservative Catholics about the gender-inclusive language employed in the first translation); and the establishment of formal diplomatic relations with the United States in 1984 and with the State of Israel in 1994. John Paul II was also the first pope to visit Rome's chief synagogue, where he acknowledged the Church's sins against the Jews. He also canonized more than 480 saints, changed the rules for papal elections, and published several books.

At the end of his first full year in office, John Paul II startled the theological community by revoking Swiss theologian Hans Küng's status as a Catholic theologian. In January 1997, a well-known Third World theologian, Tissa Balasuriya, a seventy-two-year-old Sri Lanken priest, was excommunicated for, among other things, refusing to reject the possibility that women could be ordained to the priesthood. Disciplinary actions were also instituted against various bishops. Indeed, one of the most enduring legacies of this pontificate will be the vast numbers of conservative bishops appointed to various dioceses all over the world, many times in opposition to the wishes and recommendations of the local hierarchies, priests, and people.

Beginning in 1992 a series of illnesses and accidents left the pope in a weakened physical condition. Following a series of medical setbacks in early 2005, John Paul II died in the Apostolic Palace on April 2, 2005. His funeral in St. Peter's Square was the largest on record. Soon after his election, the new Pope, Benedict XVI, suspended the required five-year waiting period and authorized the initiation of formal proceedings leading to John Paul II's eventual beatification and canonization.

263 BENEDICT XVI

German, b. 1927, pope from April 19, 2005

The sixth German-born pope in history and the first since Victor II (1055–57), Benedict XVI was a trusted adviser to John Paul II. At age seventy-eight, he is the oldest person elected to the papacy since Clement XII in 1730. Although he had been a theological adviser to Cardinal Joseph Frings of Cologne during the Second Vatican Council (1962–65) and at one time a collaborator with the Jesuit theologian Karl Rahner and a close friend and colleague of the controversial Swiss theologian Hans Küng, he gradually developed a more critical attitude toward some of the reforms of the council, especially those relating to the liturgy, and postconciliar developments in the Church, particularly those calling for additional reforms of its internal governance and for greater pluralism in theology and pastoral practice.

Born Joseph Alois Ratzinger in Marktl am Inn, a town in rural Bavaria, on April 16, 1927, the son of a police officer and a barmaid, he served for a time, under legal compulsion, as a member of the Hitler Youth and as a draftee in the German army (and later prisoner of war) during World War II. He was ordained a priest for the diocese of Regensburg in 1951 and awarded a doctorate in theology from the University of Munich in 1953 and eventually became professor of theology at several universities.

In March 1977 he was appointed by Pope Paul VI to succeed Cardinal Julius Döpfner as the archbishop of Munich and Freising, and less than three months later he was named a cardinal. Pope John Paul II appointed him in November 1981 as prefect of the Congregation for the Doctrine of the Faith, where he established a reputation as a strict enforcer of doctrinal orthodoxy and clerical discipline, being tagged with various nicknames such as "the Panzer cardinal" and "the pope's rottweiler."

Soon after the death of John Paul II on April 2, 2005, the Italian press reported that Cardinal Ratzinger enjoyed the support of at least fifty cardinal-electors, or about twenty-five fewer than the required two-thirds for election. This speculation startled many who thought the cardinal too old and too polarizing a figure to be seriously considered, much less elected. However, it became clear that key curial cardinals and others associated with the so-called new movements like Opus Dei and the Legionaries of Christ had carefully cultivated support within the body of cardinal-electors. Cardinal Ratzinger was elected on the fourth ballot.

After accepting election, the newly elected pope was immediately ready to announce his papal name. He would be called Benedict XVI, to honor Benedict XV (1914–22), who was "a courageous prophet of peace" at the time of World War I and who had worked for "reconciliation and harmony between peoples," and to honor also St. Benedict of Nursia (ca. 480–ca. 574), copatron of Europe, "whose life evokes the Christian roots of Europe" and "the centrality of Christ in our Christian life."

When Benedict XVI, at seventy-eight and with a history of at least two serious illnesses prior to his election to the papacy, began his pontificate, many Catholics were in doubt about the eventual course he would follow. His most conservative supporters expected his pontificate to be a continuation and extension of John Paul II's, if not even more hard-line with respect to limiting the range of theological dissent and liturgical development. Progressive Catholics wondered if Pope Ratzinger would govern with the same attitudes and approaches that Cardinal Ratzinger had adopted as head of the Congregation for the Doctrine of the Faith. Others in the middle asked if the responsibilities of the office would temper some of those earlier stances and whether his choice of the name Benedict suggested a desire to bring peace not only to the world, but to the Church as well. Only time and circumstances will eventually yield a pattern.

INDEX OF NAMES